Feedback from

It's the best theory book I've ever seen.
Eddie Berman, Manager of The Music Loft, Raleigh, NC

Bruce Emery has "got it right" with his gentle pace. Books like this are the product of extensive experience at the grass-roots level and should be welcomed by teachers everywhere. ***Adrian Ingram, reviewer for "Just Jazz Guitar"***

I received my copy of Volume One of the "Skeptical" series, and I must say, it is *really, really* well done!! I have taught guitar for years and have always found it difficult to present music theory for the "skeptical" student ......So, great job! ***Dale Morgan, Guitar Instructor, Crescent City, CA***

The book sells itself. ***David Willmott, Owner of Music-Go-Round, Cary, NC***

These books demystify music theory.....Should have been written ***years*** ago!
Rob Farris and Scott Miller, Sales Representatives, Fat Sound Guitar Superstore, Cary, NC

What an accomplishment! Clear---I love the clean, easy-to-follow format, too. You have made basic music theory accessible to guitarists; or should I say, you've translated it to the language of the guitar. As your former teacher, I can only sit back and smile like a Cheshire cat. Congratulations on a job well done!! ***Joanne Ryan, Guitar Instructor, Vicksburg, MS***

I devoured the two volumes in a few nights. This is the first time that I have seen this much (applied) theory condensed in so few pages, with so much humor to boot. Congratulations! ***Gert-Jan Terlouw, Amsterdam, the Netherlands***

Your book took me farther than any other book on music theory before my brain began to hurt. ***Bill Case, Madison, AL***

I bought your book because it made me laugh. ***Mike Schwartz, Montclair, NJ***

Your books are excellent and have helped me quickly grasp some principles of music that otherwise seem too complex. I, for one, am glad you decided to leave forest genetics. ***Paul Patsis, Lake Oswego, OR***

If you can teach me, you can teach anyone. ***Bob Burns, Fountain Valley, CA***

Concise and well-presented.....Your mathematical approach to the inter-relationships of chord families in conjunction with the Circle of Fifths was a revelation. Well done! ***Dan Miller, Macon, GA***

Skeptical?

In my estimation, you qualify as a Skeptical Guitarist if:

(1) You doubt that learning about music theory can have any impact whatsoever on your guitar playing. You may even think that it would cause you deep suffering.
OR
(2) You realize the value of music theory, but you've never found a book which proved to be particularly useful or easy to read. You don't expect this one to be any different.

If you are the first kind of Skeptical Guitarist, well, I do realize that the point of studying music at all is to *play songs*. But after you've learned to play several dozen songs or so, you probably begin to get that sneaking suspicion that there are some *patterns* at work, some notes and chords that sound good together, and so forth.

Yet it's common to go on learning songs as if they are isolated islands, strewn across some vast body of uncharted water that is buffetted by storms and writhing with dark peril. But a working knowledge of music theory can help you to *build bridges* among these islands, and you begin to see the myriad characteristics that these little outcroppings of music share. From that point on, you will be able to approach each new piece of music with your eyes wide open, confident that you already have a pretty good notion of what to expect.

If you are the second kind of Skeptical Guitarist, believe me, I've been there myself. When you go in and buy some new theory book, you are filled with anticipation and hope, only to have your dreams shattered *once again.* You get to about p. 10 when it dawns on you that the author has grown weary of 'splainin' it to you nice. At precisely the moment that you need a few more examples and some patience, he decides to make the jump to light speed. It's not malice; it's just that he gets carried away with the jargon.

In any case, you start to feel unworthy and musically challenged, and that's when the turbines start to shut down, the lights dim, and you suddenly feel like doing absolutely *anything* else, so long as it isn't music theory. But hope springs eternal, and before long, there's another theory book that looks enticing, and you decide to give it ***one more try***.

Well, I hope you'll give this book a try. I've been playing guitar since 1967 and teaching it full-time since 1987. I like teaching, and my students say that I do it well. Of course, they have to, or else. But I think that I've been able to identify and isolate those elements of music theory that truly have the most interest and practical value to the recreational guitarist who lives on the planet Earth and has limited study time.

In other words, I'm on your side. I want to teach you guitar music theory. If you want to learn it, then I think that some of the best odds you've got are laid out for you in the following pages.

Music Principles for the SKEPTICAL GUITARIST

Volume One: The Big Picture

Music Principles for the SKEPTICAL GUITARIST

Volume One: The Big Picture

by

Bruce Emery

Skeptical Guitarist Publications

Manufactured in the United States of America

ISBN: 0-9665029-0-6

Cover design: Marc Harkness
Copy editing: Mary Pickering

Skeptical Guitarist Publications
P. O. Box 5824
Raleigh, NC 27650-5824
(919) 834-2031

First Edition

Table of Contents

Introduction

My approach to teaching guitar is to move inward from the outside.
It's important to start with the practical, then move toward the theoretical.

A single note may be the easiest thing to play on the guitar, but chords are more useful at first. So after laying some groundwork about the Musical Alphabet, we'll jump right into chords and learn how to use them to play songs in different keys. In this **First Approach** to music theory we'll try not to get too bogged down in details and technicalities. It will be a broad survey, a reconnaissance mission to get the lay of the land.

In the **Second Approach**, we'll rewind to the beginning and start all over again with the Musical Alphabet. I'll show you, step by step, how to transform notes into scales and scales into chords. We'll delve more deeply into chord relationships within, as well as between, Chord Families as we consider the Circle of Fifths. Finally, we'll touch on Minor Scales.

A second volume will provide more detailed information that is targeted at the guitarist. You see, ***Volume One*** covers music theory topics that extend to all musical instruments: the Chromatic Scale, the Major Scale, building triads, the Circle of Fifths, and so on. We just happen to be using the guitar in the examples because we play the guitar.

But ***Volume Two*** will present many concepts that are *specific* to the guitar --- the arrangement of notes within various guitar chord *shapes* as well as the deployment of chord and scale shapes over the entire neck of the instrument. Much of this information would be of no use to anyone but a guitarist. Someone who wants to be able to arrange solo guitar pieces or wants to learn to improvise up and down the neck will find ***Volume Two*** to be pretty handy, I'll wager. ***Volume Three*** will then extend these principles to the styles known as Blues and Jazz.

I'd like to mention several things before we get started:

(1) Fretboard diagrams and Tablature diagrams, which I describe on the next page, will be used to express chords and notes in the **First Approach.** Standard music notation (the dots and stems and clefs) will be added in the **Second Approach** for those of you who are already familiar with this notation. I won't be teaching how to read standard notation in this volume; if you are interested, I have written another book that will help you out, called "A Practical Guitar Method for a Practical World." Contact me if you want it. *Everyone should learn how to read standard music notation at some point in time.*

(2) You'll run into an occasional section labeled, "***Skip It.***" This means that the following material may be a bit complex, but don't sweat it; it is non-essential. Merely a sidelight. Take a look at it, but keep in mind that you can just let it slide if you want. You'll also see some circled page number references for quick reviews.

(3) *Please try to do all the little exercises.* They aren't hard, and they really help solidify what you ***think*** you understand. *And play all of the examples!* Hearing is believing.

Fretboard Diagrams

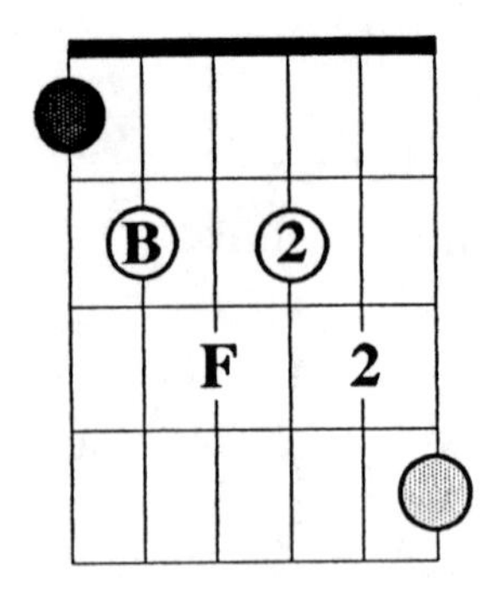

The fretboard diagram is a pictorial representation of the neck of the guitar. The darker, horizontal line at the top indicates the **nut** of the guitar, near the **tuning pegs**. The vertical lines are the 6 **strings**, and the thinner horizontal lines are the metal **frets**, or fret wires.

The notes that you'll be asked to play will be indicated in different ways. Sometimes you'll just see a dark dot on a certain string at a certain fret. Sometimes you'll see the *letter name* of the note inside a circle, or just the letter name without the circle. Other times you'll see a *number*, with or without a circle, which refers to either a certain finger or a scale degree (whatever that is, right?).

Tablature Diagrams

The Tablature diagram ("Tab" for short) is something like a tipped over fretboard diagram. Both types of diagram show the 6 strings of the guitar, but in the Tab diagram, the strings are laid out horizontally, and there are no lines that represent frets. Instead, the frets at which you can find specific notes are indicated with numbers that are placed on the "strings" and proceed from left to right (the same way we read text) to indicate melodies.

Here is a Tab diagram showing the C Major Scale:

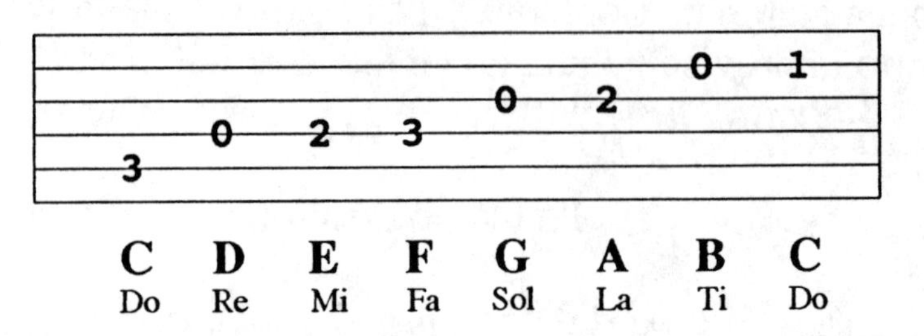

C	D	E	F	G	A	B	C
Do	Re	Mi	Fa	Sol	La	Ti	Do

The first note, "C" or "Do," is indicated by the number "3" on the 5th line from the top, which represents the 3rd fret of the 5th string. The second note, "D" or "Re," is indicated by the "0" on the 4th line from the top, representing the ***open*** 4th string. "E" and "F" are also found on the 4th string, at the 2nd and 3rd frets, respectively. And so forth.

In Standard Notation, there are only 5 lines, and there is a **treble clef** at the beginning, which distinguishes it from Tab. In Standard Notation, the lines and spaces indicate specific notes, like C, D and E, that you yourself must locate on the guitar. On the other hand, Tablature bypasses the naming of the notes and tells you *exactly where* to put your finger to play a certain note.

In the **First Approach,** the Tab will be useful in helping you find the Starting Notes for singing the musical examples.

The First Approach

Notes and Pitches

To speak the language of music, the first thing you need to know about is the **Musical Alphabet**, which is made up of 12 **notes**, or individual musical sounds, which our ears perceive as proceeding from "low" to "high." Most everyone has the natural ability to distinguish lower sounds from higher ones.

The confusing part is that, while there are 12 different notes, there are only ***7 different letters*** in the Musical Alphabet. (I'll explain later why this is so.) The 7 letters we use are A, B, C, D, E, F, and G. These are called the **natural notes.** The other 5 notes are called **accidentals** and are interspersed among the natural notes. You've probably heard the expressions **sharp** and **flat** used in a musical context, as in "F-sharp" or "B-flat." These are simply names for accidental notes. The symbol for sharp is "#" and the symbol for flat is "♭." A natural note can be called simply by its letter name.

Here's a picture of the piano keyboard. I'll bet you've fiddled around on a keyboard at some point in time. Piano keys move from "low" to "high" as you go from left to right:

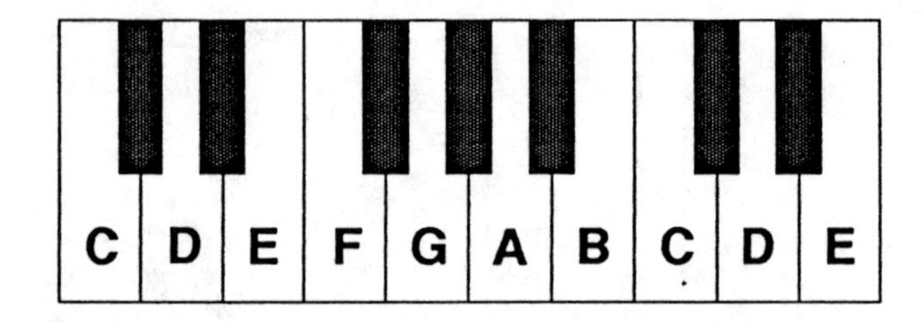

Well, the white keys are the natural notes and the black keys are the accidentals. Now, each accidental can be known as *either a sharp or a flat*. For example, the black key between the C and D notes can be called either C#, meaning one note *higher* than C, or D♭, one note *lower* than D. There is no E# (or F♭) and there is no B# (or C♭), which is why there is no black key between E and F or between B and C.

On the guitar, it isn't so easy to distinguish natural notes from accidentals since there are no white and black keys to help, just frets which look like frets which look like frets! But this can have some advantages, as you'll see later on.

So, using natural notes and sharps (rather than flats, to keep it simple), the Musical Alphabet starts at A and proceeds through G#, like this:

A - A# - B - C - C# - D - D# - E - F - F# - G - G# - A

And then it starts over, proceeding again from A to G#, only in a higher **octave**. This word comes from "octa," meaning "8." It means that the 8th letter along from the A note is another A note. So all the notes in the second octave have the same names as the corresponding notes in the first octave (and they blend together perfectly), but these notes are said to have higher **pitches**, meaning that they vibrate at higher frequencies. So, pitch increases from A to G#, then the Alphabet starts over again with A, *while the pitch continues to increase octave after octave.*

When I was a kid, I made a little cardboard wheel---I still have it---
to keep track of the notes in the Musical Alphabet. It helped me get past those
problem spots where there are no accidentals (between B and C, and E and F).
(By the way, for those of you with a little more music theory awareness,
this is ***not*** the Circle of Fifths. It's the Circle of Bruce.)

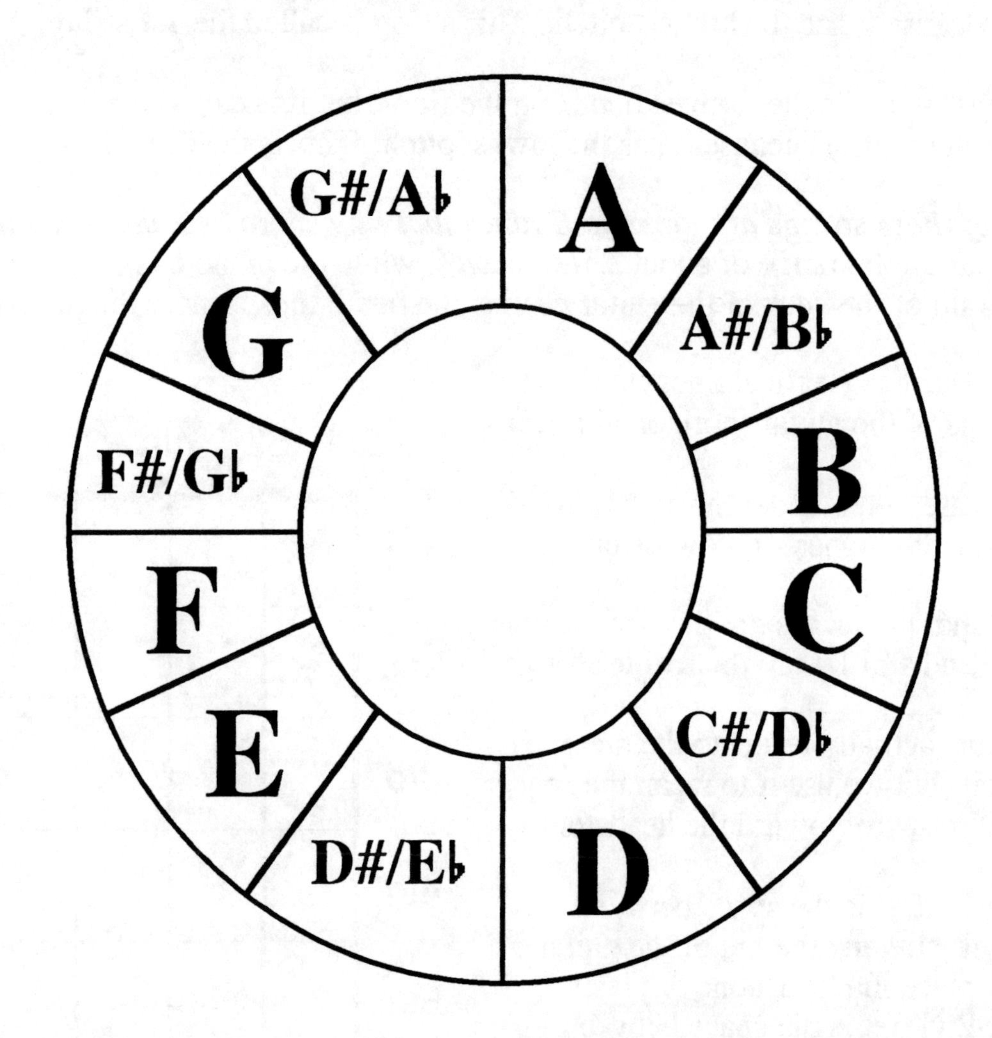

Don't get stuck on this idea of *natural* and *accidental* notes. In a way, the piano keyboard does us a disservice in sorting the notes into white and black keys. That segregation implies that there is some basic, intrinsic difference between the two classes of notes, ***and there isn't***. All 12 notes have equal status in the eyes of the musical gods. The A-flat note is ***not*** some kind of weird version of the A-natural note; rather, it is a distinct musical presence that stands on its own. The democratic structure of music is far more apparent on the guitar fretboard than on the piano keyboard.

I don't want to dwell too much on the Musical Alphabet right now. I prefer to skip ahead into the realm of **chords** rather than to dig too deeply into this area just yet. The 12 notes, to be sure, are the building blocks of chords (and scales), and you will learn more about this construction process later. But I think that it is far more rewarding to start making and using music right away. So we'll talk a little about the layout of the strings across the frets, describe how to tune the instrument, and then go on to chords.

The Layout of the Notes on the Guitar

Take your guitar. There are six strings (I hope) ranging from thinner to thicker. The **thinnest** string is the one closest to the floor, but it is called the **highest** string, because it has the highest pitch. This string is called the **1st** string.

The **thickest** string is the farthest one from the floor, but it is called the **lowest** string (guess why) because it has the lowest pitch. This is the **6th** string.

Both of these strings are tuned to E notes that happen to be 2 octaves apart.
(The guitar has a total range of about 3 1/2 octaves, while the piano has over 3 times that.)
Here's a diagram of the neck of the guitar nearest the **headstock**, where the tuning pegs are:

Here are the 6 strings (vertical lines) laid across the first 5 frets of the guitar (horizontal lines).

The strings are numbered 1 through 6 from right to left, from highest- to lowest-pitched.

The 6th, 5th and 4th strings are the **bass** strings, and the 3rd, 2nd and 1st are the **treble** strings.

The term "fret" actually refers to the metal bar, the wire itself, but we use it to mean the space *behind* the fret wire (toward the headstock).

So the 1st fret is the space between the 1st fret wire and the nut of the guitar (the crosspiece made of bone or plastic), and the 2nd fret is the space between the 1st and 2nd fret wires.

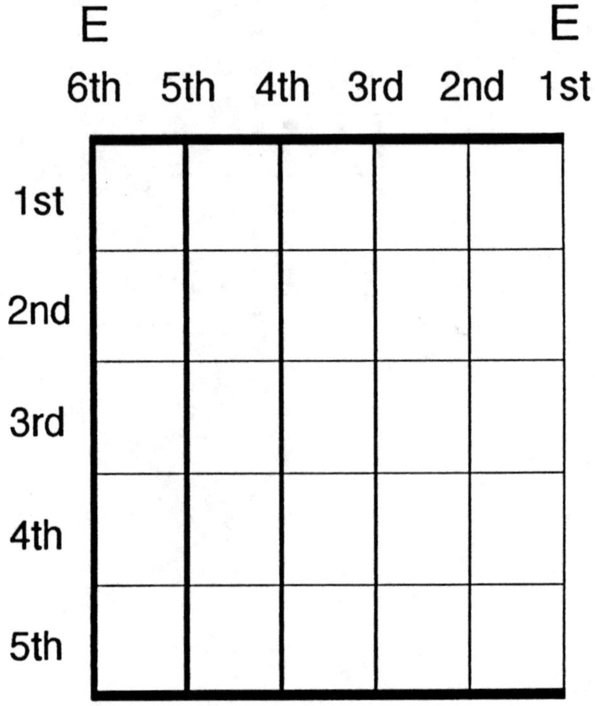

E E
6th 5th 4th 3rd 2nd 1st
1st
2nd
3rd
4th
5th

Take the low E string. Play the string open, with no left hand finger holding it down. Then hold down and play the string at the 1st fret, then at the 2nd, 3rd, 4th and on to the 12th fret, where there should be double dots on the fretboard. (There should also be single dots at the 3rd, 5th, 7th and 9th frets.)

You have just traveled one octave **up the neck**, running through all 12 notes in the musical alphabet, starting and ending with an E note. (The word "up" is used because pitch is *increasing* as you move from the 1st through 12th frets.)

Compare the sounds made by the 6th string played open and then played at the 12th fret. They are both E notes, played one octave apart. Same notes, different positions and pitches. *In fact, all 6 notes at the 12th fret are one octave above the notes found on the open strings.*

Tuning the Guitar

Probably the best way for a beginner to tune the guitar is to use an electronic tuner.
This device uses blinking lights or dials to make certain you've got the right pitch.
But, in the absence of such technology, here is a method called **Relative Tuning**.

We'll start with the 6th string.
Now, since a guitar string can be tuned to
an infinite number of slightly different pitches,
you really should have some way to know that
the 6th string is tuned approximately to E.

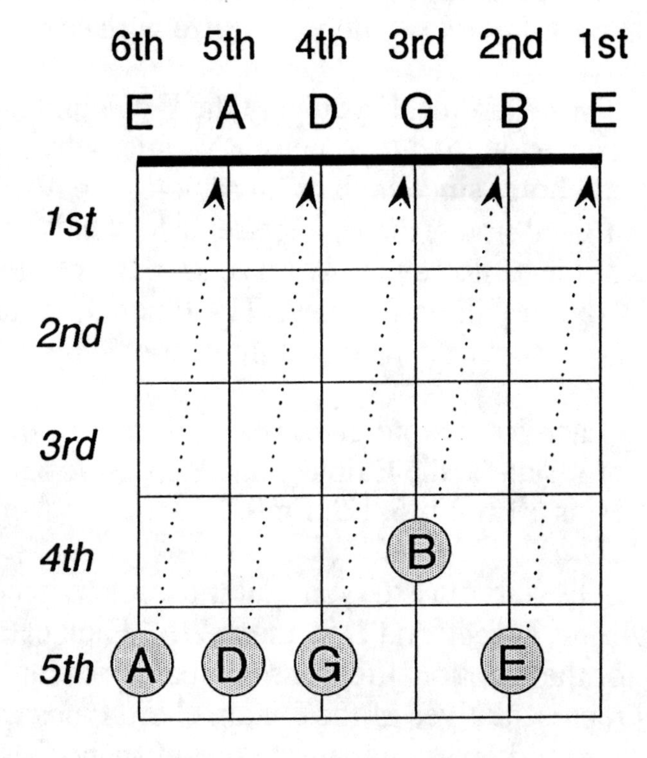

This can be done with a pitch pipe, piano
or tuning fork, but it doesn't *need* to be exact,
unless you are playing with someone else.

Now, play the **5th fret** of the 6th string.
This is an A note, which happens to be
the same note that the open 5th string
needs to be tuned to. In other words,
they need to be **in unison**.

(I've drawn arrows between all
the notes that need to be in unison
for a guitar to be in tune.)

Play the two "unison" notes at the same time. Do the 2 pitches sound close?
They'll either be right on, be off by a little or be off by a lot! Your ear can probably tell.
Tighten or loosen the 5th string until you get it to sound pretty close to the fretted 6th string.

When it gets so close that you can't quite tell whether it needs to be tightened or loosened,
you need to listen for a beating, pulsating sound, sort of an argument, between the two notes.
The closer you get, the slower the pulse. When all you get is a pure sound, you're there.

Well, this procedure is simply repeated from string to string, usually at the 5th fret.
Test the open 4th string against the fretted 5th string, the open 3rd against the fretted 4th.
Of course, every rule has an exception, and this rule is no exception. Here it is: Compare
the open 2nd string with the **4th fret** of the 3rd string. Think "2-3-4" (2nd / 3rd string,
4th fret). But then it's back to the 5th fret for the remaining pair of strings.

Remember that *the fretted note is the standard*, so the open string is adjusted to agree
with the fretted string. If you get confused, and change the *fretted string* by mistake,
you wind up in the Twilight Zone, and heaven help you. Actually, the worst thing
that could happen is that you'd need to start over. Or get an electronic tuner.

Chords and Chord Quality

So far we've only talked about the individual notes in the Musical Alphabet. All I really want to do at this stage of the game is to point out that notes are the basic building blocks of music. What is important to us at the moment is that notes can be grouped together into **chords**. A chord is just a musical structure that contains 3 or more notes that **harmonize** with each other and sound "good" when played together.

For example, if you play the E, G# and B notes together, you have made an E chord. Fair enough, but you might wonder why it is called an E chord instead of a G# chord or a B chord, since both of those notes are *also* in the chord. It is called the E chord because, of the 3 notes, the E note seems to stand out more and take charge of the chord, while the other 2 notes mainly serve to round out the sound. This is very subjective reasoning, but it will do for now. The E note is called the **Root Note** of the E chord, because it supports the chord like a root supports a plant. *Every chord has a Root Note.*

Each Root Note gives rise to dozens of different chords that are named after that note. For instance, the E note is the Root Note for such chords as E, Em, E7, Ema7, Em7, Esus2, Esus4, E6, Em6, E9, Em9, E13, and so forth. So, there are *bunches* of chords out there!

Let's start our study of guitar chords by recognizing that they fall into 3 main categories: **Major**, **Minor** and **Dominant 7th.** Each category has what is called its own **chord quality**, or the emotional response that a particular kind of chord evokes in the listener. Here are representatives of the 3 main chord types having the "E" Root Note. The numbers in the chord diagrams refer to the left-hand fingers: Index is 1st, Middle is 2nd, and so on:

The most common type of chord is the **Major chord**, which has a bright, happy sound. This is just a basic, generic, vanilla-flavored, garden variety, just-plain-old chord. When you write the symbol for a Major chord, you just use the letter name itself. So, for an E Major chord, you would simply write "E." It is assumed to be "Major."

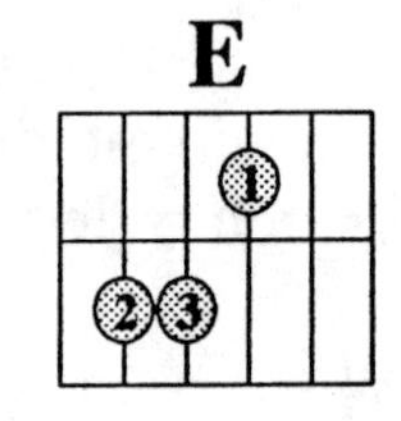

Then there is the **Minor chord**, which has a sad, blue or somber sound to it. I've also heard it described variously as the *war chord* and as the *scary chord.* The E Minor chord is written as "Em."

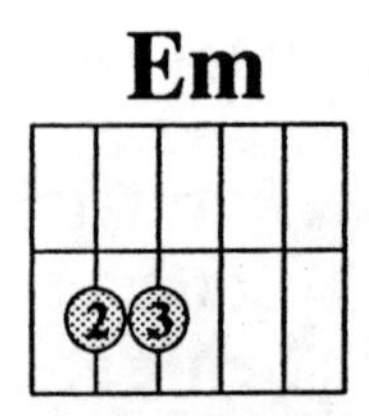

Finally, there is the **Dominant 7th chord**, also known simply as the **Seventh** chord, which has a restless, slightly dissonant sound that makes you want to keep moving on, to either a Major chord, a Minor chord, or even another Seventh chord. The E Dominant 7th chord is written as "E7."

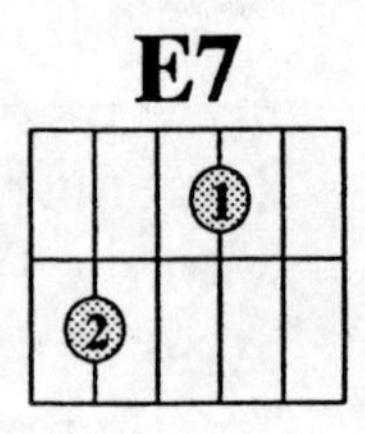

Strum the E, Em and E7 chords and listen for "happy," "sad" and "restless." Again, at this point, I'm not concerned whether you understand exactly how these chord types are constructed from the individual notes or why they sound the way they do. The main thing right now is to become accustomed to ***how they sound*** and to be able to distinguish between these different chord qualities with your ears.

Below, you'll find ***The Big Fifteen.*** Armed with these 15 chords and a **capo** (which we'll talk about later), you'll be able to get a leg up on most of the songs that you'll ever run into in the styles of folk, rock or country music. These are the most common (and easily played) chords on the guitar.

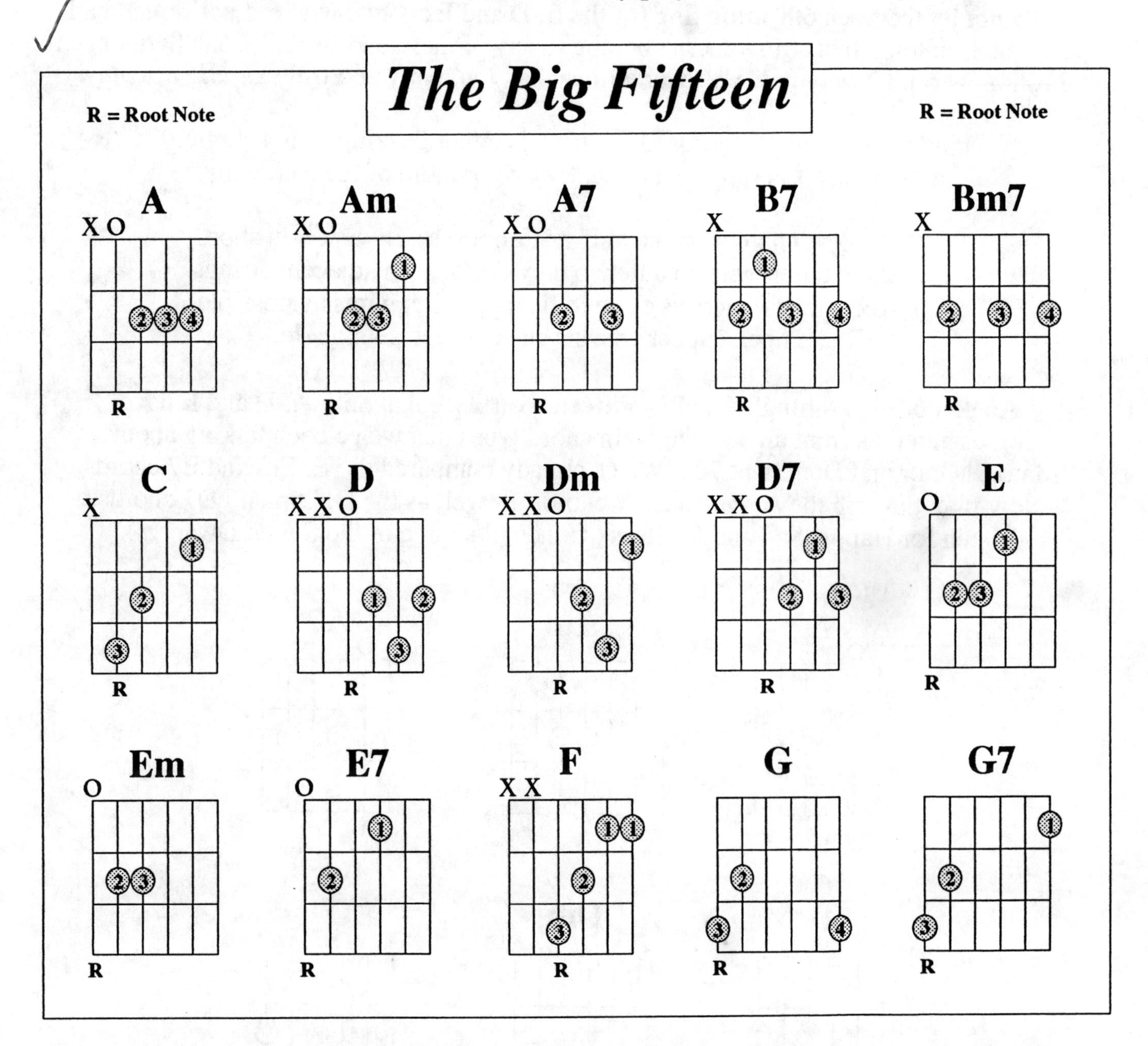

If a bass string has an "x" over it, try not to play it. If it has an "o" over it, ***try not to miss it.*** When you are strumming away, it's hard to avoid playing the open 6th string accidentally, so try to hook around your left-hand thumb so you can mute it. Just touch the string enough to deaden it, not so much that you actually play a note. It may be a stretch.

Now, the reason for avoiding or deadening certain bass strings is that, all things being equal, ***we like to hear the Root Note of a chord in the bass.*** For each chord, I've marked the string that bears the lowest-sounding Root Note:

The 6th string is allowed to ring for all the G and E chords.
The 5th string is allowed to ring for all the A, B and C chords.
The 4th string is allowed to ring for the D and F chords.

To be honest with you, it's ***okay*** to let the 6th string ring for the A and C chords, and it's ***okay*** to let the 5th string ring for the D and F chords; even though these notes are not Root Notes, at least they belong to the chords being played, and don't sound *bad.* But ***do not*** let the open 6th string ring for the B, D and F chords, where it *will* sound bad, since the E note on that string doesn't belong to any of these chords and won't harmonize. From now on, I'll only put "x's" over strings that you really and truly ***should not play.***

Play through all 15 chords. If a string is either buzzing or not ringing at all when it is supposed to be, try one or more of the following:

(1) Press down harder on the string. Callouses will visit you shortly.
(2) Stand the fingers up taller so they don't touch adjacent strings.
(3) Keep your fingers as close to the upper fret wires as possible. (Remember, "upper" means closer to the soundhole.)

As you browse through **The Big Fifteen**, you'll see that only A, D and E have representatives from all 3 of the main chord types that we've been talking about: Major, Minor and Dominant 7th. We've already compared the E, Em and E7 chords. Now play through the A, Am and A7 chords, as well as the D, Dm and D7 chords. Listen for Happy, Sad and Restless (sounds like three of the Seven Dwarves):

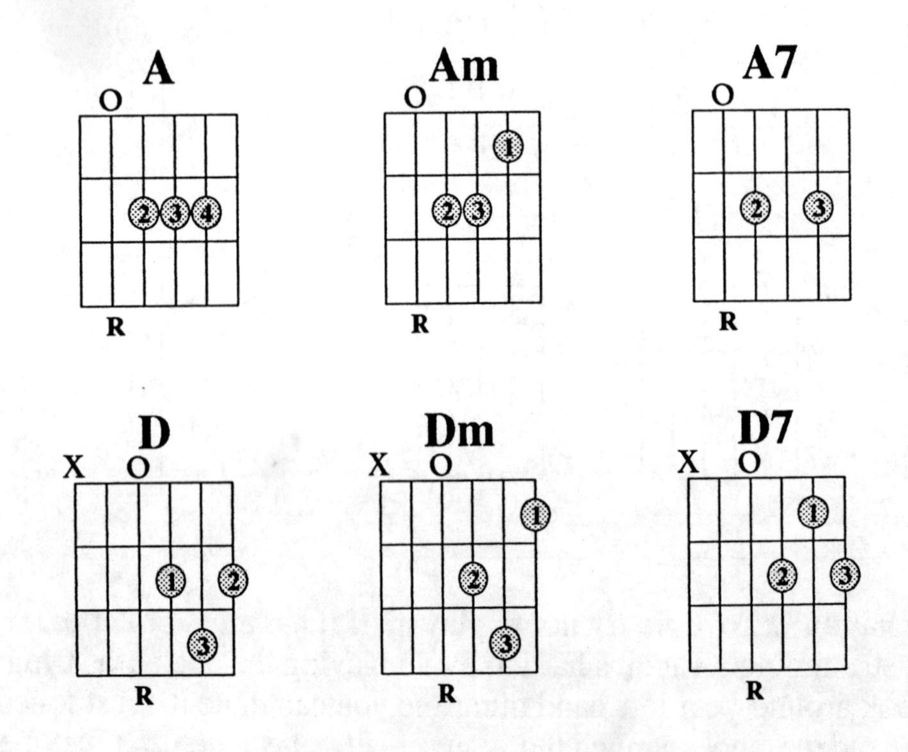

For letters other than A, D and E, not all 3 chord qualities are represented. For example, while there are only Major chord forms shown for both C and F, the Cm, C7 , Fm and F7 chords most certainly do exist (along with B and Gm). But I have omitted these from **The Big Fifteen** either because they are harder to finger, or because they don't show up all that commonly in practice.

Speaking of hard chords, this is as good a time as any to mention **barre chords**. In a barre chord, one finger, usually the 1st finger, holds down all six strings, *and that's just for starters.* As many as 3 extra fingers (all you've got left) may be required to form the rest of the chord. We'll avoid these for now.

You might have noticed that I gave you a Bm7 chord ("B-minor-seventh") instead of Bm. This chord can be seen as a **substitution** for Bm, which is one of those lousy barre chords. We'll talk about chord qualities other than the straight Major, Minor and Seventh in ***Volume Two.***

Regarding the other chords in **The Big Fifteen**, the A chord is a bit crowded, I know. There are various other ways to finger the chord, depending on the chords that come either before or after the A chord, and I'll give those as needed in the examples.

The B7 uses all 4 fingers, but the first 3 fingers look just like D7 moved over 2 strings. Then just add the 4th finger to the 1st string.

The C and G7 chords are a bit of a stretch at first; try angling your hand different ways.

Try making the G chord with the *3rd and 4th fingers* as shown, even though they hate this. These two fingers are rarely called upon in daily life to do much of anything, and they don't like being separated like this. But all it takes is persistence. I guarantee that, within several weeks, this G chord fingering will become your buddy. And it's easier to get to a C chord.

But the hardest chord on the page has got to be the F chord. The bad news is that you must hold the 1st finger ***flat*** over the 1st and 2nd strings while you ***arch*** the 2nd and 3rd fingers to avoid deadening strings; either they all want to arch or they all want to lie flat. And you mustn't let the 6th string ring open, so you either avoid it or deaden it with your thumb. If you like, there is a much easier way to finger an F, and you only lose one note: Just stand the 1st finger up on the 2nd string rather than laying it flat, and deaden the 1st string by touching is slightly with your 1st finger.

But if you want to try fingering it the right way, believe me, it's almost impossible to make a decent F chord without *flattening* the 1st joint of the 1st finger while the other 2 fingers *arch,* which demands a degree of finger independence that you may currently lack.

So, play through all these chords in different orders. See which ones you like the sound of most, and see if a chord evokes a certain feeling or reminds you of a particular song, melody or musical phrase.

Playing in Different Keys

Some chords sound good when they are played together, while others don't really seem to agree. For example, the C and G chords are quite comfortable with each other, while the C and E chords just sort of stare each other in the face, uncomprehending. Without getting too technical just yet, the chords that are the friendliest with each other, and would sound good together in a song, tend to belong to the *same musical* ***key***.

As you know, there are 12 different notes in the Musical Alphabet. It turns out that *each of those 12 notes has a key named after it.* So, for example, there is the Key of A, the Key of A-sharp (or B-flat), the Key of B, and so forth. Each key contains a number of chords that group together naturally, under the leadership of the chord that has the same name as the key. So, in the Key of A, the A chord is the boss, but there are *secondary* chords that are centered around the A chord that play supporting roles.

But confusion can arise because ***keys can overlap with each other to varying degrees,*** and may have certain numbers of chords in common. For example, in the Key of A, the 3 most important chords are A, D and E. In the Key of D, they are D, A and G. The 2 keys share 2 out of their 3 most important chords. In general, all chords take turns being primary chords in their own keys and secondary chords in some other keys.

So how do we organize this mess? First of all, let's restrict our discussion to just 5 keys, the Keys of **C, G, D, A** and **E.** These are the 5 most commonly used keys for the guitar, and we'll use the word "***C-A-G-E-D***" to refer to these keys, since that's what they spell!

Let's get to the specifics, using the ever-popular ***Key of G*** as an example. If I am playing a song in the Key of G, the G chord will take on a commanding role in the **chord progression**. It will most likely be the *first* and *last* chord, and the song will often return to the G chord, because it will radiate a sense of stability and repose, a feeling of being at *home.* In musical jargon, the G chord is called the **Tonic chord** in the Key of G.

Of course, the secondary chords will be used to make the song interesting, and it will sound good to visit these chords, like visiting friends and family, but eventually it always feels good to come *home.*

So what about these secondary chords? How do we identify them for the Key of G, or for any other key, for that matter? Well, there is a simple formula that we can apply. Lay out the 7 letters of the Musical Alphabet, starting with G, and number them 1 through 7:

G	**A**	**B**	**C**	**D**	**E**	**F**
1	2	3	4	5	6	7

Now, pick out the letters that correspond to the numbers **1, 4** and **5.**

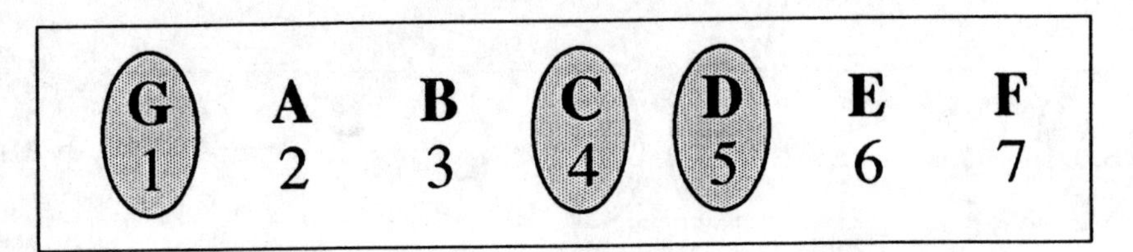

There. We have just identified the 3 most important ***Major*** chords in the Key of G. G is designated as the **1 chord** (Tonic), C is the **4 chord** and D is the **5 chord**.
As a general rule, the 1, 4 and 5 chords will be the main chords for any key.
(I'm supposed to be using Roman numerals, but I always thought they were confusing.)

Organizing chords within keys this way is called the 1 - 4 - 5 System.

The **5 chord** is a special case because it can have either a Major chord quality or a *Dominant 7th* chord quality. So in the Key of G, the **5 chord** can be either D or D7. We'll express a **5 chord** with a Dominant 7th chord quality as a **"5**7**" chord**.

Try playing the following chord progression, **1 - 4 - 5 - 1**, in the Key of G.
This is the most common chord progression in music:

G **C** X **D** **G**

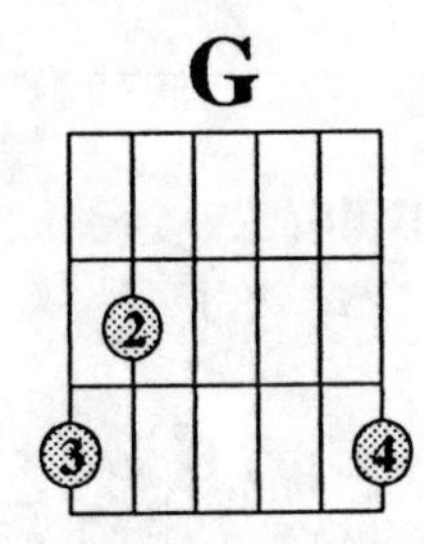

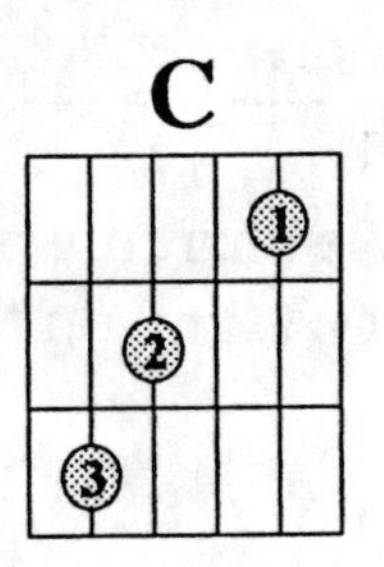

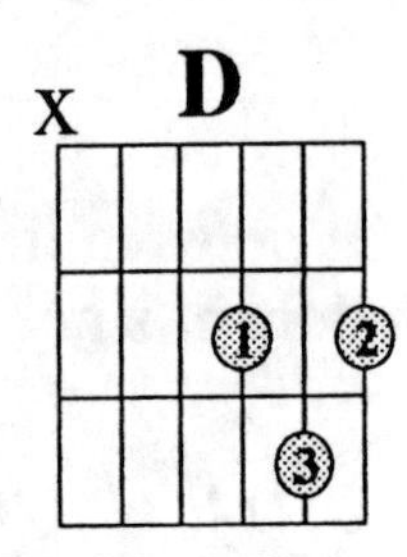

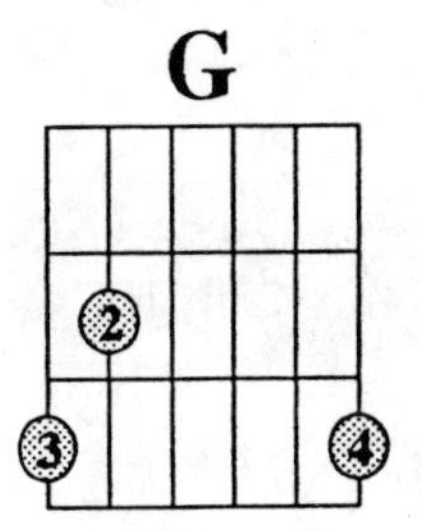

Now try it with a D7 chord (the **5**7) instead of a D. Sounds more restless and edgy.

G **C** X **D7** **G**

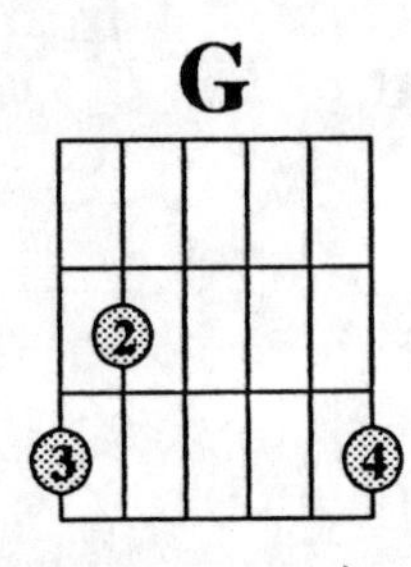

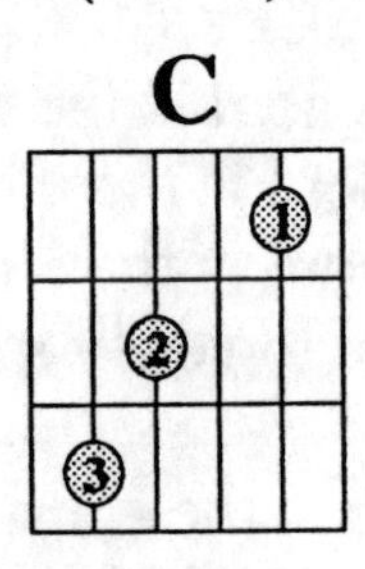

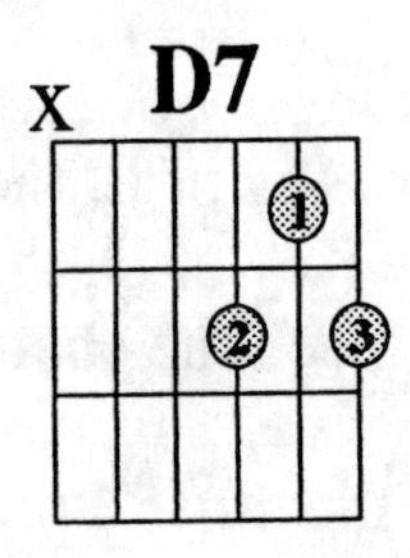

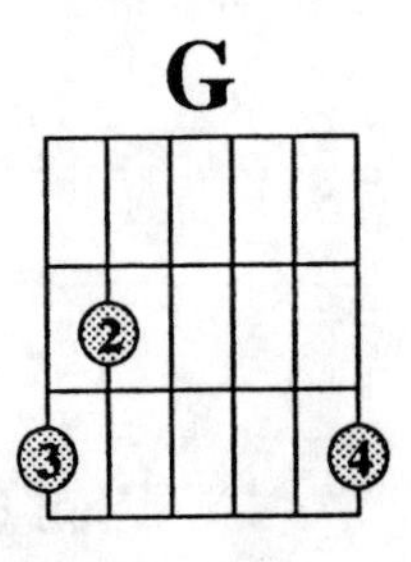

Now change around the order. Still satisfying, but not quite as *final* sounding as before.

G X **D** **C** **G**

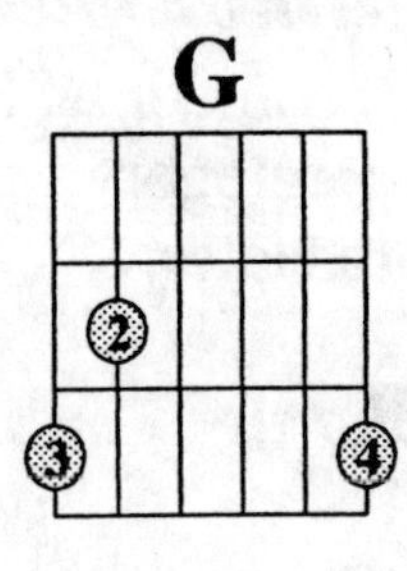

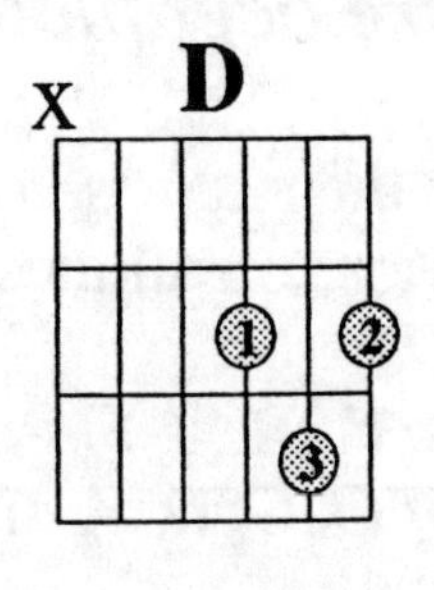

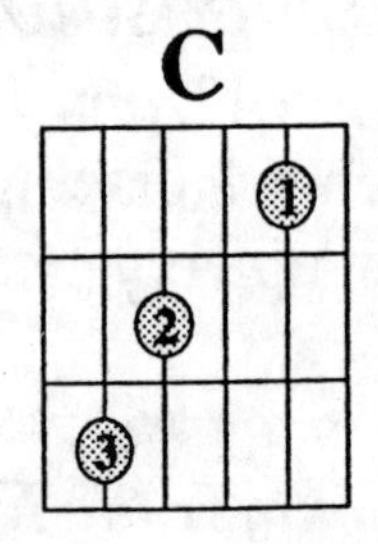

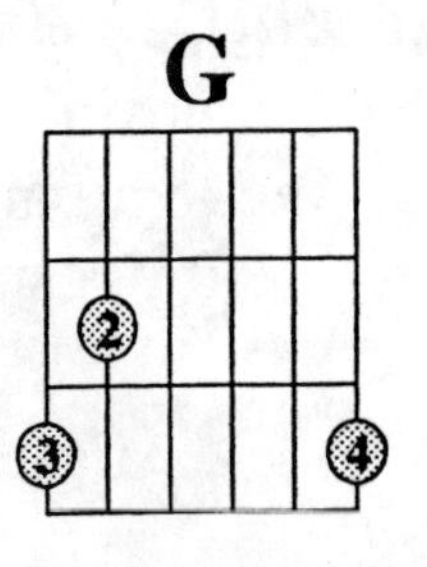

And here are the **1 - 4 - 5 chords** picked out for the 4 other *C-A-G-E-D* keys:

Key	1	2	3	4	5	6	7		Chords
Key of C:	**C** 1	**D** 2	**E** 3	**F** 4	**G** 5	**A** 6	**B** 7	→	**C, F** and **G** or **G7**
Key of D:	**D** 1	**E** 2	**F** 3	**G** 4	**A** 5	**B** 6	**C** 7	→	**D, G** and **A** or **A7**
Key of A:	**A** 1	**B** 2	**C** 3	**D** 4	**E** 5	**F** 6	**G** 7	→	**A, D** and **E** or **E7**
Key of E:	**E** 1	**F** 2	**G** 3	**A** 4	**B** 5	**C** 6	**D** 7	→	**E, A** and **B** or **B7**

(Some of the notes in the above chart are accidentals, but I've omitted them since we don't land on them anyway.)

Every Major chord occurs in 3 different keys.

In one key, it is the **Tonic chord**, where it is the boss; in another key, it functions as the **4 chord**; and in yet another key, it functions as the **5 chord**. Everybody takes turns.

So, in the Key of A, the A chord is the **1 chord.**
In the Key of E, the A chord is the **4 chord.**
In the Key of D, the A chord is the **5 chord.**
(Check the chart above to verify this.)

What about the other 4 positions in the Musical Alphabet, namely, the 2nd, 3rd, 6th and 7th? Well.....

*The 2nd, 3rd and 6th positions are occupied by **Minor** chords.*

The 7th position contains a ***Diminished*** chord, which behaves something like a Dominant 7th chord, placing it in the *restless-sounding* category. It doesn't show up very often. More on all these chords later.

On the next page, you will see the 1, 4, 5 and 57 chords laid out for the Keys of G, C, D, A and E.

Keys	1 chord	4 chord	5 chord	57 chord
KEY of G	G	C	X D	X D7
KEY of C	C	X F	G	G7
KEY of D	X D	G	O A	O A7
KEY of A	O A	X D	O E	O E7
KEY of E	O E	O A	B	X B7

Most guitarists play the B7 instead of the barred B chord.

Chord Families

These groups of chords that gather together within keys are also known as **Chord Families,** because the chords are all *related* to each other by virtue of being in the same key. And remember that Chord Families are going to overlap some, in much the same way that extended human families overlap.

You need to start getting used to playing the **1**, **4** and **5** (or **5_7**) **chords** for the *C-A-G-E-D* Chord Families. Here are the chords you'll need for an exercise. You've already seen them:

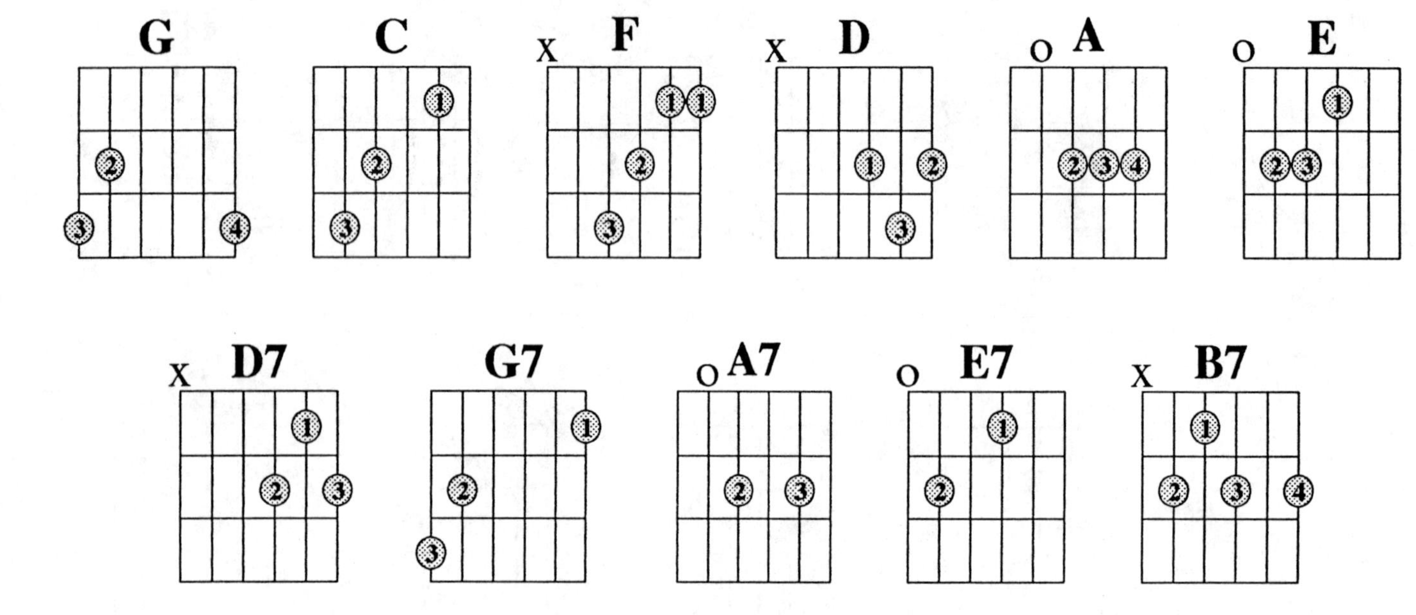

Play this simple chord progression: **1 - 4 - 1 - 5_7 - 1 - 4 - 5_7 - 1**,
as it translates into each of the five *C-A-G-E-D* keys below:

Key of G:	**G - C - G - D7 - G - C - D7 - G**
Key of C:	**C - F - C - G7 - C - F - G7 - C**
Key of D:	**D - G - D - A7 - D - G - A7 - D**
Key of A:	**A - D - A - E7 - A - D - E7 - A**
Key of E:	**E - A - E - B7 - E - A - B7 - E**

Try the first 3 keys again, this time using the ***Major*** chord quality for the **5 chord** instead of the Dominant 7th chord quality:

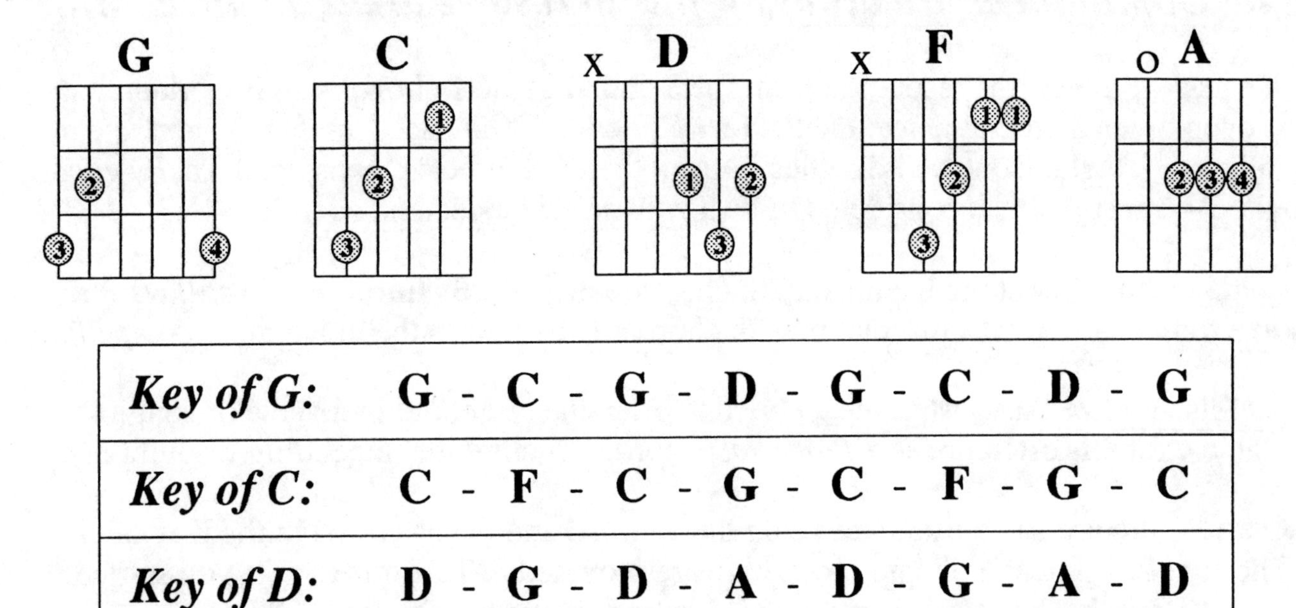

Key of G:	**G - C - G - D - G - C - D - G**
Key of C:	**C - F - C - G - C - F - G - C**
Key of D:	**D - G - D - A - D - G - A - D**

You don't quite get the same *edgy* feeling when all the chords are Major, do you? Whether you use the Major or the Dominant 7th chord quality for the **5 chord** is largely a matter of taste. Some people like the purity of using all Major chords, and some prefer the pushy aspect of the **5 chord** as a Dominant 7th. In fact, the word "pushy" is a fitting description of the Dominant 7th chord quality. We can call the **5_7 chord** a ***push chord.***

The 1 chord and the 5 chord

By now, you might be getting some sense of the *personality differences* that exist among the **1 chord**, the **4 chord** and the **5 chord**. For the next few pages, I would just like to focus on how the **1** and **5 chords** interact, since they play the most important roles in the forward propulsion of music. We'll return to the **4 chord** later.

As we've said before, the **1 chord**, also known as the **Tonic chord**, is the anchor chord, or home chord, in any key. It imparts a feeling of gravity, of a **Tonal Center**. It is the parental unit of the Chord Family---first, last and strongest.

But the **5 chord** has a certain kind of power of its own, especially when it is given a Dominant 7th chord quality. Incidentally, the **5 chord** is known as the **Dominant chord**, whether it has a 7th quality or not. Now, pay close attention to this next musical principle:

The Dominant chord always wants to "resolve" to the Tonic chord.

In music, the expression "to **resolve**" means "to come to rest," if only briefly. Now, we don't always *allow* the **5 chord** to resolve to the **1 chord**; nevertheless, the tension created by the **5 chord** makes us *want* to let it resolve to the **1 chord**.

Come to think of it, this principle is so universal that it bears repeating:

The Dominant chord always wants to resolve to the Tonic chord.

In classical music, the resolution from the **5 chord** to the **1 chord** is so important that it is even given a special name: the **Perfect Cadence.** "Cadence," in this context, means "a falling off," where one chord settles into another. ("Perfect" means, well, *really good.)* So the **5 - 1** resolution is considered to be a *downward* movement, as in "**5** - 4 - 3 - 2 - **1**."

Again, even without the Dominant 7th chord quality, the **5 chord** would *still* want to resolve to the 1 chord; it's just that the 7th chord quality makes the move more *compelling*.

Also realize that, just as the **1 chord** is often the last chord in a verse or song, the **5 chord** is often the *next-to-the-last* chord, signaling the impending resolution.

Okay. Here are some examples using the **1 chord** and the **57 chord** in the Key of G. The first few notes for singing each tune are provided in Tablature to get you started. (Refer back to the Introduction if you're not sure how to read Tablature.)

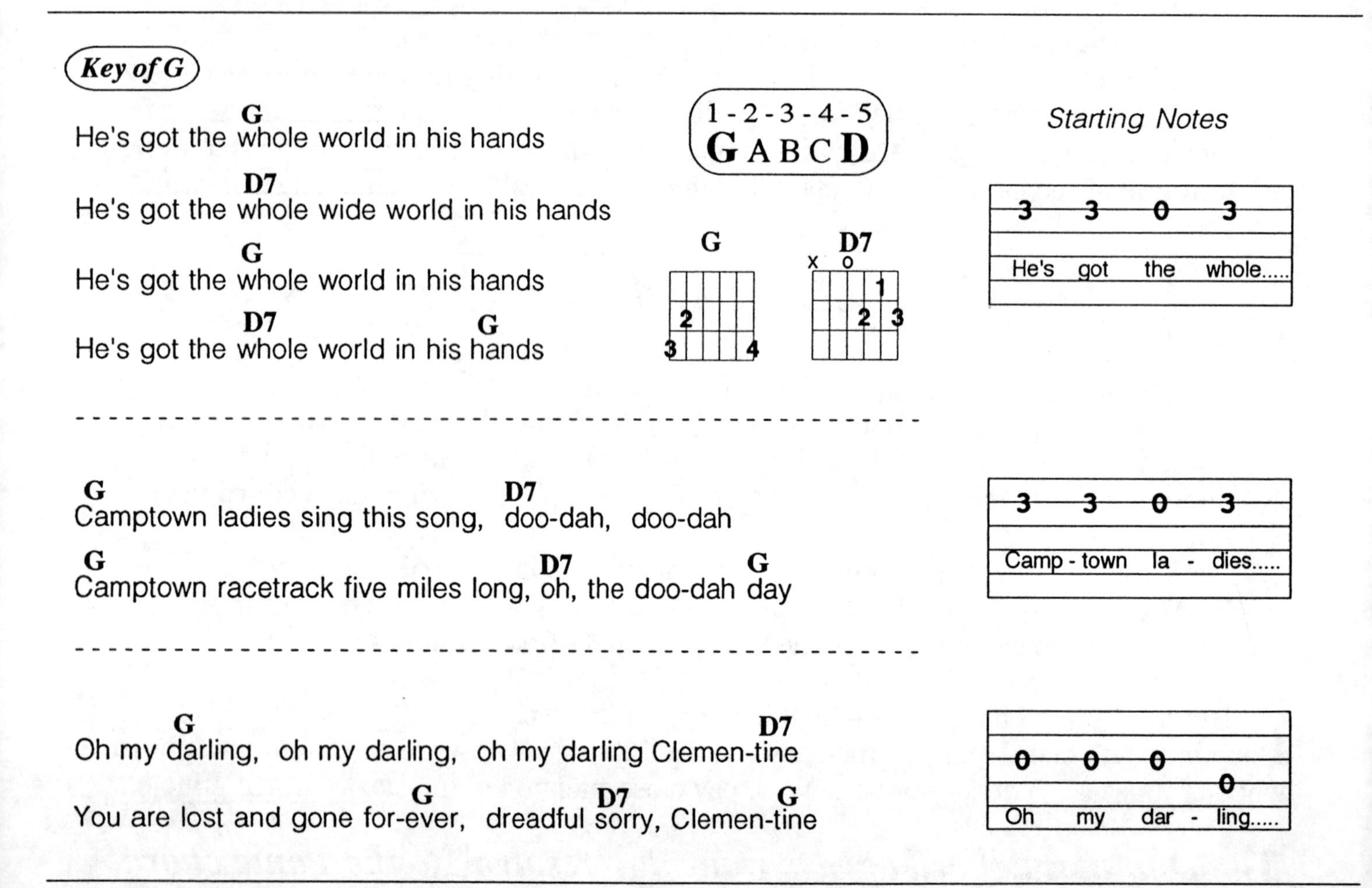

Try using the *Major* chord quality for the **5 chord** instead of the 7th. They both work fine.

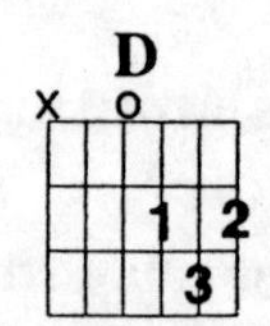

On this page, you'll see the same 3 songs **transposed** to the Keys of C and D.
Please play through these examples......Hearing is believing.

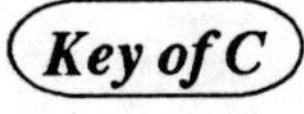

1 - 2 - 3 - 4 - 5
C D E F G

C
He's got the whole world in his hands

G7
He's got the whole wide world in his hands

C
He's got the whole world in his hands

G7 C
He's got the whole world in his hands

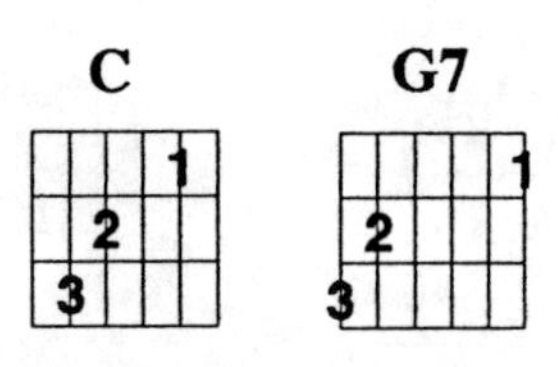

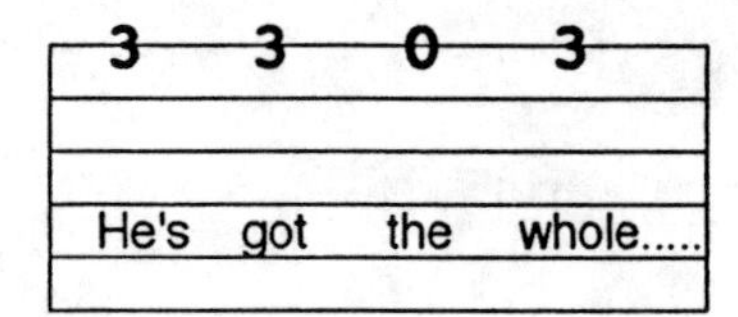

C G7
Camptown ladies sing this song, doo-dah, doo-dah

C G7 C
Camptown racetrack five miles long, oh, the doo-dah day

3 3 0 3
Camp - town la - dies.....

C G7
Oh my darling, oh my darling, oh my darling Clemen-tine

C G7 C
You are lost and gone for-ever, dreadful sorry, Clemen-tine

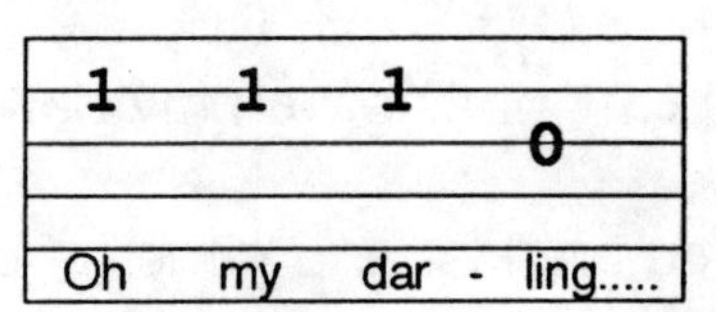

Key of D

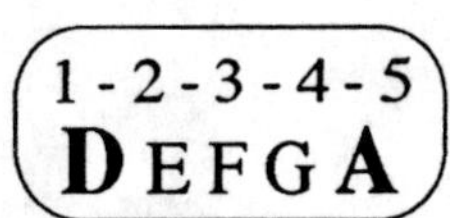

D
He's got the whole world in his hands

A7
He's got the whole wide world in his hands

D
He's got the whole world in his hands

A7 D
He's got the whole world in his hands

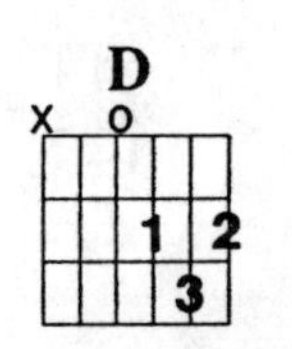

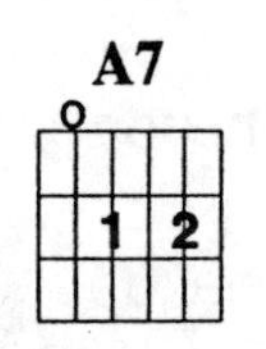

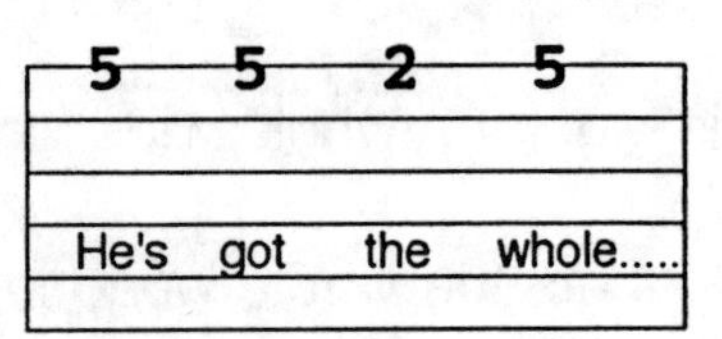

D A7
Camptown ladies sing this song, doo-dah, doo-dah

D A7 D
Camptown racetrack five miles long, oh, the doo-dah day

5 5 2 5
Camp - town la - dies.....

D A7
Oh my darling, oh my darling, oh my darling Clemen-tine

D A7 D
You are lost and gone for-ever, dreadful sorry, Clemen-tine

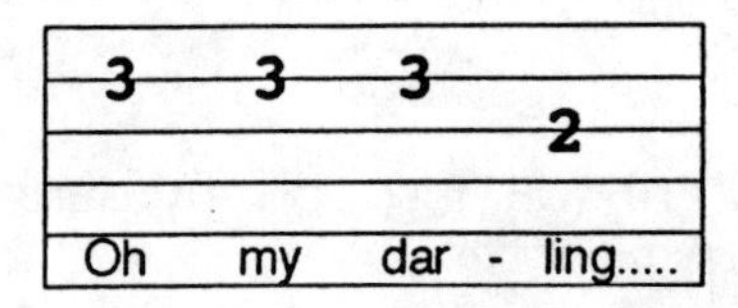

On this page, the same songs are transposed to the Keys of A and E.

Key of A

1 - 2 - 3 - 4 - 5
A B C D **E**

A
He's got the whole world in his hands

E7
He's got the whole wide world in his hands

A
He's got the whole world in his hands

E7 **A**
He's got the whole world in his hands

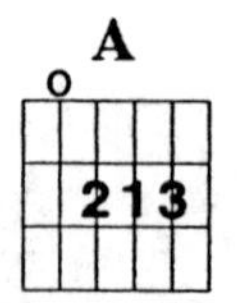

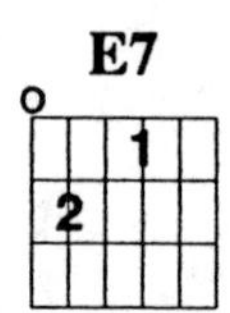

0 0 2 0
He's got the whole.....

- -

A **E7**
Camptown ladies sing this song, doo-dah, doo-dah

A **E7** **A**
Camptown racetrack five miles long, oh, the doo-dah day

0 0 2 0
Camp - town la - dies.....

- -

A **E7**
Oh my darling, oh my darling, oh my darling Clemen-tine

A **E7** **A**
You are lost and gone for-ever, dreadful sorry, Clemen-tine

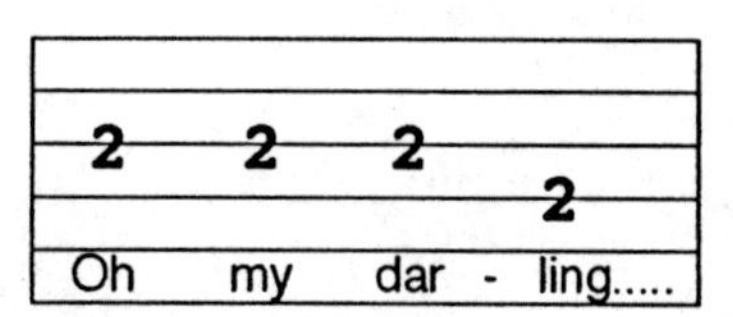

Key of E

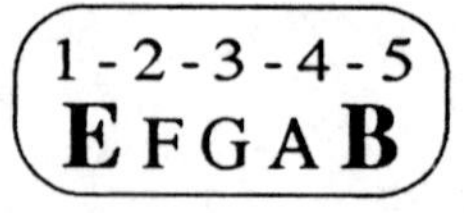

E
He's got the whole world in his hands

B7
He's got the whole wide world in his hands

E
He's got the whole world in his hands

B7 **E**
He's got the whole world in his hands

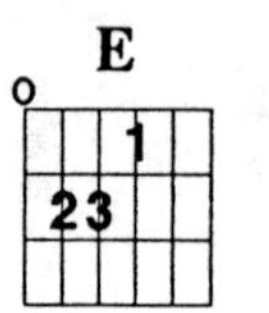

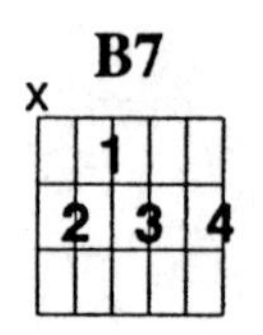

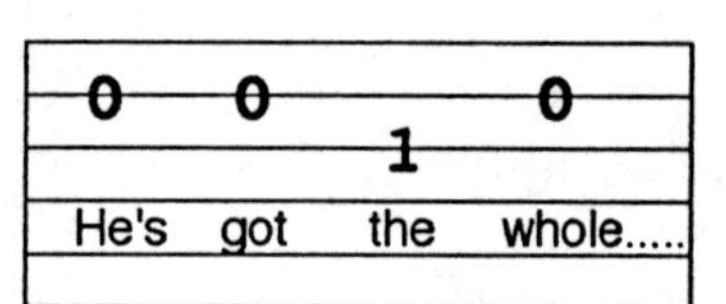

- -

E **B7**
Camptown ladies sing this song, doo-dah, doo-dah

E **B7** **E**
Camptown racetrack five miles long, oh, the doo-dah day

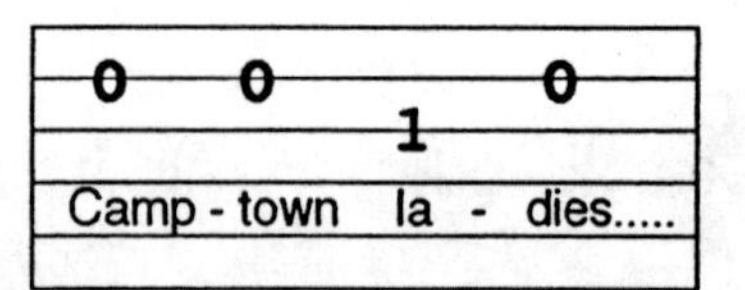

- -

E **B7**
Oh my darling, oh my darling, oh my darling Clemen-tine

E **B7** **E**
You are lost and gone for-ever, dreadful sorry, Clemen-tine

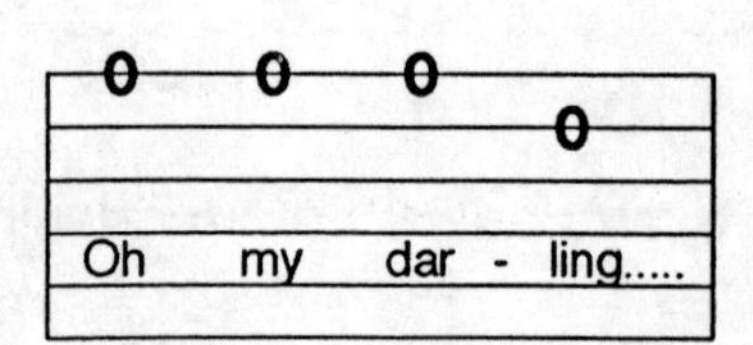

The 1 chord, the 4 chord and the 5 chord

So by now, you have (presumably) played through bunches of little musical phrases involving the **1 chord** and the **5_7 chord** in our favorite guitar keys, *C-A-G-E-D.* What do you think of those little *push* chords? I find it difficult to resist that Dominant-to-Tonic resolution, which leads me to declare a universal truth:

The music of western civilization is based on two main factors: (1) the harmonic tension created by the Dominant 7th chord; and (2) the resolution of that tension felt in the Tonic chord.

So where does the **4 chord** fit into all of this? Well, the **4 chord**, which is known as the **Subdominant chord**, is a friendly sort of chord with regard to the **1 chord**. It seems to me that we can travel back and forth between these two chords all day without any sense of urgency or particular direction. It feels like a stress-free exchange, a cordial dialogue. That is, until the **5 chord** comes along and says, "Let's get moving, people."

I don't mean to paint the Dominant chord as a bad boy. We truly need the propulsion that is provided by the Dominant chord to keep us moving through a musical composition.

So, the ***1 chord*** *is stable, the* ***4 chord*** *is friendly and the* ***5 chord*** *is pushy.* These 3 personality types function together to tell interesting musical stories. It's amazing how many folk, rock and country songs have been written using just these three chords.

This might be a good time for a little side trip. How would it sound if we started off playing in one Chord Family and then abruptly switched to a different Chord Family in midstream? Let's hear some examples:

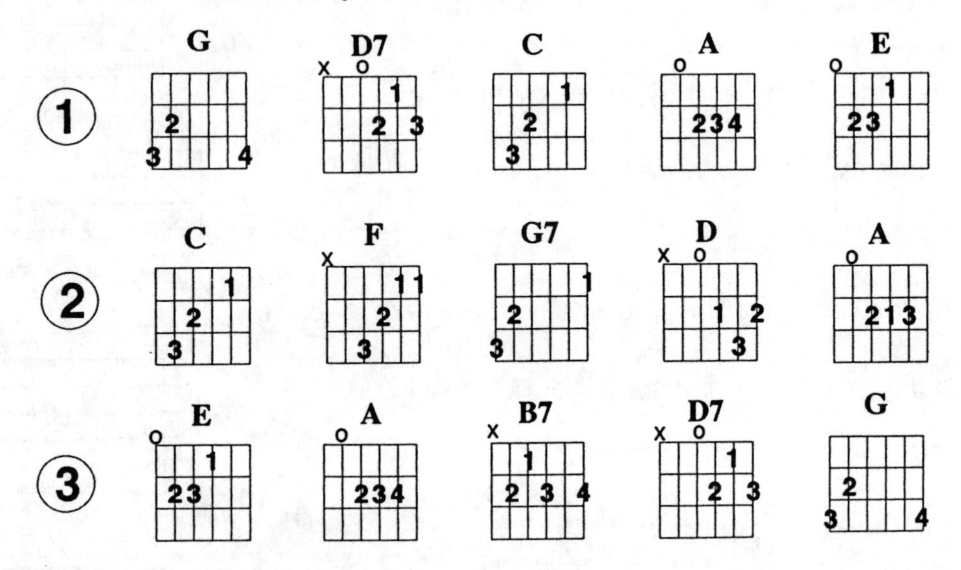

In each example, the key change came after the 3rd chord, and I'll bet that your ear detected the aberration. Already you can discern a musical tragedy! To me, it just seems as if we took a very wrong turn and wound up somewhere we hadn't intended to go.

Let's return to the harmonious world of 1 - 4 - 5. Here are some more snippets of songs, presented in the Key of G, that show the interplay among the G, C and D7 chords.

Key of G

1 - 2 - 3 - 4 - 5
G A B **C D**

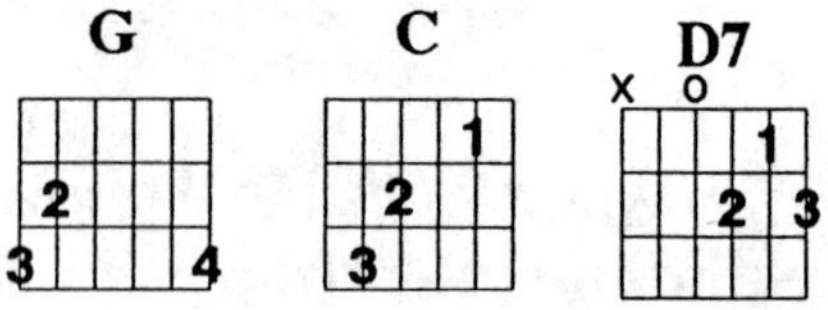

G C D7

Starting Notes

G C
Oh, give me a home where the buffalo roam
G D7
Where the deer and the antelope play
G C
Where seldom is heard a dis-couraging word
G D7 G
And the skies are not cloudy all day

Oh, give me.....

- -

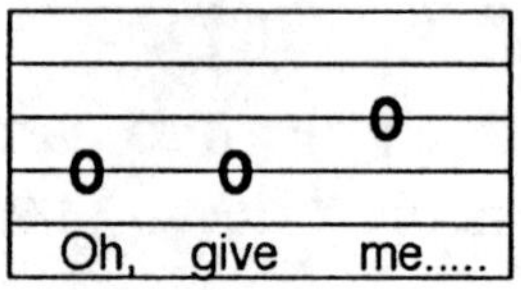

G C G D7
My bonnie lies over the ocean, my bonnie lies over the sea
G C G C D7 G
My bonnie lies over the ocean, oh, bring back my bonnie to me

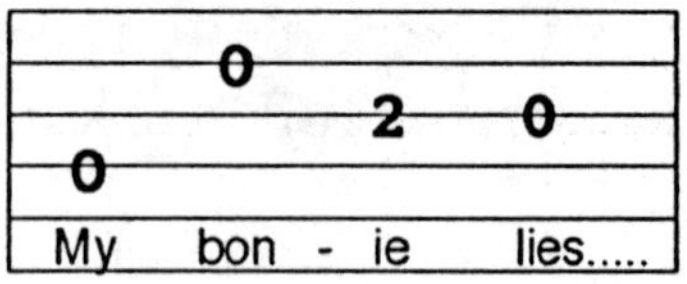

My bon - ie lies.....

- -

G C G
Jingle bells, jingle bells, jingle all the way
C G D7
Oh, what fun it is to ride in a one-horse open sleigh, hey!
G C G
Jingle bells, jingle bells, jingle all the way
C G D7 G
Oh, what fun it is to ride in a one-horse open sleigh

Jing - le bells.....

- -

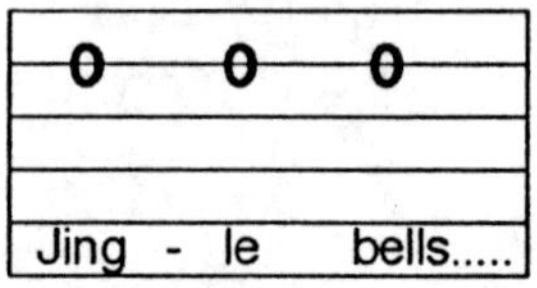

G C G
Will the circle be unbroken, by and by, Lord, by and by
D7 G
There's a better home awaiting in the sky, Lord, in the sky

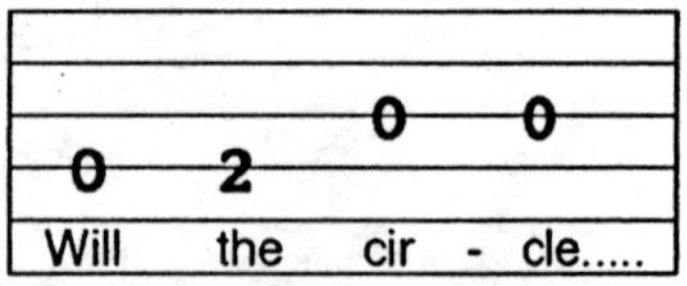

Will the cir - cle.....

- -

G C G D7
Amazing grace, how sweet the sound, that saved a wretch like me
G C G D7 G
I once was lost, but now I'm found, was blind, but now I see.

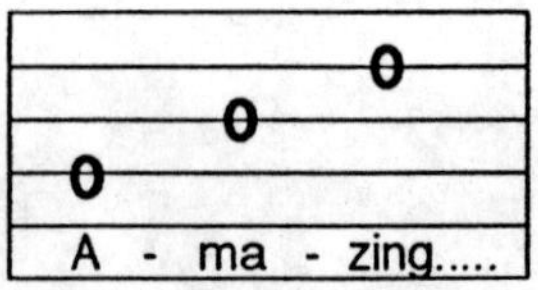

A - ma - zing.....

- -

G
Well, I wish I was in the land of cotton
C
Old times there are not forgotten
G D7 G
Look a-way, look away, look a-way, Dixie land

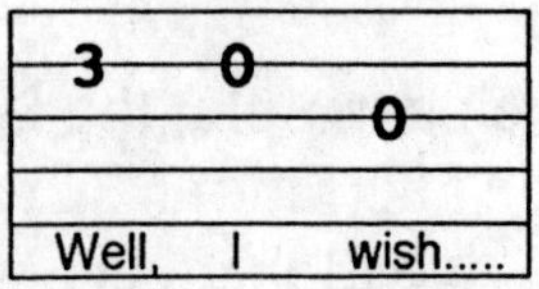

Well, I wish.....

Next, the Keys of C and D:

Key of C

1 - 2 - 3 - 4 - 5
C D E **F G**

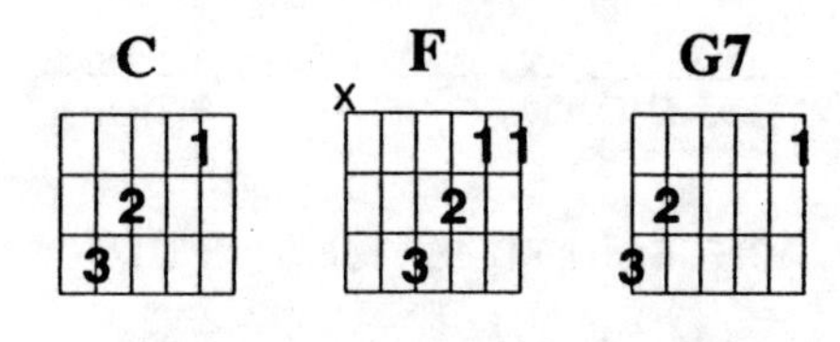

C F
Oh, give me a home where the buffalo roam

C G7
Where the deer and the antelope play

C F
Where seldom is heard a dis-couraging word

C G7 C
And the skies are not cloudy all day

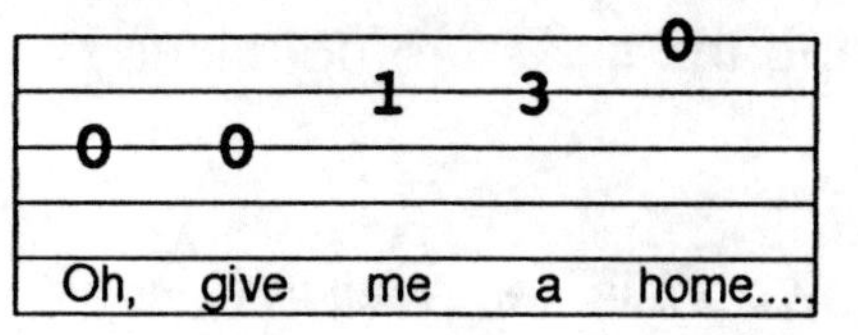

- -

C F C G7
My bonnie lies over the ocean, my bonnie lies over the sea

C F C F G7 C
My bonnie lies over the ocean, oh, bring back my bonnie to me

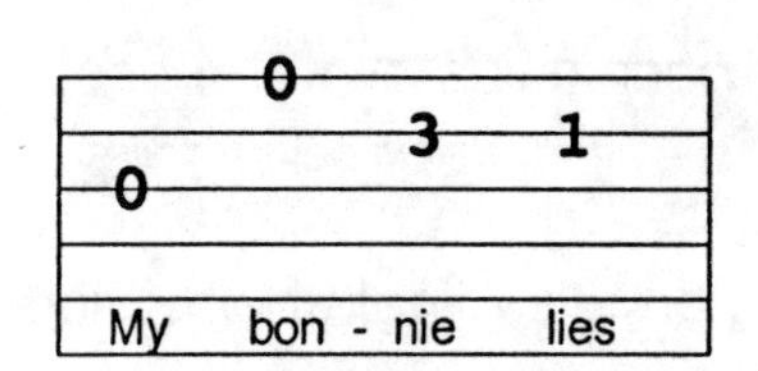

- -

C F C
Jingle bells, jingle bells, jingle all the way

F C G7
Oh, what fun it is to ride in a one-horse open sleigh, hey!

C F C
Jingle bells, jingle bells, jingle all the way

F C G7 C
Oh, what fun it is to ride in a one-horse open sleigh

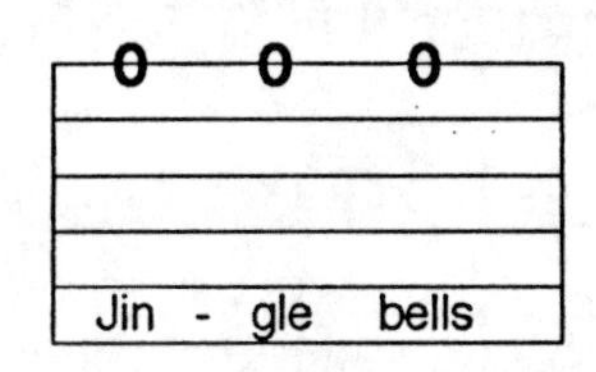

Key of D

1 - 2 - 3 - 4 - 5
D E F **G A**

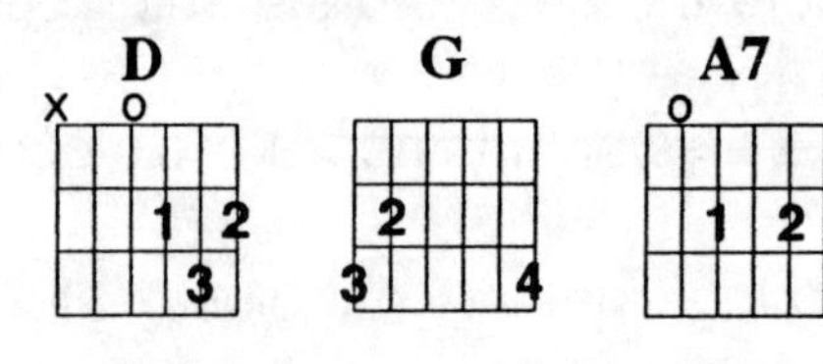

D G
Oh, give me a home where the buffalo roam

D A7
Where the deer and the antelope play

D G
Where seldom is heard a dis-couraging word

D A7 D
And the skies are not cloudy all day

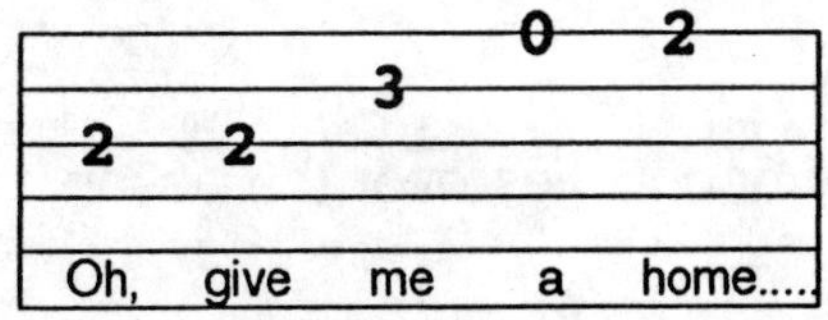

- -

D G D A7
My bonnie lies over the ocean, my bonnie lies over the sea

D G D G A7 D
My bonnie lies over the ocean, oh, bring back my bonnie to me

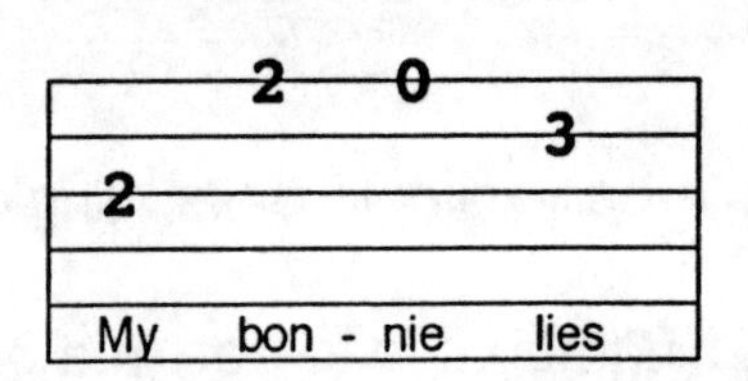

- -

D G D
Jingle bells, jingle bells, jingle all the way

G D A7
Oh, what fun it is to ride in a one-horse open sleigh, hey!

D G D
Jingle bells, jingle bells, jingle all the way

G D A7 D
Oh, what fun it is to ride in a one-horse open sleigh

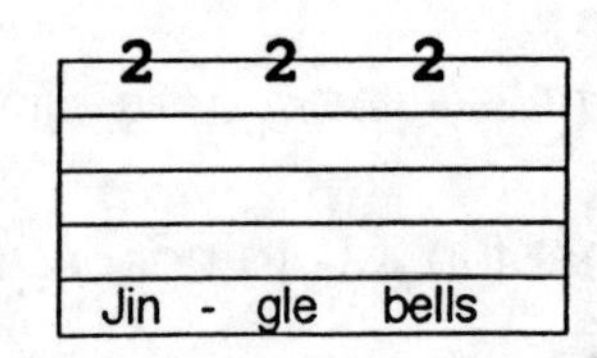

And the Keys of A and E:

Key of A

1 - 2 - 3 - 4 - 5
A B C D E

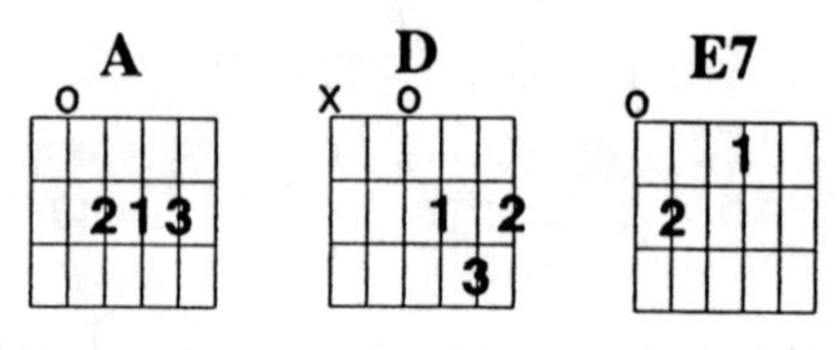


```
   A                                 D
Oh, give me a home where the buffalo roam
               A                      E7
Where the deer and the antelope play
          A                     D
Where seldom is heard a dis-couraging word
          A              E7     A
And the skies are not cloudy all day
----------------------------------------

   A          D       A                                E7
My bonnie lies over the ocean,  my bonnie lies over the sea
   A          D       A         D              E7        A
My bonnie lies over the ocean,  oh, bring back my bonnie to me
--------------------------------------------------------

A                               D     A
Jingle bells,  jingle bells,  jingle all the way
D                  A              E7
Oh, what fun it is to ride in a one-horse open sleigh, hey!
A                               D     A
Jingle bells,  jingle bells,  jingle all the way
D                  A             E7                 A
Oh, what fun it is to ride in a one-horse open sleigh
```

Oh, give me a home....

My bon - nie lies

Jin - gle bells

Key of E

1 - 2 - 3 - 4 - 5
E F G A B

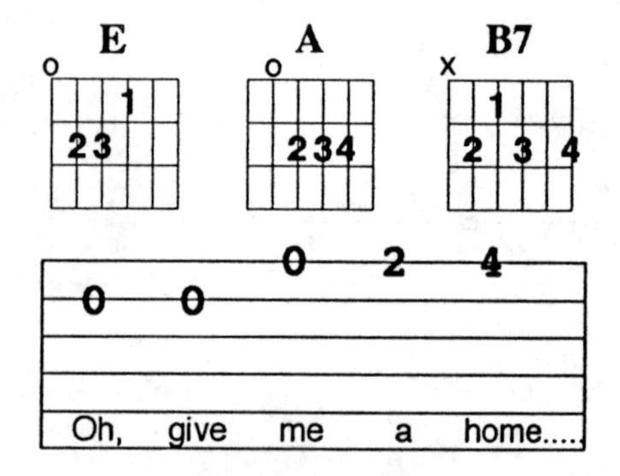


```
   E                                 A
Oh, give me a home where the buffalo roam
               E                      B7
Where the deer and the antelope play
          E                     A
Where seldom is heard a dis-couraging word
          E              B7     E
And the skies are not cloudy all day
----------------------------------------

   E          A       E                                B7
My bonnie lies over the ocean,  my bonnie lies over the sea
   E          A       E         A              B7        E
My bonnie lies over the ocean,  oh, bring back my bonnie to me
--------------------------------------------------------

E                               A     E
Jingle bells,  jingle bells,  jingle all the way
A                  E              B7
Oh, what fun it is to ride in a one-horse open sleigh, hey!
E                               A     E
Jingle bells,  jingle bells,  jingle all the way
A                  E             B7                 E
Oh, what fun it is to ride in a one-horse open sleigh
```

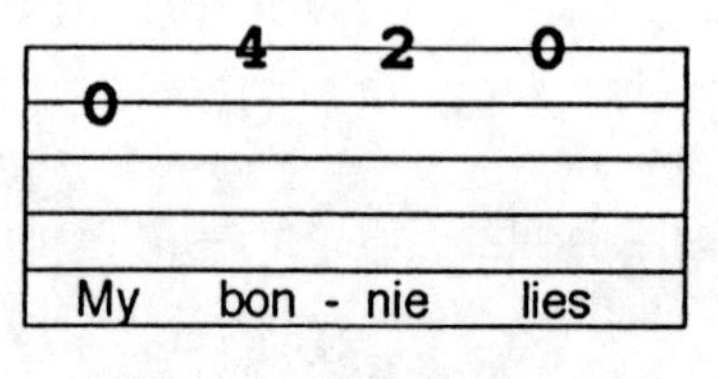

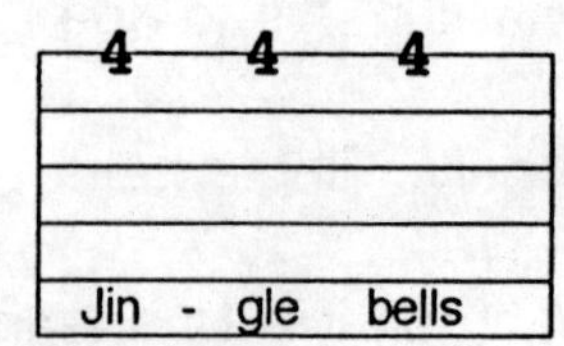

In **"Silent Night,"** the **5₇ chord** shows up *before* the **4 chord**, right in the 1st line. Next comes a friendly exchange between the **1 chord** and **4 chord** in the 2nd line, and then more *push* chords in the last line. ***Play and sing through each version.*** The Chord Families appear in alphabetical order (they get "higher" as you go).

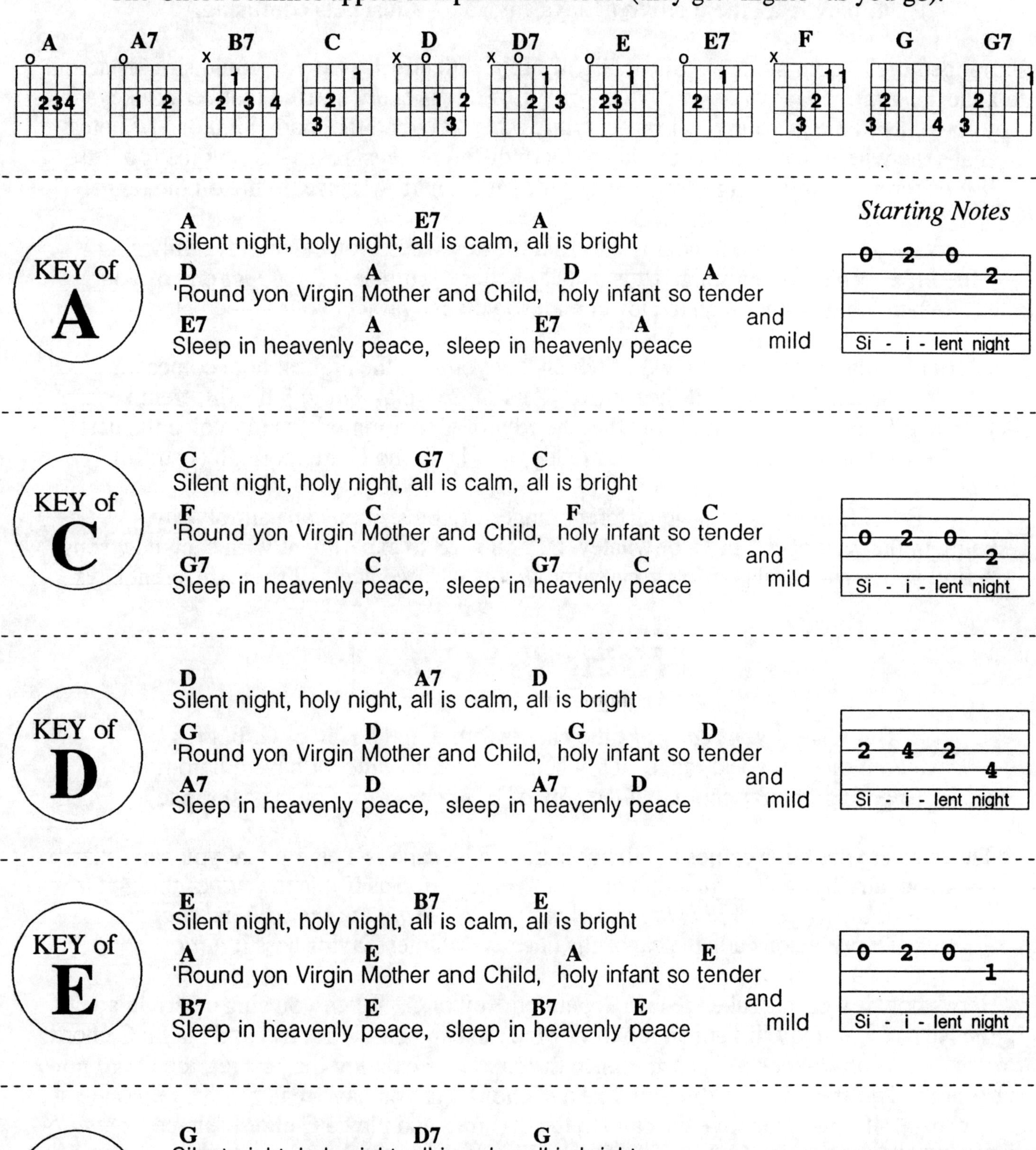

G   D7   G
Silent night, holy night, all is calm, all is bright
C   G   C   G
'Round yon Virgin Mother and Child, holy infant so tender and mild
D7   G   D7   G
Sleep in heavenly peace, sleep in heavenly peace

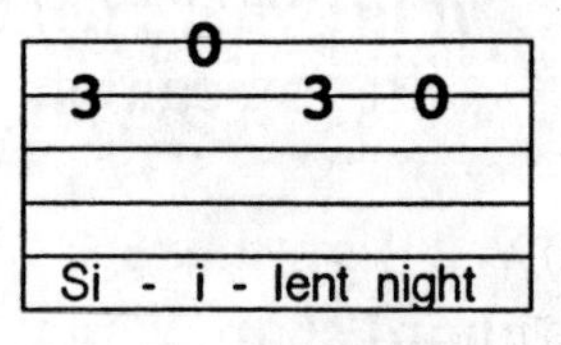

Choosing the Right Key

I suppose the one issue we haven't addressed yet is why we need to learn to play in all these different keys anyway---it just gets confusing.

I arranged the five versions of "Silent Night" alphabetically so that you could sing, hear and feel the song moving *from lower to higher keys*. You probably noticed that certain keys felt more comfortable in your vocal range, while other keys had too many high or low notes. That's the whole reason for bothering to learn different keys. Everyone's voice is a little bit different --- high range, low range, wide range, narrow range, home on the range.

Specifically, your quest should be to find the key where you can comfortably sing the ***highest note*** in the song. (It is usually better to sing near the upper end of your vocal range rather than the lower end, so you can project your voice better.)

For "Silent Night," regardless of which key you use, the highest note comes on the first syllable of the word "heavenly." As I myself play through the different keys, with my deeper vocal range, I find that the Key of C accommodates my voice the best. The Key of A is too low (I sound muddy) and D, E and G are too high (I strain).

But different songs have different ranges of notes. You can't simply say, "I sing in the Key of A," or C, or whatever. You need to experiment with each new song to find your own vocal comfort zone. And *that* is why we need all these different keys.

Using the Capo

But what if you *really like* the chords found in the Key of G, but it's way out of your vocal range? Or what if you *really hate,* or have a hard time fingering, the B7 chord, but the Key of E is perfect for your vocal range?

That's where the ***capo*** comes in mighty handy. The capo is a clamp that you can set at just about any fret on the guitar. You then treat the capo as if it is the ***nut*** of the guitar, *thus allowing you to play in several higher keys using the same* ***chord shapes.*** Doc Watson calls the capo "the cheater." James Taylor uses it *a lot.*

Here's how it works: Take the fairly common Key of C. When you sing a certain song in the Key of C, it may just sound too low. Slap the capo on the 1st fret and play a C chord, *except that it's no longer a C chord.* Since the capo is occupying the 1st fret, the chord now starts at the *2nd* fret. It may still look like a C chord, but you have really moved up one key, to C-***sharp*** . If you then move the capo to the 2nd fret, and play a C chord "shape," *actually* it is (what's next in the Alphabet?) a D chord, even though it doesn't *look* like a D chord. So you can play in higher and higher keys without changing the chord shapes you like.

We'll get back to this issue later. For now, if you need a higher key but don't want to change chord shapes, just put the capo where you need it and don't worry about what key it *really* is.

Quiz Time for the 1 - 4 - 5's

If you ever find that you need to do a lot of key-changing to accommodate other singers or musicians, you might find it helpful to analyze the songs you are playing in terms of the **1 - 4 - 5 chord** structure, rather than memorizing chord progressions in specific keys.

By now, your ear is probably doing a fairly good job of distinguishing among the three Major chord family members, regardless of which key you are playing in. What remains to be done is to commit to memory:

*The 1, 4 and **5 chords** for each of the five C-A-G-E-D chord families.*

Time for a little exercise. Down below, instead of making it easy and giving you 5 different versions (one for each key) for the 3 songs we'll look at, I've given you ***one version*** with the numbers "1," "4" and "5" over the appropriate lyrics.

(It's like in algebra, where they give you a general formula using letters, like "y = ax + b," and then you fill in the actual numbers to calculate a numerical answer. Well, here it's just reversed: I give you the *numbers* and you figure out the corresponding *letters.)*

There's a chart of the **1 - 4 - 5's** to help out, and you can use either the **5** or the **5$_7$ chord.** Try this exercise two different ways: First, play one song in all 5 keys before going on to the next song; then, pick one key and play all 3 songs in that key before going on to the next key.

On your own, try to find the Starting Notes for singing each song in each key. If this is hard to do, check out the method for finding Starting Notes given on the next page.

```
1      4    5              1      4     5
Bam  - ba,  Bamba,         Bam  - ba,  Bamba

1                        5      1               5
Yankee Doodle went to town,   riding on a pon-y
1                   4               5           1
Stuck a feather in his hat and called it maca-roni

         1                     5            1                    4
Should auld acquaintance be forgot and never brought to mind
         1                     5           4         5           1
Should auld acquaintance be forgot, and days of Auld Lang Syne
```

1	4	5
G	C	D
C	F	G
D	G	A
A	D	E
E	A	B7

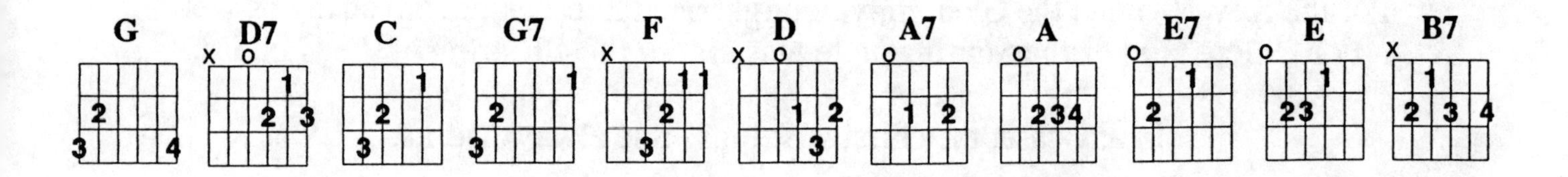

Skip It

Finding the Starting Note

Not everyone can sense exactly what note to start singing some song on.
One way to do it is to play through the chord progression and *just jump in,*
grab a note with your voice, and see if you can stumble onto the melody that way.
I know, this sounds like a hit-or-miss kind of operation that *might* work for a person
who has already developed an "ear for music." Since you are probably still working on
your musical ear, here is a way to track down the Starting Note by a process of elimination.

Identify the **1 chord**. Again, it'll probably be the first, last and most common chord.

*The Starting Note for singing a song can be found
on either the 1st, 2nd, 3rd or 4th strings of the 1 chord.*

This amounts to just simple trial and error. Play one of the notes in the chord, by itself.
Try to match the note with your voice, then try to sing the song starting on that note
while playing through the chord progression. If it sounds good, you have found
the Starting Note. If it doesn't, pick another string and try again.
One of these 4 notes must be the Starting Note.

Take "Silent Night" in the Key of D and finger a D chord, which is the **1 chord**.
Play the 1st string, match it with your voice and sing the song with the chords.
Does it work? No way, sounds awful. It's not even close.

Try the 2nd string. That's not it either. Again, it's not even a *question* of being wrong.
Try the 3rd string. Aha! That's the one. Now you can get on with the rest of the song.

Try this approach with each of the other keys.
Different songs will have different Starting Notes.
Here are the right Starting Notes for "Silent Night" in our 5 keys.
Hold down the tonic chords and play the strings indicated:

Key of G --- G chord --- 4th string.
Key of C --- C chord --- 3rd string.
Key of D --- D chord --- 3rd string.
Key of A --- A chord --- 1st string.
Key of E --- E chord --- 2nd string.

By the way, the "First 4 Strings" rule can be modified a little. It turns out
that for the Keys of D, C, A and E, you only need to check the first *3 strings.*
For the Key of G and the G chord, you might need to check the 4th string as well.
For "Silent Night," the Starting Note *was indeed* the 4th string in the G chord.

In any case, the "First 4 Strings" rule always works.

Adding the Minor Chords

Next we come to the Minor chords (the sad ones). Minor chords are not as prevalent as Major chords, but they certainly help us to express a broader range of moods and emotions.

As I said before, Minor chords occupy the ***2nd, 3rd*** and ***6th*** positions in the Musical Alphabet for whatever key you are playing in, while Major chords occupy the **1st**, **4th** and **5th** positions.

The **6m chord** is the most important Minor chord in the Chord Family, and is designated the **Relative Minor**. This means that the **6m chord** is the Minor chord that is most closely related to the Tonic chord, and may even substitute for the Tonic chord in some instances. The **2m chord** is a close second in popularity, and the **3m chord** is a distant third.

To keep matters simple for now, we'll look at examples in the Keys of G and C only. So here are the **2m, 3m** and **6m chords** presented along with the Major chords for two keys. Again, we'll use the Bm7 instead of the Bm chord in order to avoid the mean old barre chord. When you play the **1 - 2m - 3m - 4 - 5 - 6m chords** in order, it makes a nice little progression.

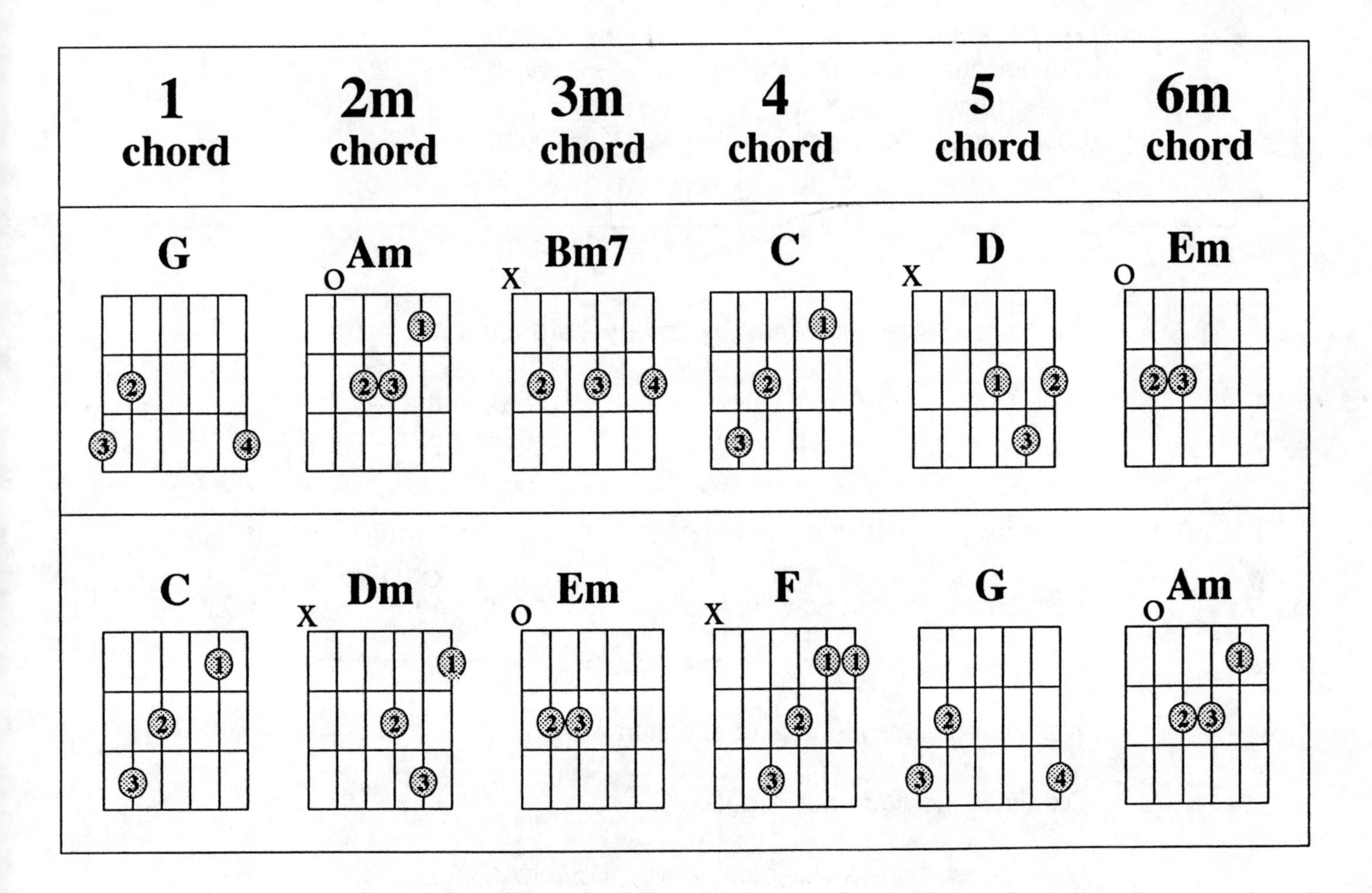

Let's get right to some examples. In these first 2 songs, which we've used before, we're just going to substitute Minor Chords into sections of the songs that had been occupied by Major chords in the previous examples.

The 3rd example, "Dixie," has been modified to include all 3 Minor chords in sections where there were only Major chords before. Sounds better, I think.

Leave out the Minor chords the first time through, then go back and put them in.

KEY of G

```
              G                          C                       G
Will the circle be unbroken,  by and by, Lord, by and by

                                 Em                G          D7      G
There's a better home a-waiting in the sky, Lord, in the sky
- - - - - - - - - - - - - - - - - - - - - - - - - - - - - - - - - - - - - -

  G                        C            G                                  D7
Amazing grace, how sweet the sound,  that saved a wretch like me
   G                       C          G                 Em             D7     G
I once was lost, but now I'm found,  was blind, but now I see
- - - - - - - - - - - - - - - - - - - - - - - - - - - - - - - - - - - - - -

           G                      Bm7
Well, I wish I was in the land of cotton
C                           Am
Old times there are not forgotten
          G                  Em                D7              G
Look a-way,  look a-way,  look a-way, Dixie land
```

Em: o, 1 2

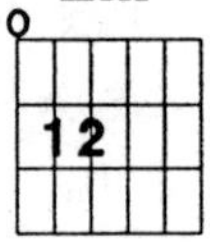

Am: o, 1, 2 3

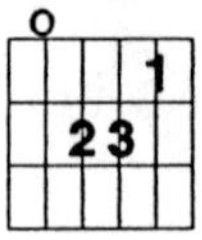

Bm7: x, 2 3 4

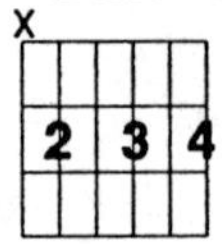

KEY of C

```
              C                          F                       C
Will the circle be unbroken,  by and by, Lord, by and by

                                 Am                C          G7      C
There's a better home a-waiting in the sky, Lord, in the sky
- - - - - - - - - - - - - - - - - - - - - - - - - - - - - - - - - - - - - -

  C                        F            C                                  G7
Amazing grace, how sweet the sound,  that saved a wretch like me
   C                       F          C                 Am             G7     C
I once was lost, but now I'm found,  was blind, but now I see
- - - - - - - - - - - - - - - - - - - - - - - - - - - - - - - - - - - - - -

           C                      Em
Well, I wish I was in the land of cotton
F                           Dm
Old times there are not forgotten
          C                  Am                G7              C
Look a-way,  look a-way,  look a-way, Dixie land
```

Am: o, 1, 2 3

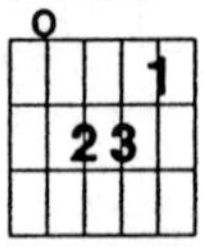

Dm: x o, 1, 2, 3

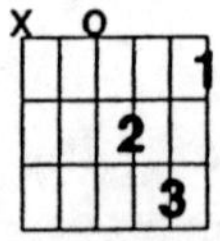

Em: o, 1 2

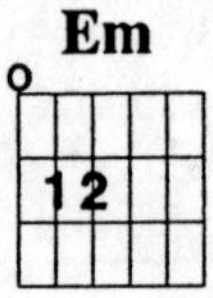

Minor Chords and "Rhythm Changes"

There is one chord progression involving Minor chords that stands out from all others, especially in jazz and early rock music. It has even been given a name by jazz musicians ---"Rhythm Changes"---because it fits the first line of the song "I've Got Rhythm." Here it is:

1 - 6m - 2m - 57

I've got rhythm, I've got music

Sometimes the **4 chord** is substituted for the **2m chord**, giving us **1** - **6m** - **4** - **5**, but we'll leave it like it is, since we're doing Minor chords here. So here are some examples in the Key of G, recycling mostly previous material.

```
G                  Em               Am        D7
Camptown ladies sing this song,  doo-dah,  doo-dah
G                      Em               Am      D7      G
Camptown racetrack five miles long,  oh the doo-dah day
```

```
G                           C
Oh, give me a home where the buffalo roam
         G             Em        Am    D7   (G)
Where the deer and the antelope play
```

```
G         Em          Am   D7
Take me out to the ball - game
G         Em          Am    D7
Take me out to the crowd
```

```
       G         Em           Am      D7       G              C
Should auld ac-quaintance be for-got and never brought to mind
       G         Em           Am      D7      C       D7       G
Should auld ac-quaintance be for-got and days of Auld Lang Syne
```

See how smoothly that chord progression works? We'll discuss exactly *why* it works in a later chapter. Now let's look at the first several lines of "Morning Has Broken." An extra chord, Bm7 (the **3m chord**, right?), has been inserted into the Rhythm Changes, and by golly, that works, too! Ain't life grand?

```
                G    Am  D7            C    G
Morning has bro - ken,  like the first mor - ning
G                  Bm7   Em   Am          D7     (G)
Blackbird has spo  -  ken,  like the first bird
```

Starting Notes

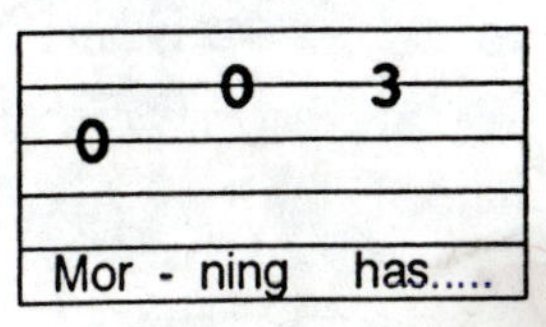

And here are those last 4 examples transcribed into the Key of C.
Please play through them. (Remember, I'm watching you,
so you'd *just better do it.)*

```
C                        Am                 Dm        G7
Camptown ladies sing this song,  doo-dah,  doo-dah
C                          Am                Dm      G7        C
Camptown racetrack five miles long,  oh the doo-dah day
```

```
     C                          F
Oh, give me a home where the buffalo roam
          C                 Am        Dm     G7  (C)
Where the deer and the antelope play
```

```
C           Am           Dm     G7
Take me out to the ball - game
C           Am           Dm      G7
Take me out to the crowd
```

```
            C         Am            Dm       G7         C                       F
Should auld ac-quaintance be for-got and never brought to mind
            C         Am            Dm       G7        F        G7          C
Should auld ac-quaintance be for-got and days of Auld Lang Syne
```

```
                C    Dm   G7              F     C
Morning has bro - ken,  like the first mor - ning
C                Em      Am   Dm              G7     (C)
Blackbird has spo  -  ken,  like the first bird
```

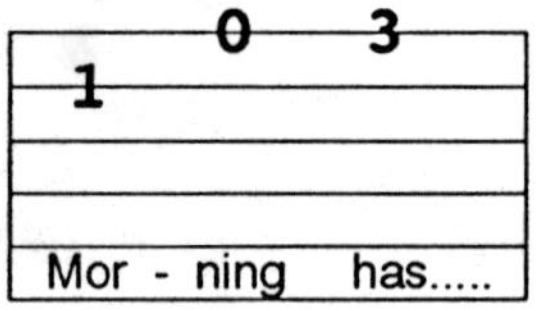

```
      0    3
--1-----------
--------------
--------------
--------------
Mor - ning  has.....
```

Here's a list of hit songs that rely on the **1 - 6m - 2m - 5**7 chord progression:

Blue Moon
Heart and Soul
Unchained Melody
House At Pooh Corner
You Make Me Feel Like Dancing
Where Have All the Flowers Gone?
All I Have to Do Is Dream
I Will Always Love You
Carolina in My Mind
You Send Me

Sherry
Y. M. C. A.
Stand By Me
The Tide Is High
Big Girls Don't Cry
Stay (Just a Little Bit Longer)
Why Do Fools Fall in Love?
Please Mr. Postman
Crocodile Rock
Hungry Heart

.............just to name a few.

Secondary Dominants

In every Chord Family, there is only one Dominant chord, only one **5 chord**. But it is very possible to borrow a Dominant chord from an *overlapping* Chord Family and insert it into the present family. But there are rules governing the selection of these **Secondary Dominant** chords.

Here's what you do: Take a Tonic chord from some key, then go up to the 5th position and find that key's Dominant 7th chord. (Done there, been that.)

Now go up to the 5th position ***above that*** *5th position.*

This new chord is a Secondary Dominant 7th chord with regard to the key you started in. This chord is also known as the ***Fifth of the Fifth (5/5)*** and it comes from *outside* the Chord Family. Where does this chord want to go? Well, it wants to resolve back to the **5 chord**, which in turn wants to resolve to the **1 chord**. Duck soup.

Here is the chord progression **1 - 5/5 - 5 - 1** for the five *C-A-G-E-D* Chord Families, using the Dominant 7th chord quality for both the **5 chord** and the **5/5 chord**:

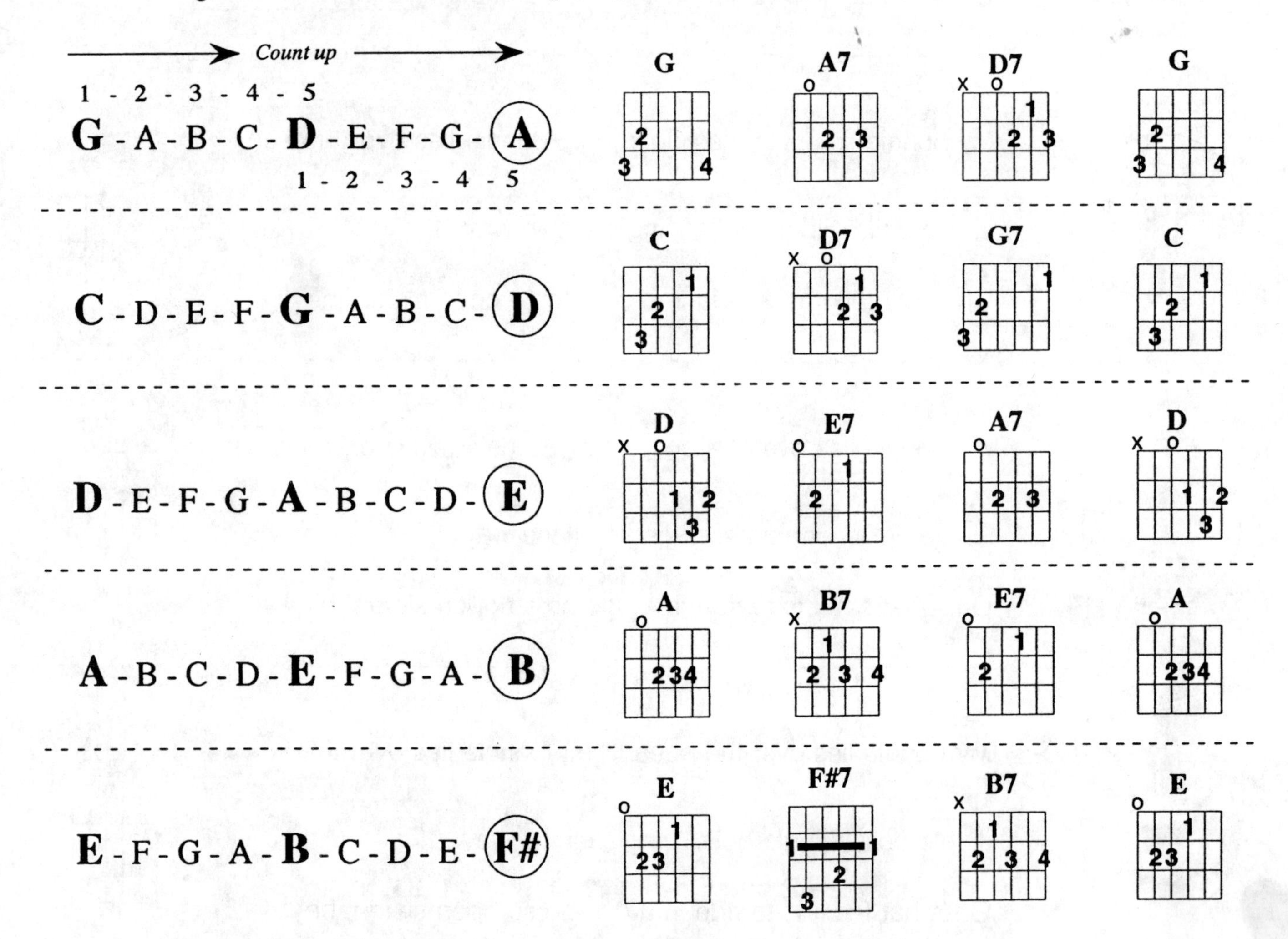

Have you noticed a ***shortcut*** to this Secondary Dominant business?

Go up one letter from the key note, and that'll wind up being the 5/5 chord.

For G, the **5/5 chord** is up one letter to A. For C, the **5/5 chord** is up one letter to D.

Here come some more fascinating examples of Secondary Dominant chord function. See how these **5/5 chords** can add a little zip to several songs we've seen before.

G C G A7 D7
My bonnie lies over the ocean, my bonnie lies over the sea

G C G
Jingle bells, jingle bells, jingle all the way

C G A7 D7
Oh, what fun it is to ride in a one-horse open sleigh, hey!

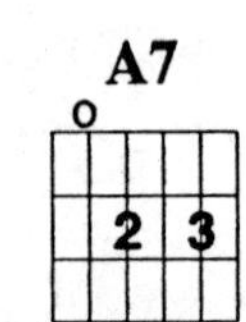

C F C D7 G7
My bonnie lies over the ocean, my bonnie lies over the sea

C F C
Jingle bells, jingle bells, jingle all the way

F C D7 G7
Oh, what fun it is to ride in a one-horse open sleigh, hey!

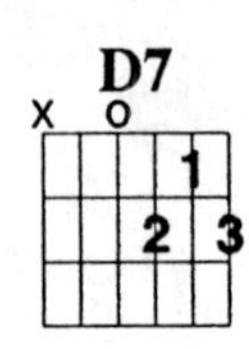

D G D E7 A7
My bonnie lies over the ocean, my bonnie lies over the sea

D G D
Jingle bells, jingle bells, jingle all the way

G D E7 A7
Oh, what fun it is to ride in a one-horse open sleigh, hey!

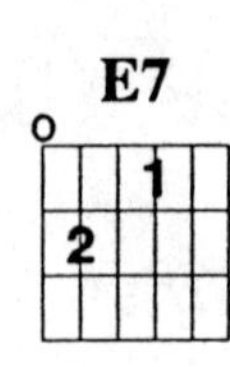

A D A B7 E7
My bonnie lies over the ocean, my bonnie lies over the sea

A D A
Jingle bells, jingle bells, jingle all the way

D A B7 E7
Oh, what fun it is to ride in a one-horse open sleigh, hey!

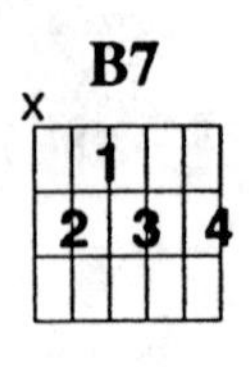

E A E F#7 B7
My bonnie lies over the ocean, my bonnie lies over the sea

E A E
Jingle bells, jingle bells, jingle all the way

A E F#7 B7
Oh, what fun it is to ride in a one-horse open sleigh, hey!

Bunches of Useful Chords

It's time to present *Bunches of Useful Chords.* So far, you have only had The Big Fifteen, which include the most common and simple Major, Minor and Dominant 7th chords. But this is only the tip of the iceberg, as you can well imagine.

On the following pages, you'll see a broader selection of interesting chords, which are grouped by Root Note in alphabetical order (A chords first, then B chords, and so on.) View this as a *chord smorgasbord.* Just browse through it and see what sounds good to you. We'll continue to use the broad classifications of Major, Minor and Dominant 7th chords, but within each of these classes, you'll be introduced to "chords of color."

Under the ***Major chord heading,*** there are **sus2** and **sus4** chords. These are **suspended** chords, which impart a dangling feeling. They like to resolve to the Major chord with the same letter. There are Major Seventh and Major Ninth chords (**ma7** and **ma9**) that sound rather jazzy. Then there are the Major Sixth chords (**6**) that sound contemplative and almost Minor.

Under the ***Minor chord heading,*** you'll find the pure Minor chords as well as variations like Minor Sixths (**m6**), Minor Sevenths (**m7**), Minor Ninths (**m9**) and Minor Elevenths (**m11**). Each one of these has its own personality, but they are all noticeably Minor in quality.

Under the ***Dominant chord heading,*** you'll see Sevenths, Suspended Sevenths (**7sus4**), Ninths (**9**) and Thirteenths (**13**). (Elevenths are the same as **7sus4's**.) All of these chords display that restless, dissonant quality of the Dominant 7th chord (a **57 chord** wanting to resolve to a **1 chord**). Ninths and Thirteenths sound particularly rich and jazzy.

Within these 3 classes, you can generally switch around and substitute chords for each other to make things interesting. For example, an Em7 or an Em9 chord could stand in for Em. Go back to the musical examples we used before and see what sounds good.

You will also see some **slash chords**, such as "G-slash-B" (**G/B**) and "C-slash-G" (**C/G**). Here's a situation where you actually want ***some other note than the Root Note in the bass.*** **G/B** indicates, for example, that the chord is a G *chord* that has a B *note* in the bass. So the letter on the left is a chord name and the letter on the right is a single note. Slash chords sound rather ambiguous and usually function as **passing chords.**

Again, my philosophy is doing first and comprehending later. Don't get overwhelmed by all these new chord qualities. I promise we'll go back to them later and explain how they work. The most important thing now is to learn how to finger these chords, to listen to them, and to try to decide for yourself *how they sound.* Try comparing all the Minor Seventh chords to each other. Listen to all the Suspended chords; do you like them? Try to figure out how a Ninth chord makes you feel. If a chord is too hard to finger, just skip it.

There will be a number of barre chords. Try them, but don't sweat them. A number may appear to the side of the chord, such as "3rd," indicating which fret the barre finger should be holding.

A Chords

The A Major chord can be fingered a number of different ways, depending on the other chords in the progression. Here are the common ones:

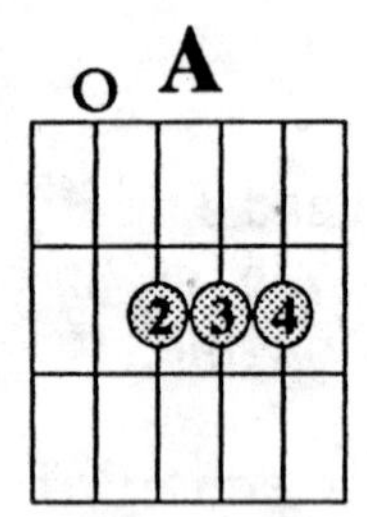

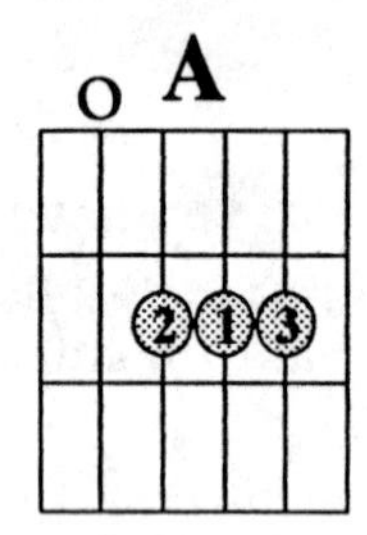

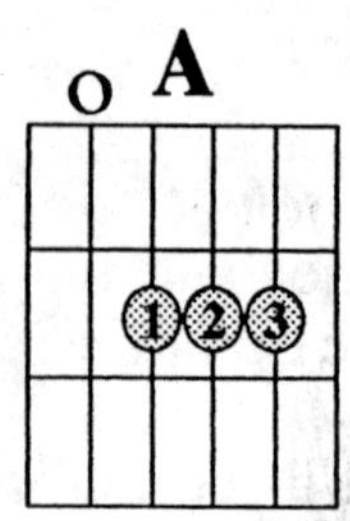

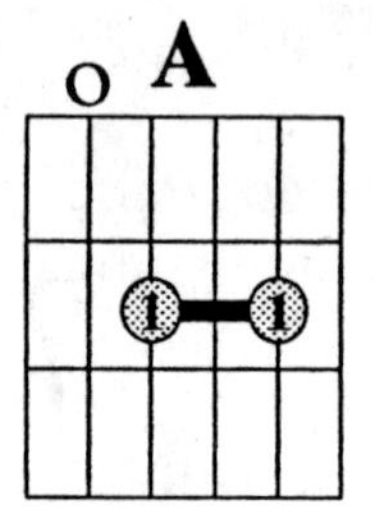

Play the 5th string in the bass, since this is the Root Note.
The 6th string can either be avoided or deadened with the thumb.
Here are some variants of the A Major chord:

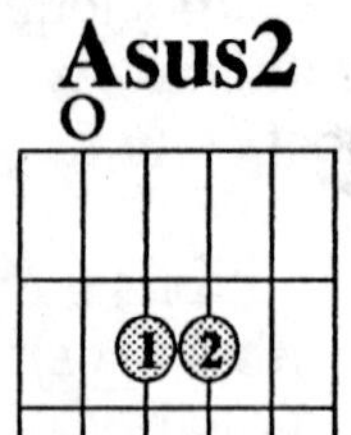

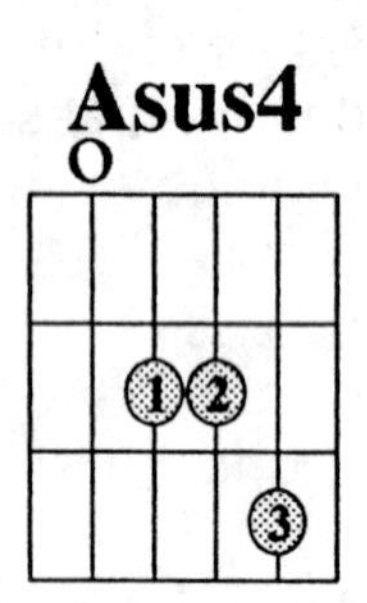

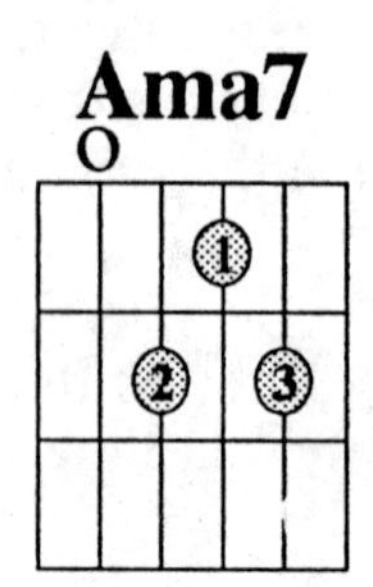

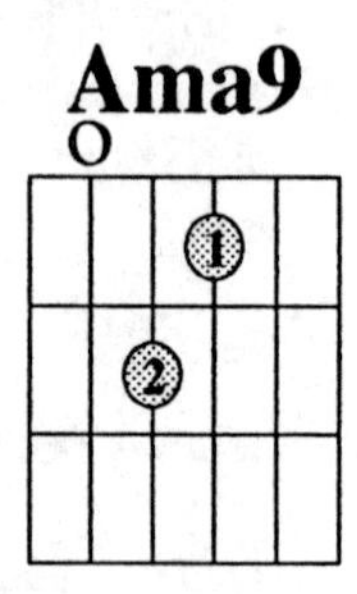

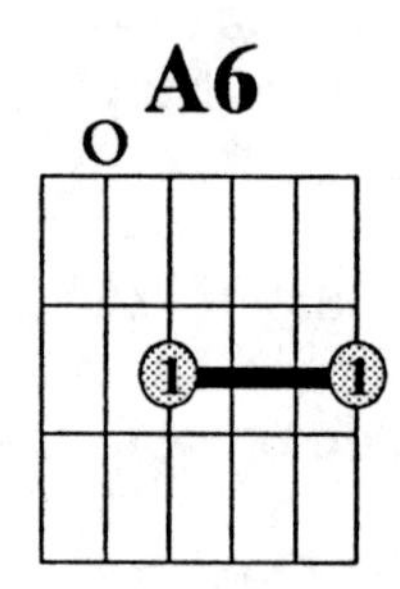

Here are several A Minor chord variants:

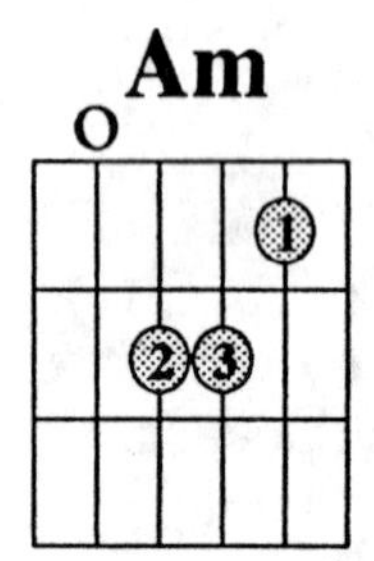

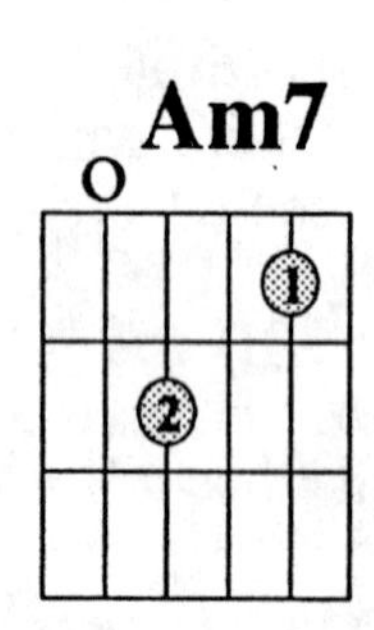

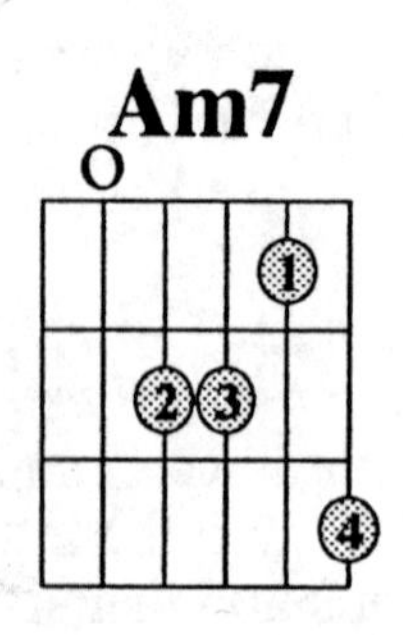

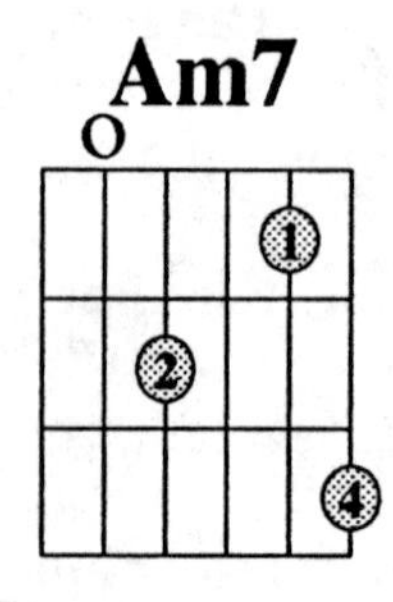

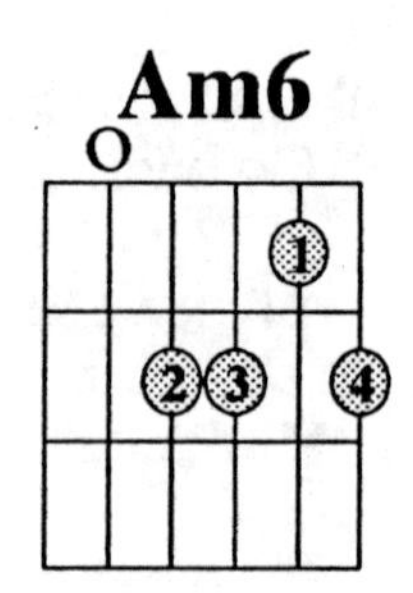

And here are some A Dominant 7th chord variants:

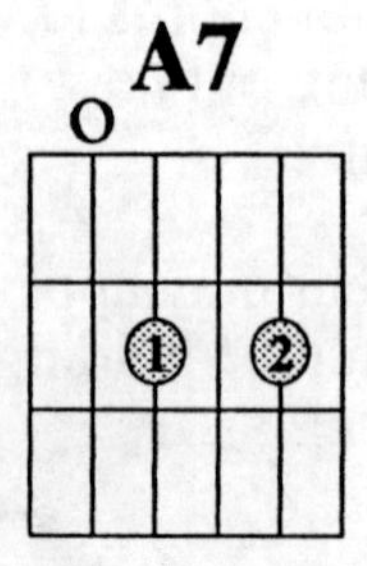

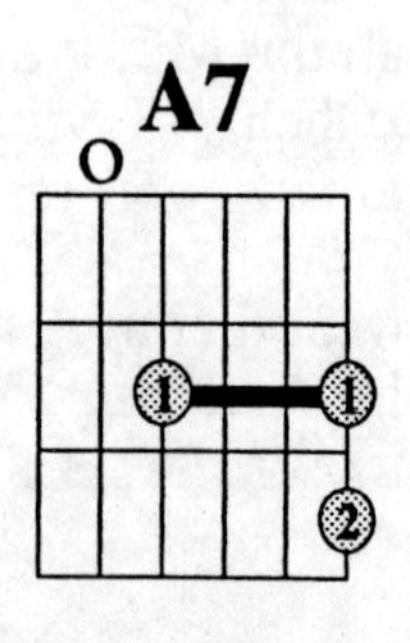

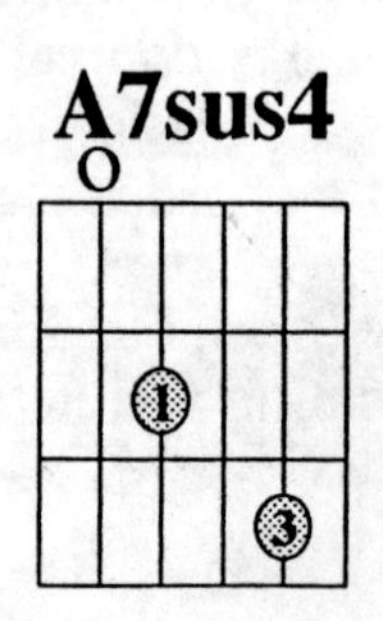

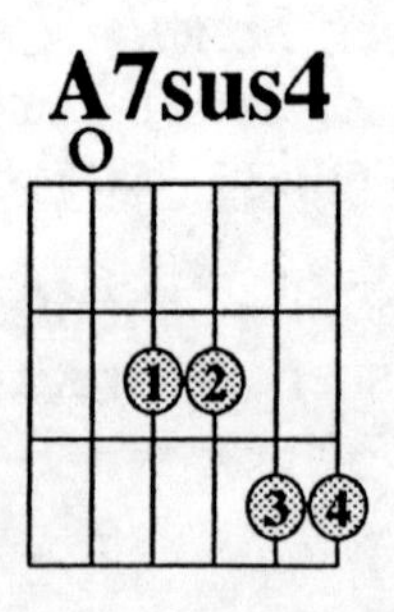

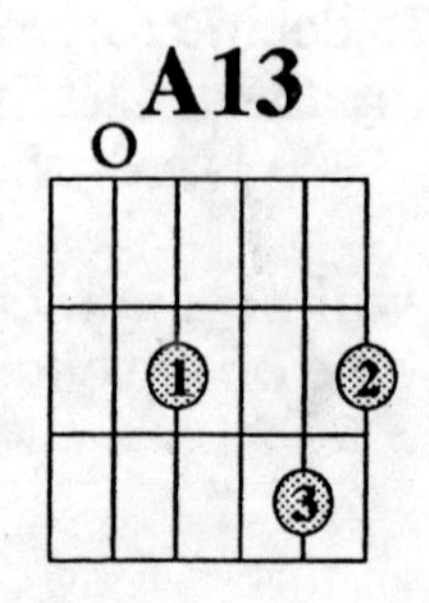

B Chords

On the guitar, B chords are not the easiest chords to play. Usually, the B Major chord is played as a barre chord; in fact, one version has both a 1st *and* 3rd finger barre. **Play the 5th string in the bass, since this is the Root Note.**

You can either deaden the 6th string with the tip of your 1st finger, or just avoid it. Or you could just go ahead and barre all the way across to the 6th string F# note, even though this isn't the Root Note. It won't hurt too much.

Here are the most common B Major chord variants:

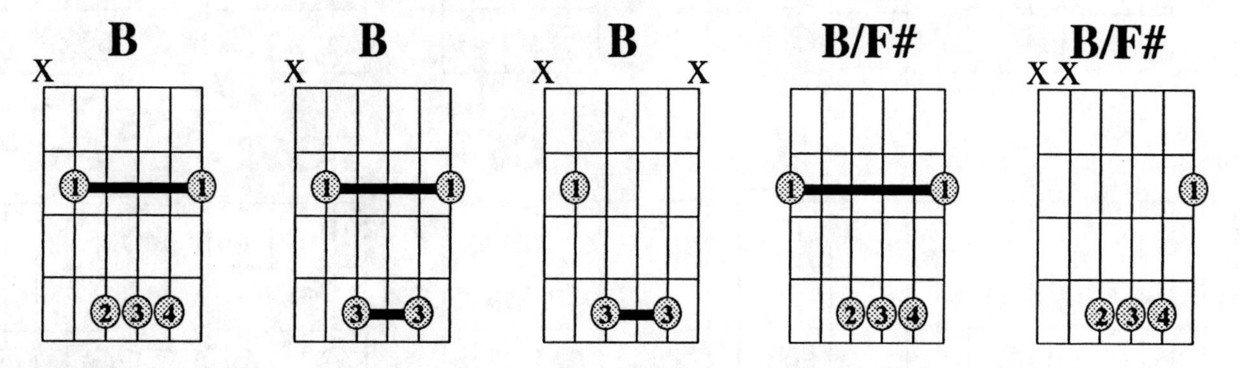

The B Minor chord is also a barre chord, for which we've been substituting an easier Bm7:

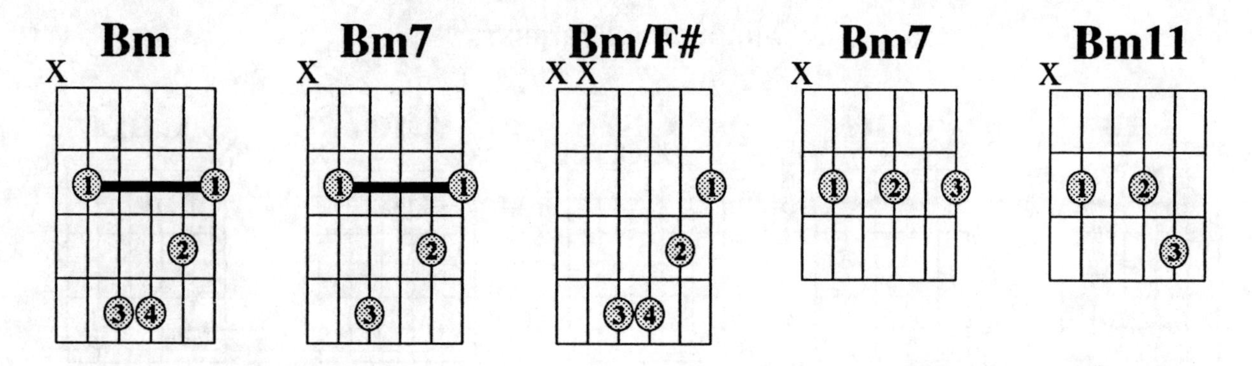

For the B Dominant 7th chord variants, the 6th string can be deadened with the thumb:

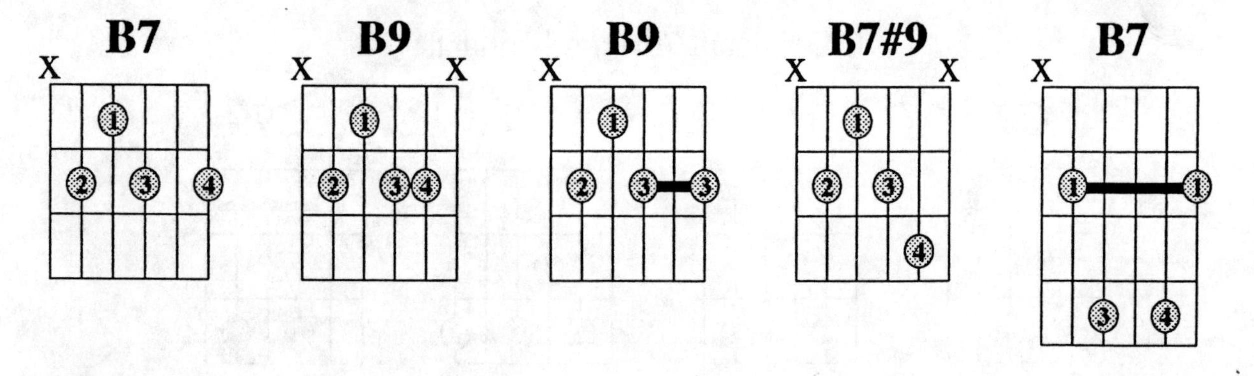

C Chords

Play the 5th string in the bass, since this is the Root Note.
You can deaden the 6th string with the thumb. But there are several slash chords that actually *use* the 6th string.

C Major chord variants:

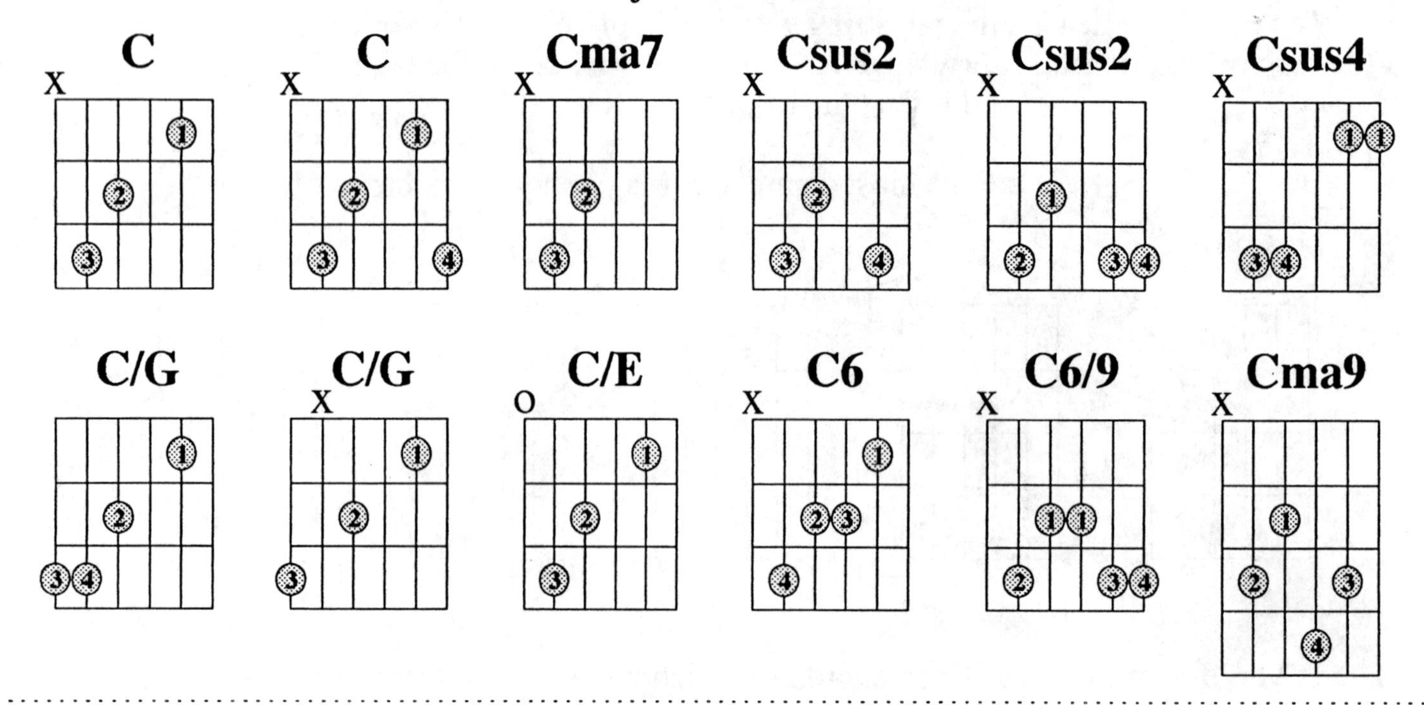

C Minor chord variants:

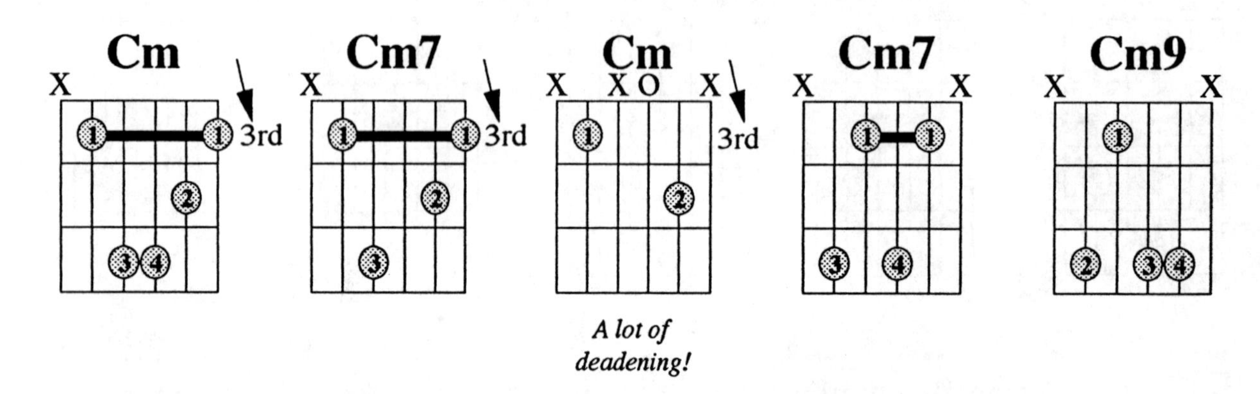

C Dominant 7th chord variants:

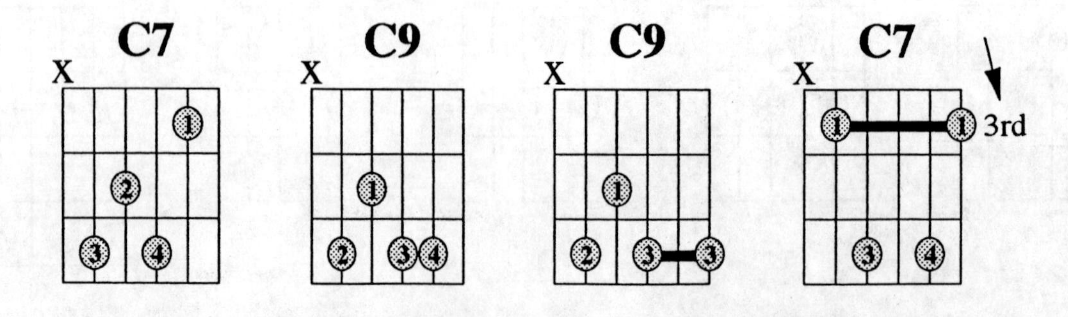

D Chords

The D Major chord is probably the most commonly played chord on the guitar.
Play the 4th string in the bass, since this is the Root Note.

Playing the 5th string in the bass is also acceptable, even though it isn't the Root Note.
At least the 5th string has a lower pitch so it actually sounds *bassier* than the 4th string.
In any case, you still want to either deaden or avoid the 6th string, unless it's a slash chord.

D Major chord variants:

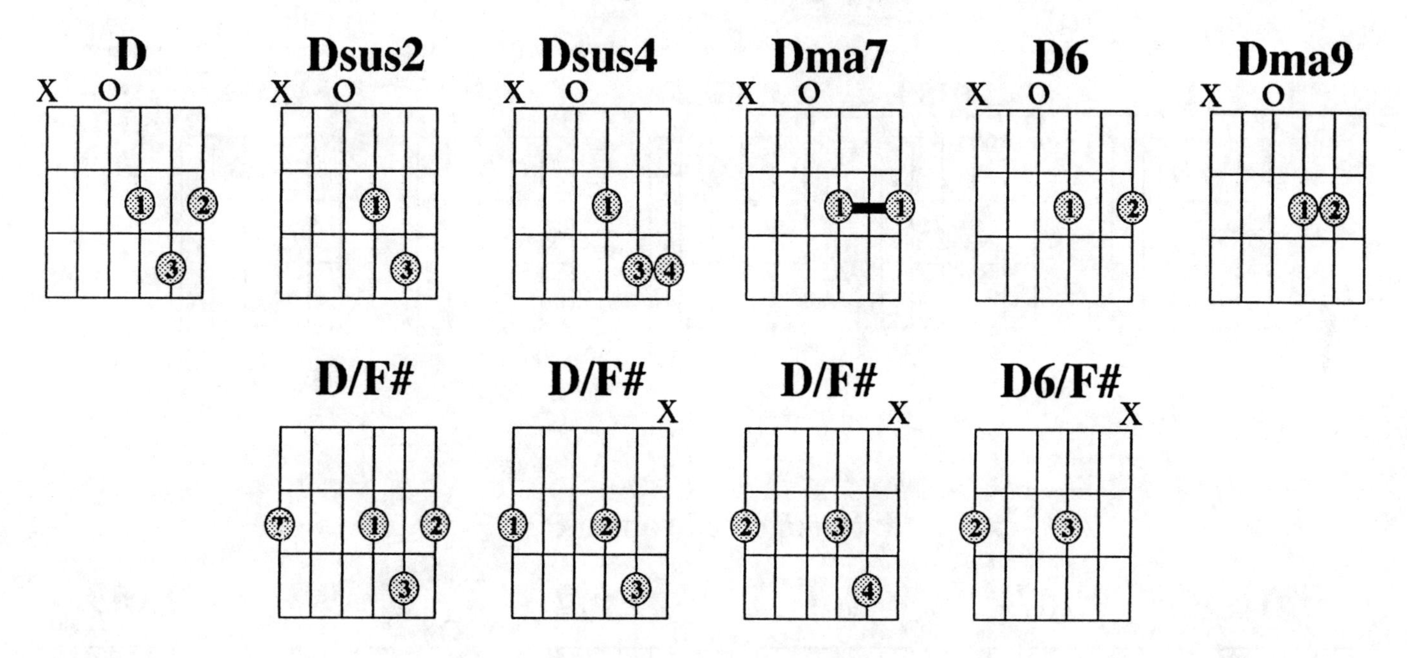

D Minor chord variants:

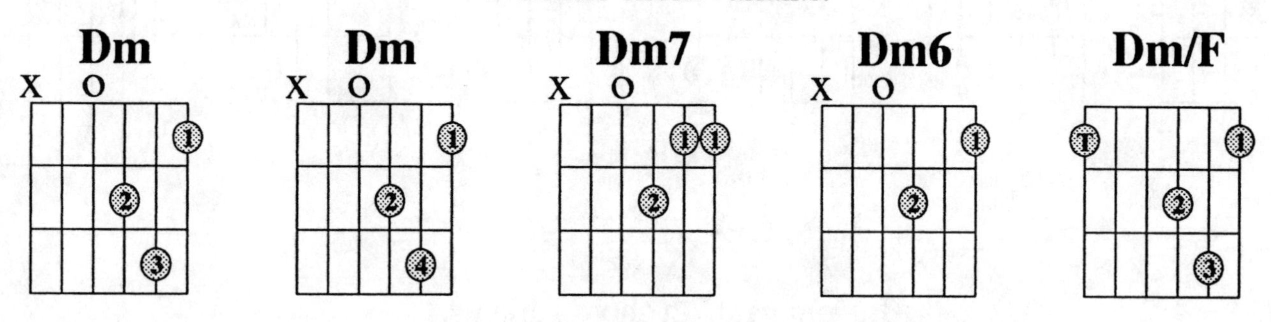

D Dominant 7th chord variants:

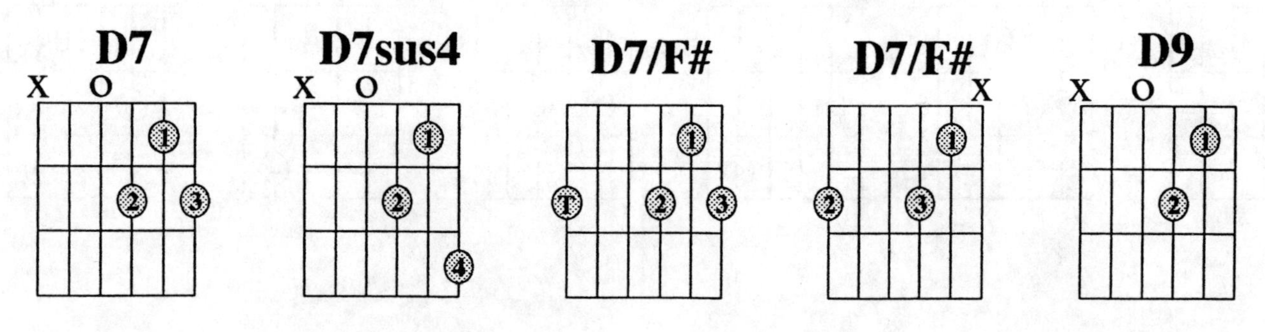

E Chords

E chords are the strongest chords on the neck of the guitar in standard tuning.
Play the 6th string in the bass, since this is the Root Note.

These are chords where you actually ***want*** to play the open 6th string in the bass, instead of trying to deaden it, as in most other chords. Oh, happy day!

E Major chord variants:

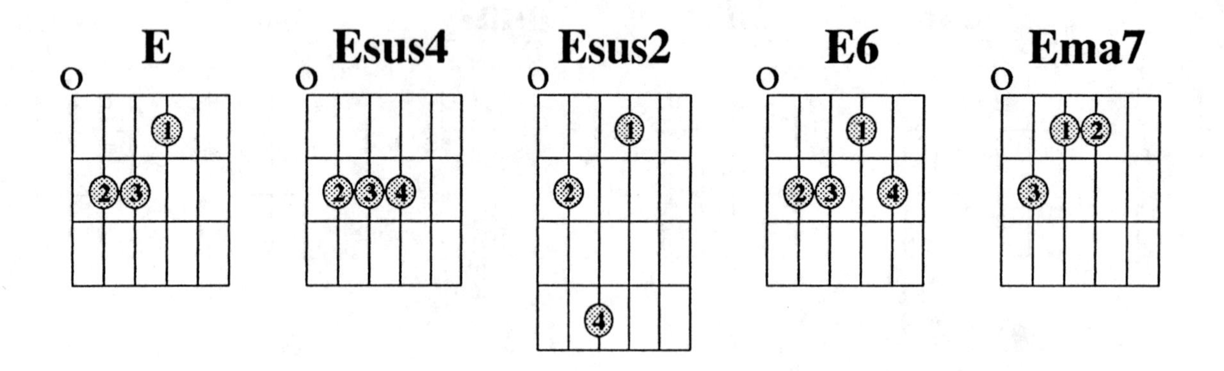

E Minor chord variants:

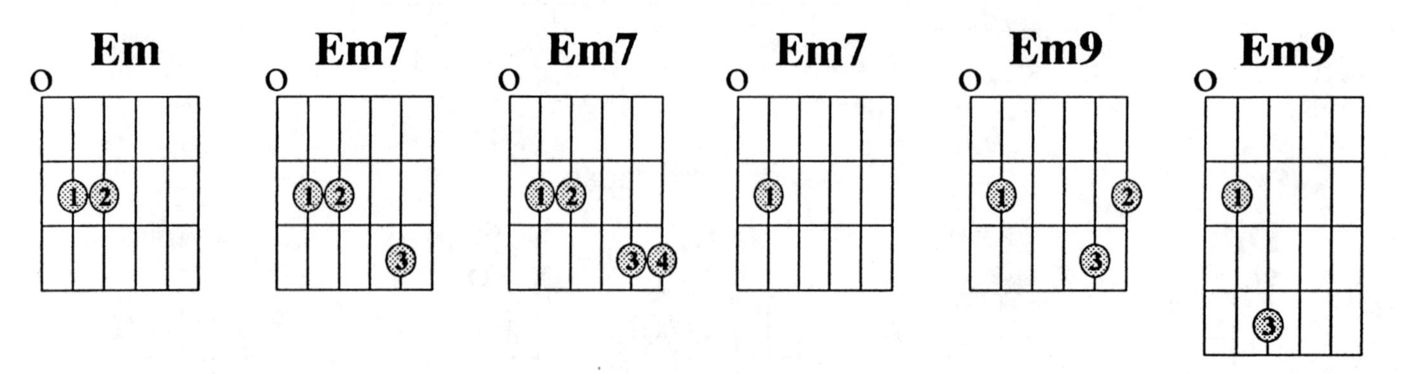

E Dominant 7th chord variants:

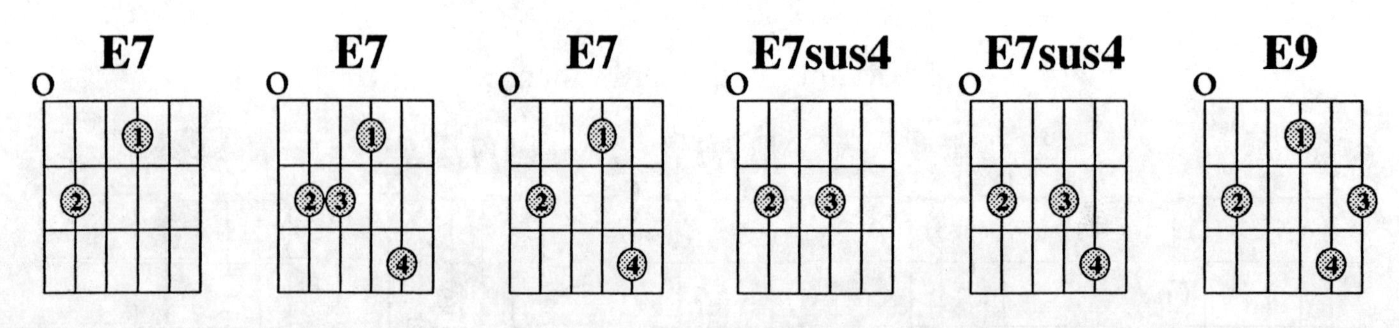

F Chords

F chords, whether they have a Major, Minor or Dominant 7th chord quality, are no picnic. Learning to play the F chord is the closest thing I know of to a ***rite of passage*** on the guitar. But as hard as that 4-string F chord is to play, there is yet another fingering for the F chord that includes all 6 strings and usually involves a 1st-finger barre at the 1st fret.

The diagram for that F barre chord appears in the top row at the far right, and it's real tough to get all 6 strings ringing, so don't beat yourself up over it. **Play either the 4th or the 6th string in the bass, since they are both Root Notes.**

Other F Major chord variants use the left-hand thumb to hold down the F note at the 1st fret of the 6th string. Even if you can't quite get enough pressure on that note to make it ring, perhaps you can just use your thumb to deaden the dissonant open 6th string. And it's okay to hear the open 5th string ringing; it's just not preferable. Sounds weak.

F Major chord variants:

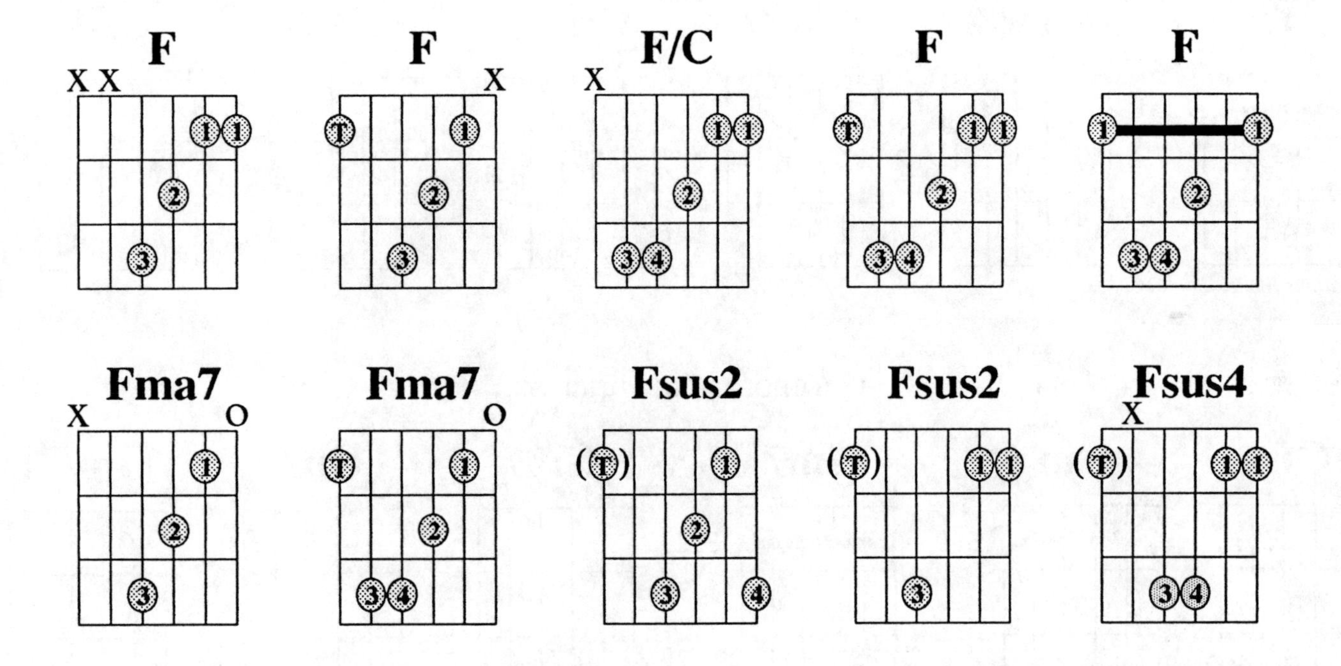

F Minor chord variants:

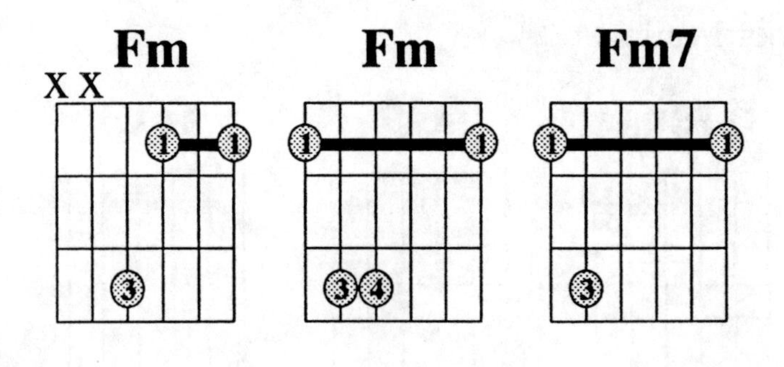

F Dominant 7th chord variants:

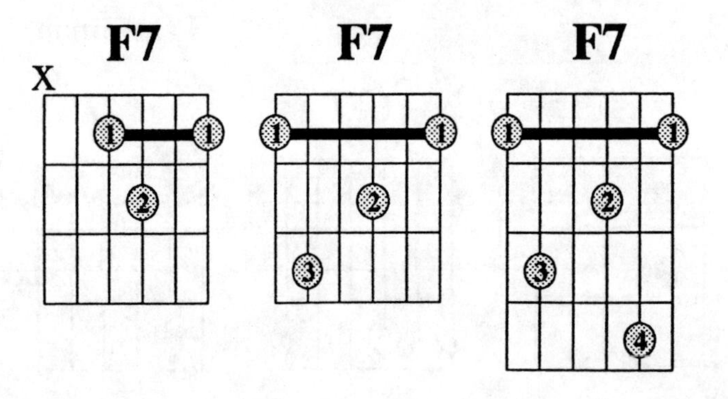

G Chords

The G chord is another strong-sounding chord on the guitar.
Play the 6th string in the bass, since this is the Root Note.

The main thing to decide about a G chord is whether or not you like to hear the *5th* string note. If you do, hold it down. If you don't (like me), *deaden* it by leaning your 3rd finger against it, which is pretty easy to do. Actually, it's hard *not* to do it.

G Major chords variants:

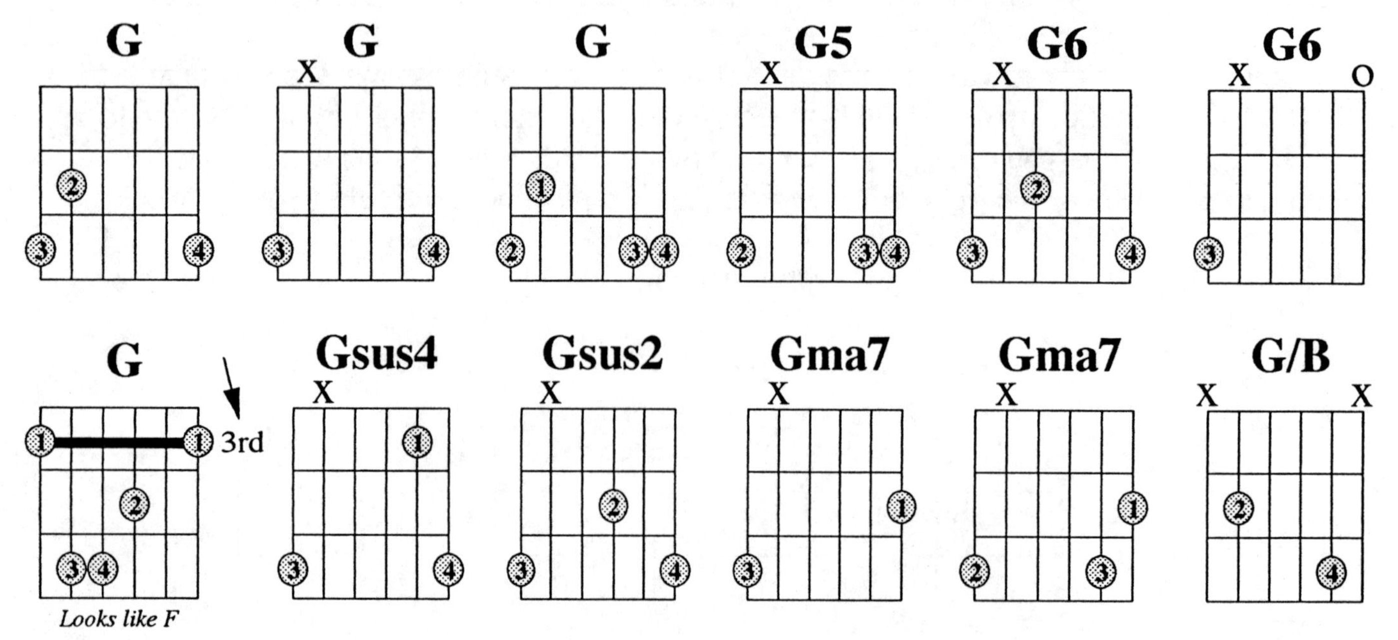

G Minor chord variants:

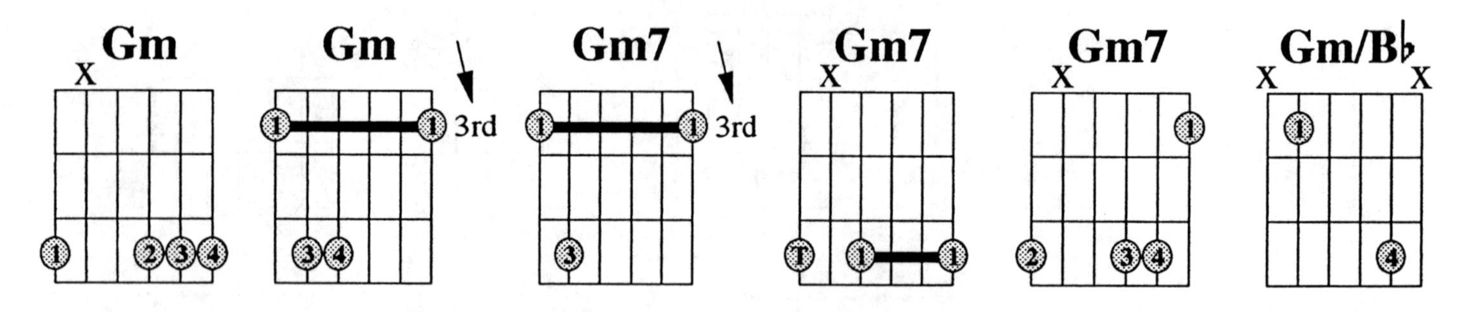

G Dominant 7th chord variants:

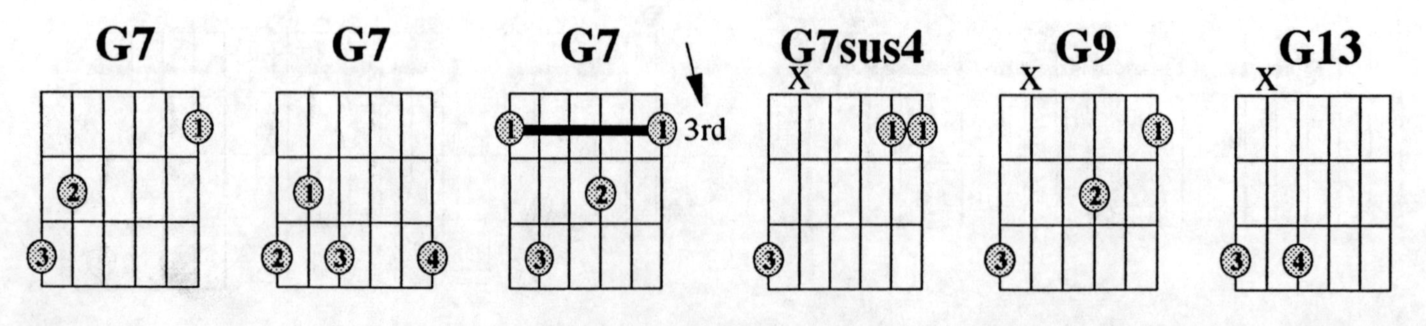

Other Common Chords

Here are some other common chords that have accidental Root Notes (#'s and ♭'s).
These chords show up from time to time and are supposed to be played as barre chords.
I also give some non-barre possibilities that may not sound as good but are easier to play.

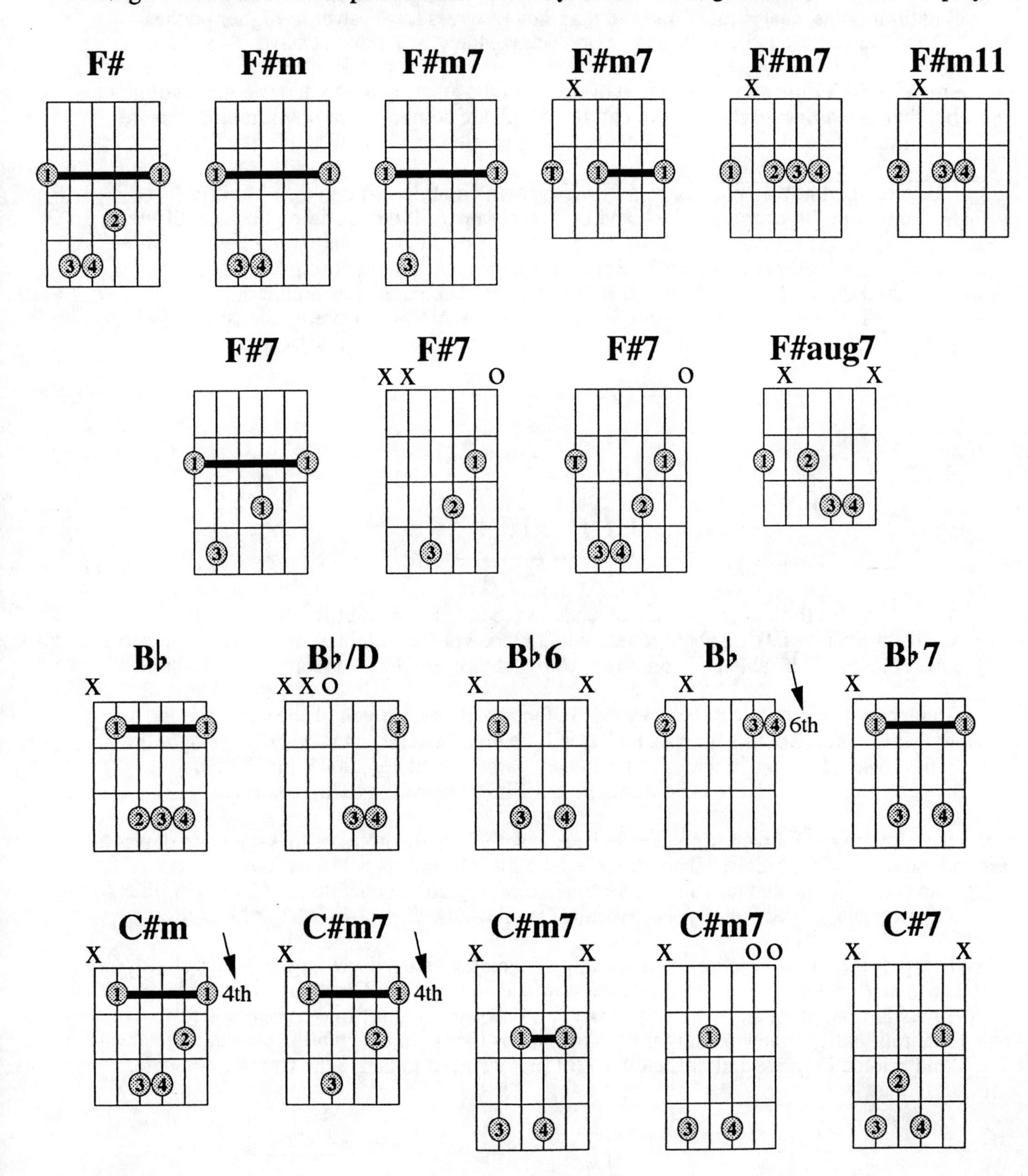

Review

So first we talked about the 12 notes in the Musical Alphabet, saying that there were natural notes, sharps and flats, and that they progress from lower to higher pitches. We said that all 12 notes fit inside one octave, then the Alphabet starts over again.

We mentioned a little about the layout of notes on the guitar and how to tune the instrument, but then we moved right along to chords, which are comprised of notes, and which are immediately useful to us in accompanying singing and in entertaining generally.

You learned how to play the Big Fifteen; how to distinguish between Major, Minor and Dominant 7th chord qualities; and how to organize all those chords into the different *C-A-G-E-D* Chord Families. We talked about chord progressions within keys, such as the **1 - 4 - 5** progression, the **1 - 2m - 6m - 5** progression, involving Minor chords, and the **1 - 5/5 - 5 - 1** progression, involving Secondary Dominant chords. Finally, you were exposed to bunches and *bunches* of pretty chords. You now have a fairly good overview of the business end of music.

Preview

Now it's time to go all the way back to the beginning and fill in the details. We'll start off by talking about notes again. Once you've seen how notes are organized into **scales**, we'll be able to figure *exactly* how chords are derived from individual notes.

Some of this material will be a review; in fact, we'll cover much of the same ground as we did before. But this time around, it will be presented more technically, using more of the standard music theory concepts and jargon. But hey, that won't bother you, now that you've been through your **First Approach** to this material.

We'll start with the **Chromatic Scale** and see exactly how the notes of this scale are deployed around the neck of the guitar. Then we'll see how the all-important **Major Scale** is derived from the Chromatic Scale, and how the Major Scale can be used to generate the Chord Families for various keys, particularly our personal favorites, the *C-A-G-E-D* Chord Families.

We'll explore the **1 - 4 - 5 chord** relationships in greater detail, throw in the Minor chords and Dominant 7ths, and then move on to the powerful and sublime **Circle of Fifths**, which will help us to realign all these scales and keys and chords and stuff into a coherent system of tonal rationality, a new paradigm for harmonious living, in which all people can prosper and rejoice in peace and musicality. But first we need to tackle the Chromatic Scale.

The Second Approach

The Chromatic Scale

As you may recall, there are **12 different notes** in the music of Western civilization. It helps to think of them as being laid out in a sequence, from left to right, where each successive note to the right is a little higher in **pitch** than its predecessor.

The 12 notes are named after letters of the alphabet. But instead of using 12 different letters, we use only 7 letters, A-B-C-D-E-F-G, to represent the **natural** notes, and then squeeze in 5 more characters among these, called **accidentals**, to come up with the necessary 12. Accidentals come in two different versions, **sharps** ("#") and **flats** ("♭").

This sequence of 12 notes is called the **Chromatic Scale**. (The word "scale" comes from the Latin word "scala," meaning "ladder.") When you reach the 13th note, you just start over again from the beginning.

Each accidental note has two names. The note known as "A-sharp," which means one note higher than A, is exactly the same note as "B-flat," which means one note lower than B. C# is also D♭, D# is also E♭, and so forth. We'll talk later about why we need both sharps and flats; anyway, here's the Chromatic Scale:

A - A# - B - C - C# - D - D# - E - F - F# - G - G# - A...
(expressed as natural notes and sharps)
or
A - B♭ - B - C - D♭ - D - E♭ - E - F - G♭ - G - A♭ - A...
(expressed as natural notes and flats)

Remember that there are no accidental notes between **B and C** and **E and F**.

You might be wondering why we *don't* just use the 12 letters A through L, which would provide a different letter for each of the 12 notes. Well, it turns out that the Chromatic Scale is ***not*** the most important scale in music. We would almost never use all 12 notes together in the same song. Really, the Chromatic Scale is no more than a sequential listing of all the notes that are in the Musical Alphabet. It contains all of the raw material of music.

The really *important* scale to become familiar with is the **Major Scale** which is made up of a ***subset*** of 7 out of the 12 notes in the Chromatic Scale. And since the Major Scale is much more useful than the Chromatic Scale, it makes more sense to use the 7 different letters instead of 12. We'll come back to the Major Scale shortly.

Here is the layout of the 12 notes of the Chromatic Scale on the 6th (lowest-pitched) string of the guitar. We start with an open ***E note*** and proceed alphabetically. At the 12th fret, the scale starts over again with another E note that is one **octave** higher than the low E note.

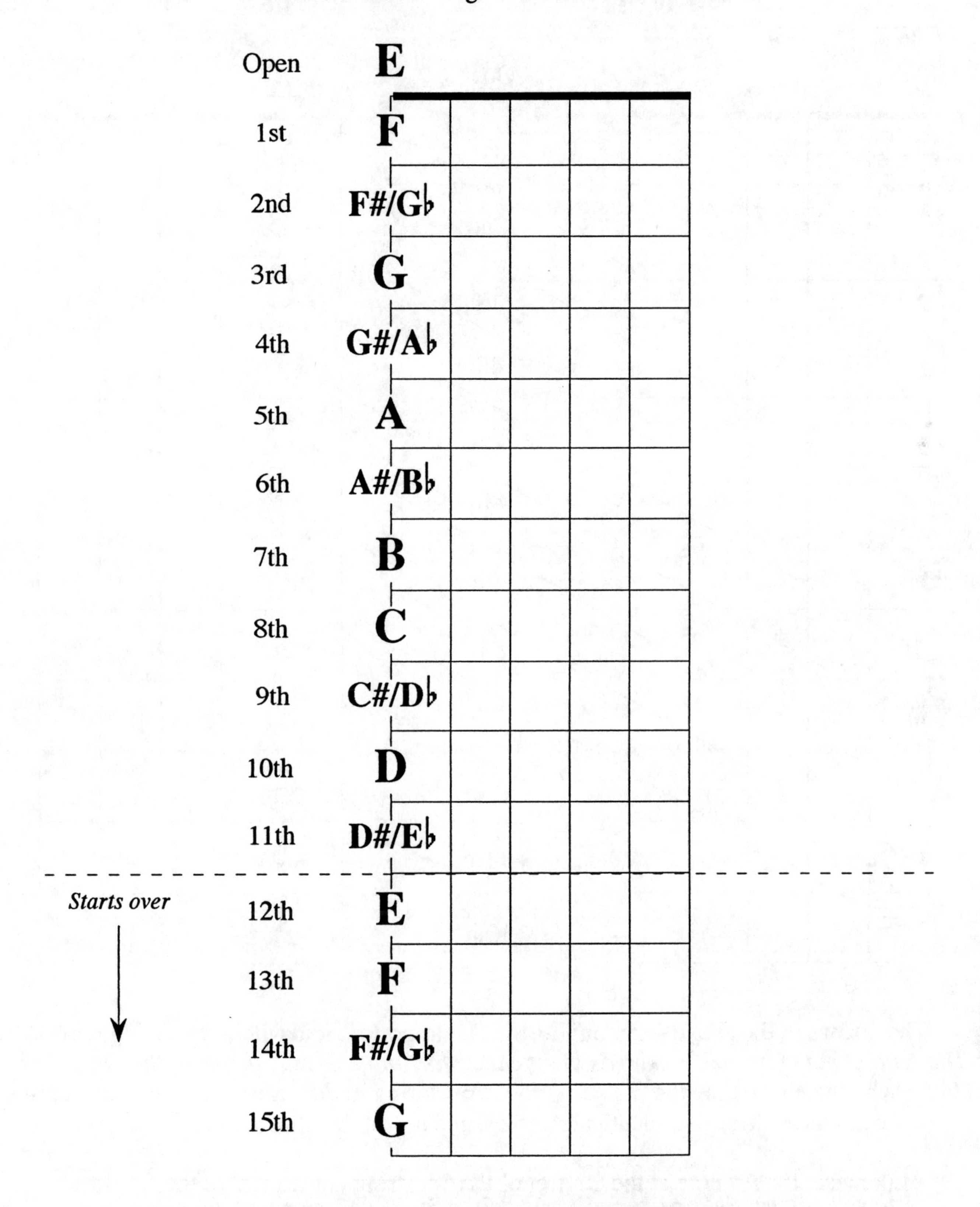

Again, there is no accidental between E and F, and there is no accidental between B and C.

Let's compare the layout of notes on the 6th string to the layout of notes on the 5th string.
This time, we'll omit the "flat" designations and keep the "sharp" designations:

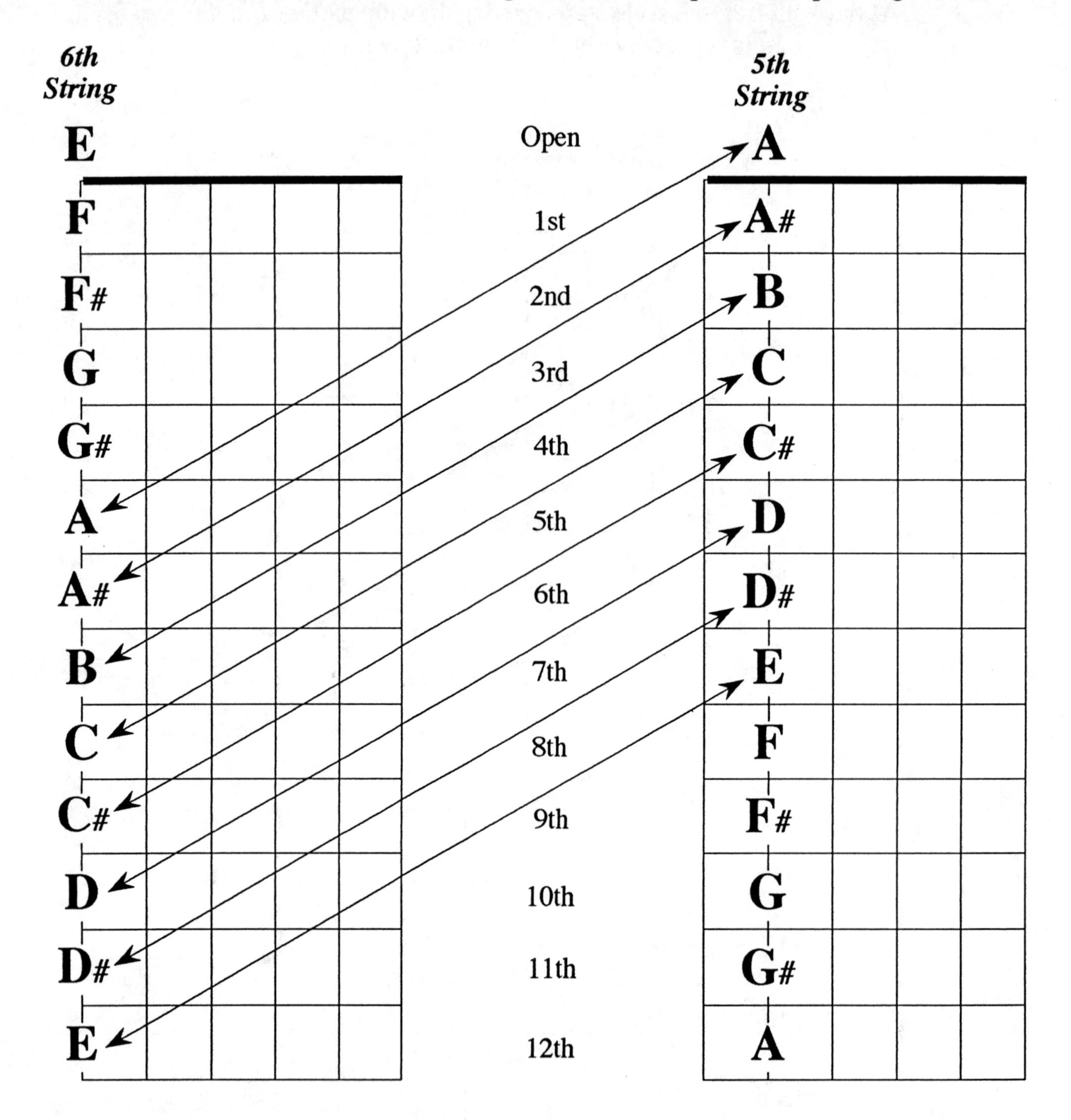

The arrows in the above diagram illustrate an important idiosyncrasy of the guitar. *The A note on the open 5th string is **identical** to the A note at the 5th fret of the 6th string.* This is why, when we tune the 5th string to the 6th string in the process of Relative Tuning, we compare these two identical A notes, and adjust the 5th string accordingly.

Likewise, the A# note at the 6th fret of the 6th string is identical to the A# note at the 1st fret of the 5th string, and so on up the neck. Only the 1st five notes on the 6th string (E, F, F#, G and G#) can be found on *only* the 6th string.

Next we'll add the 4th string, and notice how the first few notes on the 4th string (D, D#, E, F, F# and so on) can also be found starting at the 5th fret of the 5th string, *as well as* at the 10th fret of the 6th string. Play all three D notes (circled below) and you'll hear the same note with the same pitch. This feature of the guitar can lead to some confusion, but it also creates a veritable plethora (!) of opportunities.

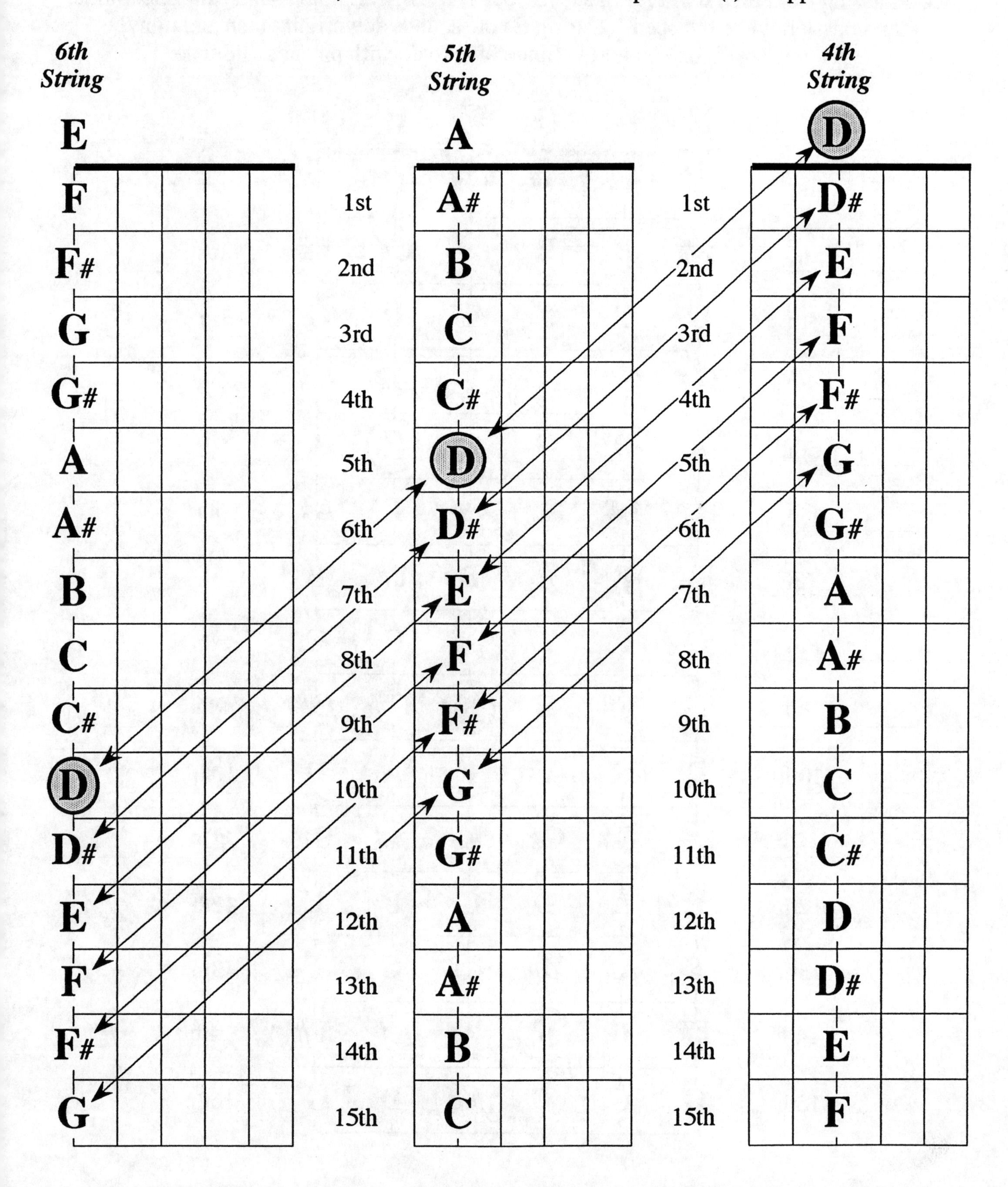

So, here's the layout of all the notes in the Chromatic Scale up to the 15th fret, with the accidentals expressed as sharps. This diagram is here for easy reference.

I'd like to show the multiple locations of *one more note:* the high open E. Play all 4 positions of this note (circled below) and listen to the **tonal quality** of each. As you proceed up the neck, moving from the 1st to the 4th string, each successive E note sounds thicker, warmer and bassier, while the open 1st string E note sounds downright brash and tinny, yet they are all unison notes. Something to do with physics. I dunno.

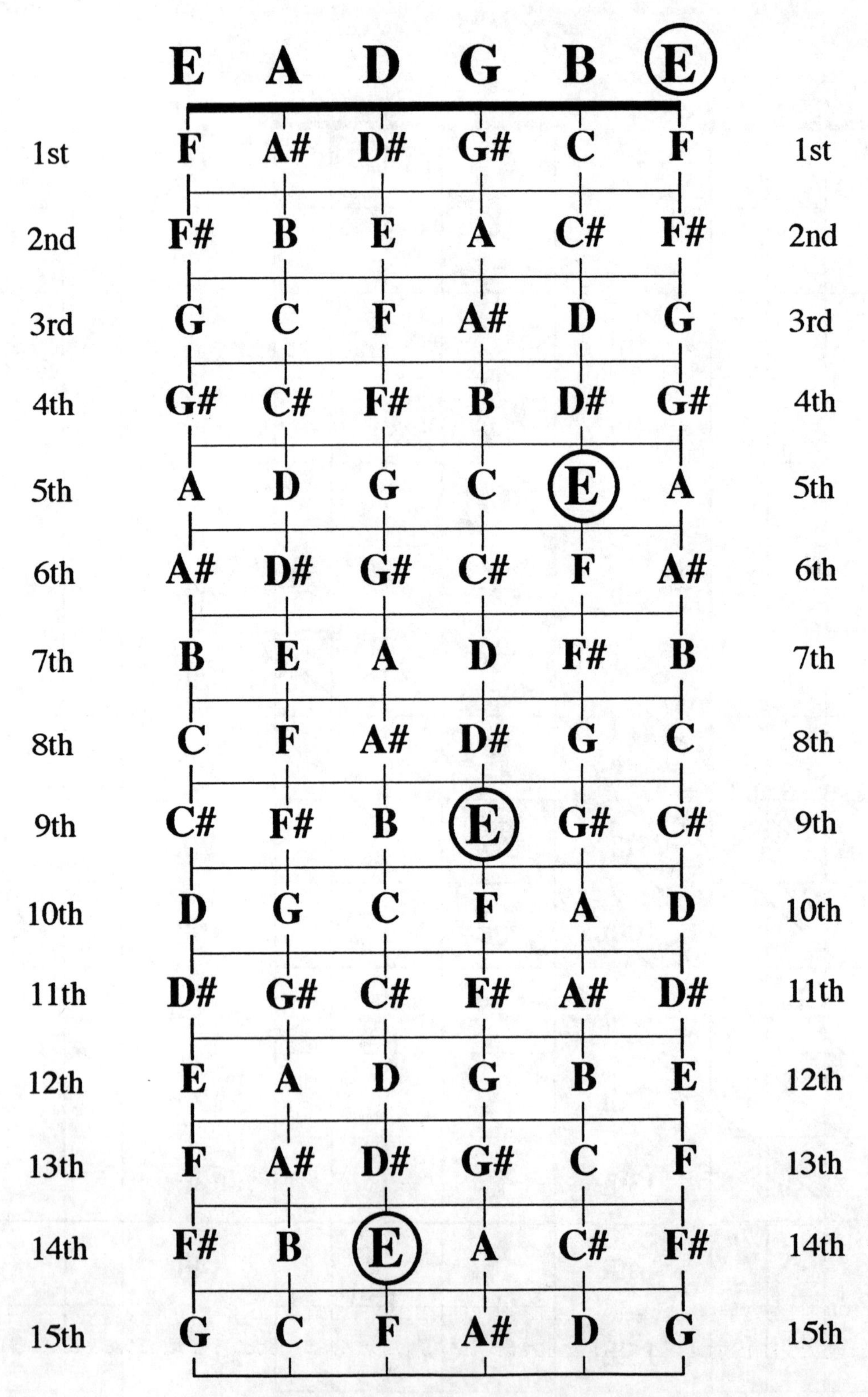

The Major Scale

We'll start with the **Chromatic Scale** and see how to use it to create a **Major Scale**. Technically, there are *12 different Chromatic Scales*, each one starting on a different note in the Musical Alphabet. So, there is an A Chromatic Scale, which starts and ends on the A note; a B Chromatic Scale, which starts and ends on the B note, and so forth. This is redundant in a way, since all 12 notes appear in all 12 scales; it's just that they have different starting and ending notes.

But it actually *is* helpful to distinguish between different Chromatic Scales, because for each Chromatic Scale there is a corresponding *Major* Scale, ***and no two Major Scales have all the same notes in common.***

Each Major Scale consists of a subset of 7 notes out of the 12 notes found in the Chromatic Scale with the same letter name. But before we can figure out exactly which notes to select to create a Major Scale, we need a way to talk about the *musical distance,* or **interval**, between two notes. We need to define the **Half-step** and the **Whole-step**:

A **Half-step** is the distance between two consecutive notes in the Chromatic Scale, a difference of **one fret** on the guitar (and one key on the piano). Example: from A to A#. This is the smallest interval in our music system.

A **Whole-step** is equal to two half-steps (**two frets**). Example: from A, skipping over A#, to B.

Using these new tools for measuring the distances between notes, there is a **formula** that we can apply to any Chromatic Scale in order to derive the infinitely more useful Major Scale. ***And here it comes, the Golden Rule, the absolute foundation of Western Music:***

Starting on the first note of any Chromatic Scale, travel
2 Whole-steps, a Half-step, then 3 Whole-steps and a Half-step.
The resulting group of notes is a **Major Scale**.

If you never learn another blessed thing about music theory, ***learn this!*** Sometimes this rule is abbreviated: *2 Wholes and a Half, 3 Wholes and a Half.*

Let's see right away how this works, using the A Chromatic Scale to create the A Major Scale. Below, you see the A Chromatic Scale laid out with the Whole-step and Half-step intervals marked just beneath it. Remember, when you travel a Whole-step, you ***skip over*** the next note in the sequence, but for a Half-step, you go ***to*** the next note:

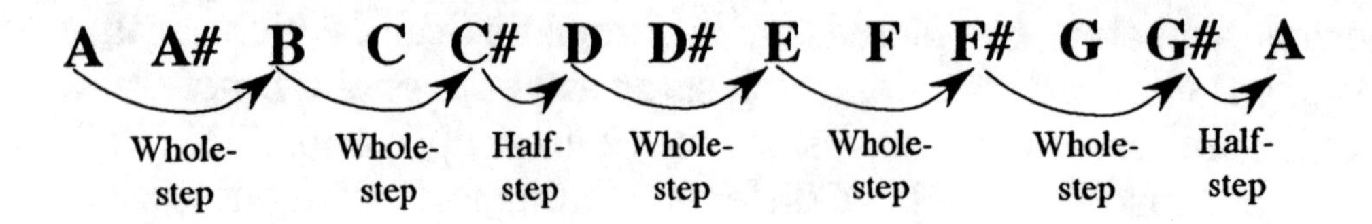

The notes that we have picked out of the A Chromatic Scale by applying the Golden Rule are as follows: A-B-C#-D-E-F#-G#-A. That's the A Major Scale.

Let's briefly go through the process 2 more times, not to really analyze it yet, but to see how it's done. Here's the B-flat Major Scale, which uses the flat names for the accidentals, and the B Major Scale, which uses the sharp names. (I really ***will*** explain why we need both flavors of accidentals soon.)

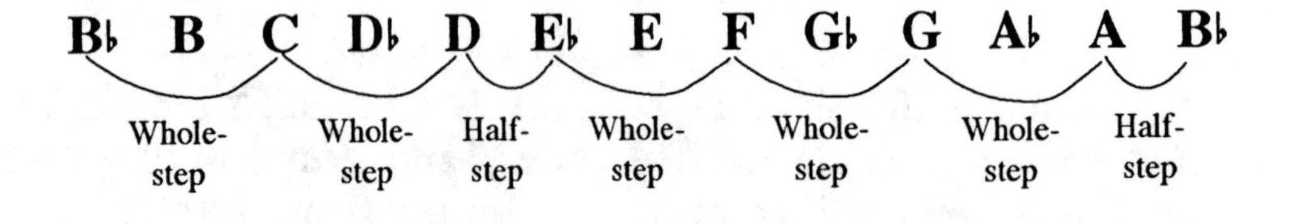

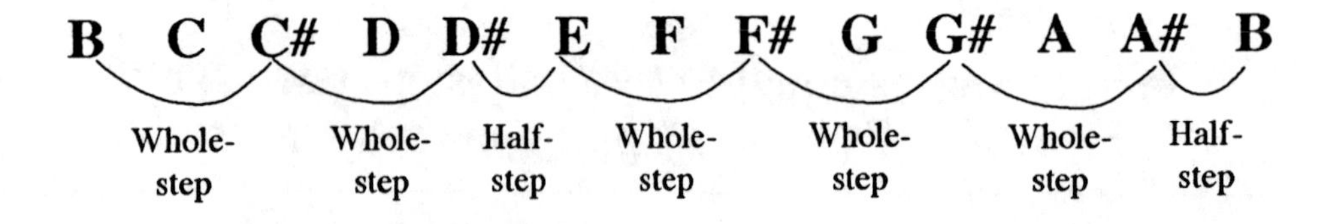

I could run through this process for the other 9 Chromatic Scales to generate the other 9 Major Scales (and will do so later), but I think you can see how our Golden Rule works.

But as we press onward, there is one very special key that we'll focus on to the exclusion of all others for awhile, and that is *(drum roll)* the **Key of C** *(trumpet fanfare).* Here's the Golden Rule applied to the C Chromatic Scale:

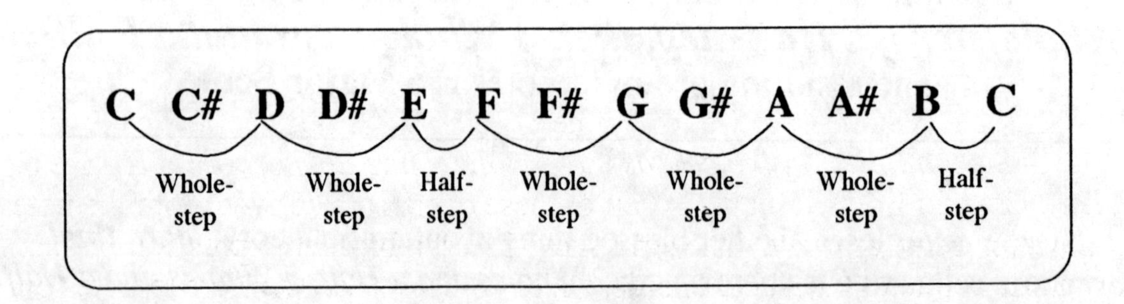

You might notice something interesting as you gaze upon the layout of the C Chromatic Scale: ***No accidentals are selected in the Whole-step / Half-step process.***

Now, this is not a chance occurrence. The reason for it goes back to the piano keyboard. Somebody, somewhere, when designing the keyboard, must have decided that natural notes would occupy the white piano keys and accidentals would occupy the black piano keys. Then there would be *one musical key* (not to be confused with a *piano* key!) to receive the honor of having all natural notes (and therefore all white keys), and it would be the Key of C. Every other musical key would receive some combination of white and black piano keys. How did C get picked? I have no earthly idea.

I'm sure that the history is more complicated than this, but it doesn't really matter ***why*** all of this is the way it is. It just ***is***, and we're stuck with it. This is not to say that this arrangement is bad; in fact, it's probably the simplest way to organize this whole mess. It's just a structure that we need to become familiar with, and the best way to learn music theory is to start with the simplest scale, the all-white-key C Major Scale (despite the fact that all of the notes on a guitar all look alike *anyway).*

You might as well see what the C Major Scale *does* look like on a piano keyboard:

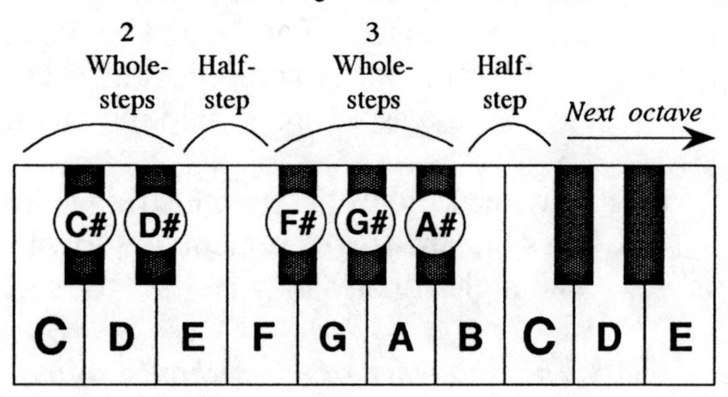

The notes on the keyboard are laid out in the form of one giant Chromatic Scale. For the C Major Scale, it is always a black key that get skipped whenever there is a Whole-step. And at those two points in the scale where there need to be Half-steps, there is no black key. So the Key of C is the easiest key to play on the piano.

On the guitar fretboard, something else determines ease of playing: *how many open strings you get to play*. Considering that criterion, the five *C-A-G-E-D* keys are the easiest to play on the guitar. So the battle plan is to start with the Key of C, dissecting and analyzing it as much as we need to, and then move on to our 4 other favorite keys.

I've been using the terms "key" and "Major Scale" interchangeably. Strictly speaking, the C Major Scale is simply a series of 7 notes: CDEFGAB. But the *Key* of C consists of that C Major Scale *plus all of the chords that belong to the C Chord Family,* like C, F, G, Am, Dm, Em and Bdim. But really, all of these chords are derived from the notes in the C Major Scale anyway. The term "key" is just a broader expression. So........ "Key of C" refers to notes and chords, while "C Major Scale" refers to notes only.

The Key of C

Here again is the diagram showing the process of picking out the notes for the C Major Scale from the C Chromatic Scale:

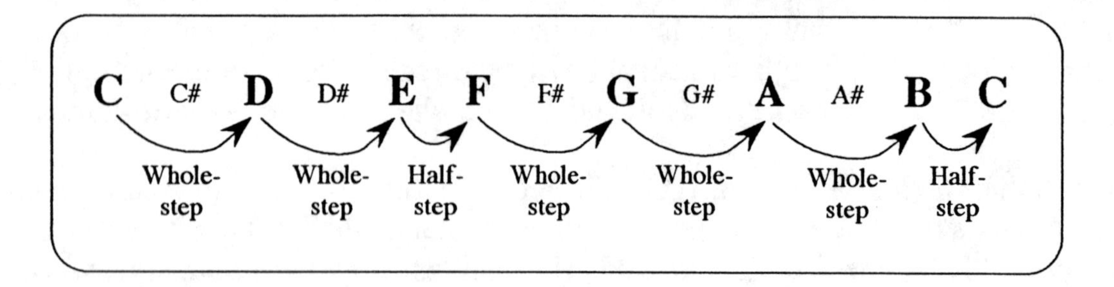

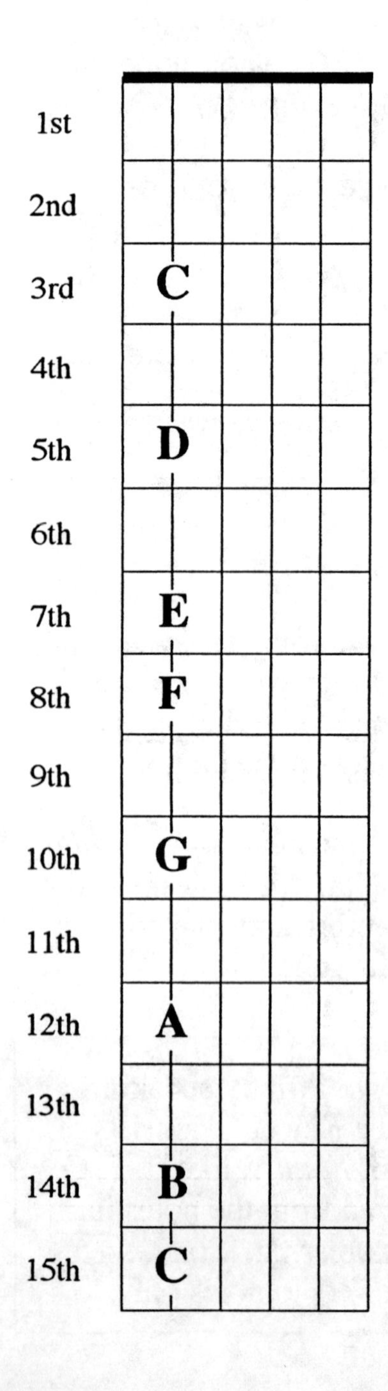

To the left, you see the C Major Scale (all the natural notes) laid out on the 5th string from the 3rd up to the 15th fret. You can actually see the sizes of the Whole-step (2-fret) and the Half-step (1-fret) intervals here. The Half-steps are between frets 7 and 8 and between frets 14 and 15. Major Scale structure is fairly easy to see when the notes are all laid out on one string.

Play these notes up the 5th string starting on the low C (that's the 3rd-fret C; remember, down is up, low is high). The highest notes may be hard to reach on your guitar.

This sequence of notes should sound familiar to you, since the Major Scale is none other than the beloved

"Do - Re - Mi - Fa - Sol - La - Ti - Do."

You've been hearing this particular pattern of notes all your life in millions of songs, perhaps without even knowing that it has a name. But it is the basis of all our music.

You can generate any other Major Scale the very same way. Just pick any note to start with, and travel (all together now...) *2 Whole-steps, then a Half-step, then 3 Whole-steps, then a Half-step.*

Again,what is so special about the C Major Scale is that when you follow this pattern, you manage to skip over all the accidental notes. Every other Major Scale has either one or more sharps or one or more flats. (There are ***no*** scales having combinations of both sharps *and* flats.)

But the truth is that, in practice, you'd never really play a scale using all the notes on the same string. The reason we have multiple strings on the guitar is so that we don't *need* to travel up and up and up the same string in order to play higher and higher notes.

Below, you see a fretboard diagram showing the C Major Scale spread out over 4 strings, while staying in what is called **Open Position**, where both fretted and open strings are used.

The C Major Scale

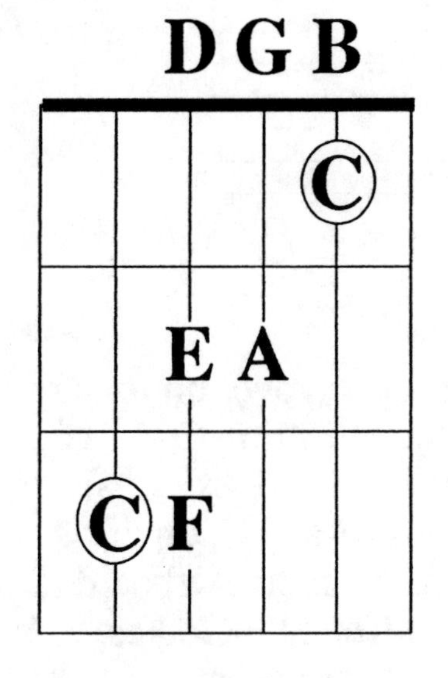

Try playing the C Major Scale alphabetically, starting at the C note on the 5th string / 3rd fret; proceeding to the D note on the open 4th string; the E note at the 2nd fret; and on to the C note one octave higher. Try not to move your hand---use different fingers at different frets.

By changing strings, there is a lot less jumping around, but there is a minor complaint: When we change strings, we lose the ability to ***discern*** the Whole-step / Half-step structure of the Major Scale. The notes sound the same as when you traveled up the same string, *but now you can't really* ***see*** *the intervals* ***between the strings.***

I mean, we know that there is a Whole-step between C and D, but because we need to *change strings* to go from C to D, we don't get to ***see*** the expected 2-fret difference. We just have to know that it really is there. Meanwhile, we actually ***can*** see the 2-fret Whole-step from D to E.

There are two other ways, along with the fretboard diagram, of representing notes on the guitar. One is called **Standard Notation** and the other is called **Tablature Notation.**

In Standard Notation, the horizontal lines and spaces in the **staff** correspond to the actual letter names of the notes. The 1st line, at the bottom, indicates an "E" note, the 1st space indicates "F," then the 2nd line is "G," and so forth, proceeding alphabetically to the top line, which is "F" again, one octave above the "F" at the 1st space.

We can use **ledger lines** to add more notes both above and below the staff. And the **treble clef** (the wiggly thing) always appears at the left end of the staff. The note symbol itself consists of a **head** (the oval part) and a **stem** (the vertical line). Here are the notes on the treble clef and the C Major Scale written in Standard Notation:

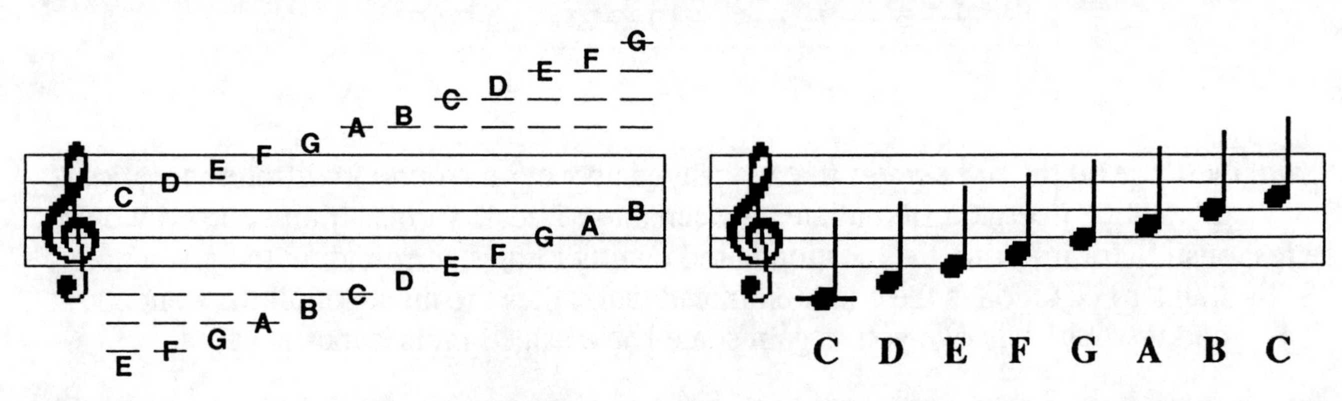

As you've seen before, in **Tablature Notation** ("Tab"), there are 6 horizontal lines that represent the 6 strings of the guitar (6th string at the bottom and 1st string at the top).

The numerals that appear on the lines in the diagram indicate which ***fret*** to hold down on a particular string in order to play the desired note. The "0" indicates an open string, "1" is the 1st fret of whatever string it appears on, "2" is the 2nd fret, and so forth. Here is the C Major Scale expressed in Tablature, next to a fretboard diagram.

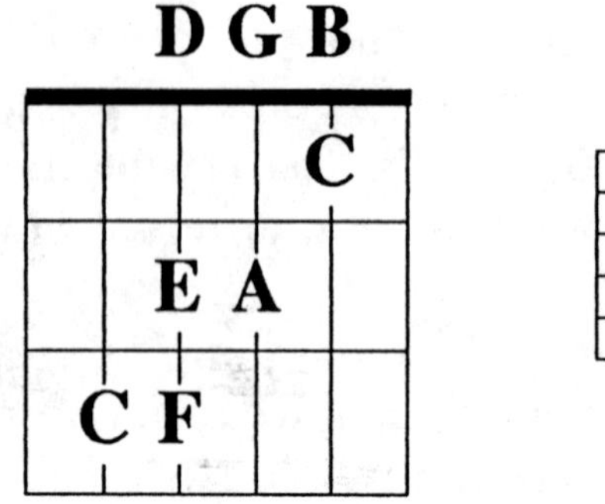

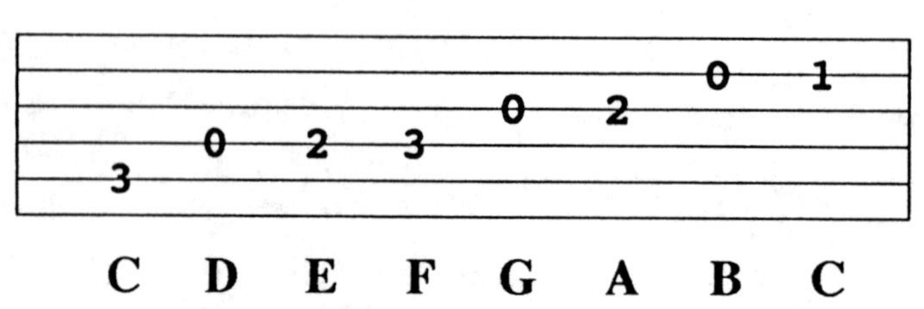

The Tab diagram can be viewed as a fretboard diagram that has been tipped over on its side. That low C note is the only note in our C Major Scale that falls on the 5th string (3rd fret). Then there are 3 notes, D, E and F, that fall on the 4th string (open, 2nd and 3rd frets); 2 notes, G and A, on the 3rd string (open and 2nd fret); and 2 notes, B and C, on the 2nd string (open and 1st fret). But the Tab diagram is more helpful than the fretboard diagram since it can show different ***sequences*** of notes found in different melodies. The fretboard diagram just shows a bunch of notes without regard to sequence.

For our purposes, Tablature has a certain advantage over Standard Notation, too. As you've already seen in the previous chapter, most notes can be found in more than one location on the neck of the guitar. (Do you remember the example of the E note on the open 1st string, which could also be found at the 5th fret of the 2nd string, at the 9th fret of the 3rd string, and at the 14th fret of the 4th string?)

Standard Notation only gives you the name of the note, then you need to figure out which ***position*** of that note you are supposed to play. Tablature tells you the exact location of that note. If we did decide to play the C Major Scale all on the 5th string, we could express it this way in Tab:

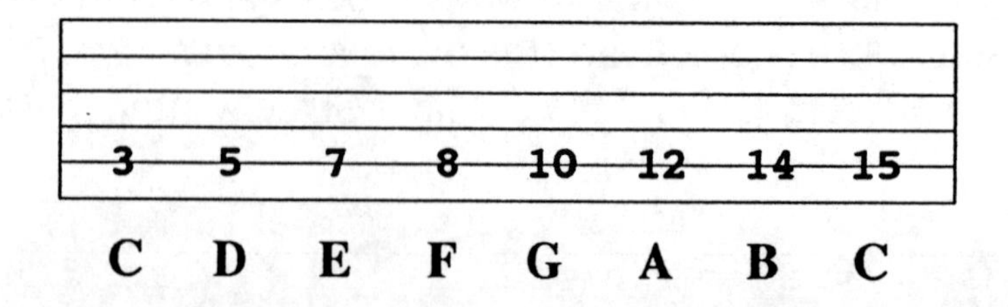

Again, these are all the ***same notes*** that we played above, just found in different locations. Standard Notation doesn't differentiate between these 2 scale forms. You yourself would be responsible for inferring the location based on other notes surrounding the given note. Still, Standard Notation is the common thread that unites the music of all instruments, and it would behoove you to gain some knowledge in this important area.

Let's proceed with our discussion of the C Major Scale using both Tab and Standard Notation:

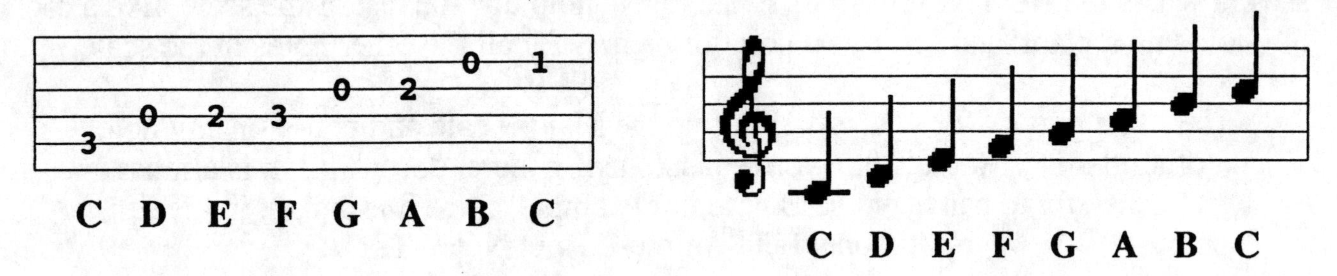

Play the scale over and over and up and down: *Do - Re - Mi - Fa - Sol - La - Ti - Do.* (The Major Scale is known as a **Diatonic Scale** because it consists of 2 ("dia") different types of intervals, Whole-steps and Half-steps.) There are many other kinds of scales, but they mostly trace their origins back to the good ol' Major Scale.

As I say, you've been hearing this scale all of your life. You even know, instinctively, when something is "wrong" with it. Try the following examples:

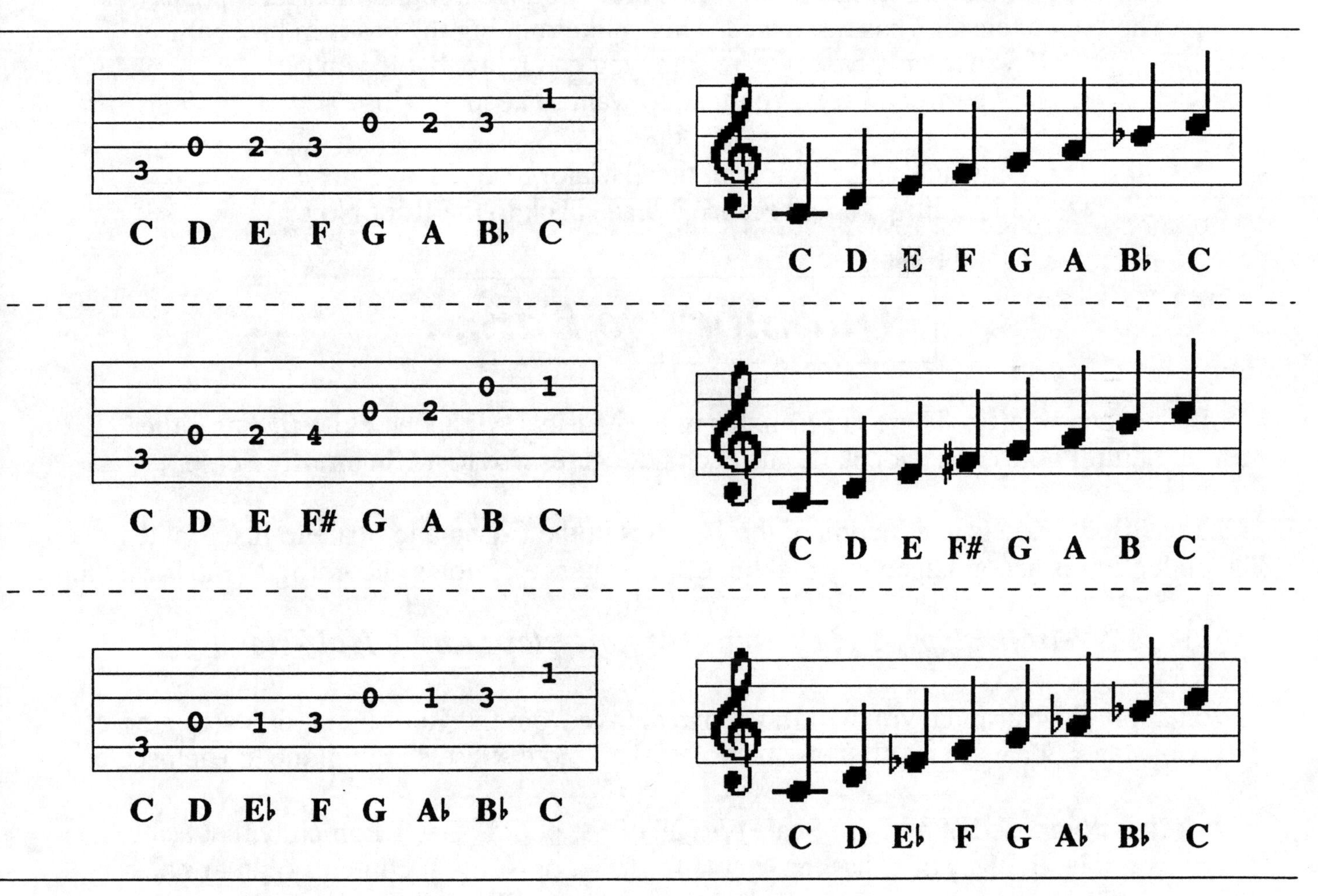

These 3 scales are all C scales, because they start and end on C, but they are not C **Major** Scales, since they all contain at least one accidental note, and as you must know by now, if there is an accidental on board, it is definitely *not* a C Major Scale. The first scale is, in fact, a C Mixolydian Scale; the second is a C Lydian Scale; and the third is a C Minor Scale. I'm telling you this now simply to show off.

Okay, back to the C Major Scale. We need to review some terminology. The two C notes are known as the **Root Notes** of this scale; they "hold up" the rest of the scale, like a root holds up a plant, and serve as a point of ***gravity*** for all the other notes in the scale.

Hear this gravity for yourself. Start up the Major Scale and pause on any note other than C. Sounds like you're just hanging there, doesn't it? It is almost *stressful* to pause on the B note, for example, since it is caught in the "gravitational field" of the C Root Note. Try it:

Now land on the C note at the 1st fret. Ahh! You have found musical repose. The "scale tension" has dissipated. This is like running the bases in baseball. If you're on a base, you're safe, you can relax, but if you're between bases, you tend to want to keep moving.

Incidentally, the B note in the C Major Scale is known as the **Leading Tone**, because it leads back to the Root Note.

Our Story So Far.....

Let's recap briefly. There are 12 notes in the Musical Alphabet, classified as either natural notes or accidentals, and each note gives rise to a **Chromatic Scale.**

The **Major Scale** is a reduction of the 12 notes in the Chromatic Scale to just 7 notes. This reduction is accomplished by picking off a sequence of notes according to the formula:

2 Whole-steps, 1 Half-step, 3 Whole-steps and 1 Half-step.

If you apply this formula, you will travel one **octave** from the **Root Note**, or starting note. No two Major Scales share all the same notes; the 7-note subsets are unique to each scale.

A **key** is composed of a Major Scale *plus* all of the chords that accompany that scale. For example, the Key of C has the C note for its Root Note. It contains 6 other notes, namely D, E, F, G, A, and B, from the C Major Scale. It also contains 7 **chords** that are constructed from each of the 7 notes in the C Major Scale, namely C Major, D Minor, E Minor, F Major, G Major, A Minor and B Diminished. (We'll work through the construction of these chords shortly.)

Any note in the Musical Alphabet can serve as the Root Note for a key. The other notes in the key will pay homage to that dominating Root Note.

Scale Degrees and Keys Other Than C

To address keys other than C, it would be helpful to start talking in terms of **numbers** rather than **letters**. Instead of Do - Re - Mi, or A - B - C, we'll use 1 - 2 - 3. Again, a Major Scale contains 7 different notes, with the 8th note the same as the 1st.

Let's assign the numbers 1 through 7 to the notes in *any* Major Scale, and we'll call these numbers the **7 degrees** of the Major Scale. Think of these degrees as *positions*, or slots, within the scale, which will be occupied by different notes in different keys. For example, in the Key of C, the 3rd degree holds the E note, but in the Key of G, the 3rd degree is B.

So, every Major Scale has 7 degrees that are occupied by a unique set of notes, which is where the *accidentals* will soon come into play. First, here is the setup for the Key of C:

Chromatic Scale	C	C#	D	D#	E	F	F#	G	G#	A	A#	B	C
Formula		*W*		*W*		*H*	*W*		*W*		*W*		*H*
Major Scale	C		D		E	F		G		A		B	C
Scale Degree	1		2		3	4		5		6		7	8

Across the top, I've laid out the Chromatic Scale starting on C. Next I've applied the Golden Rule (what is it?---*2 wholes and a half, 3 wholes and a half)* and pulled down the notes that belong to the Key of C. The scale degrees are given in the bottom row.

There is a **Whole-step** from the 1st to the 2nd degree, from C to D, skipping over the C#.

Then another **Whole-step** from the 2nd to the 3rd degree, from D to E, skipping over the D#.

Next comes a **Half-step** between the 3rd and 4th degree, from E to F. Nothing to skip here.

Then a **Whole-step** from the 4th to the 5th degree, from G to F, skipping F#.

A **Whole-step** from the 5th to the 6th degree, from G to A, skipping G#.

Yet another **Whole-step** from the 6th to the 7th degree, from A to B, skipping A#.

Finally, a **Half-step** from the 7th to the 8th degree, from B to C, with nothing to skip.

Once we have established the 7 notes that occupy the 7 degrees of the scale, we attach no further significance to whether Half-steps or Whole-steps were used to pick them off, and we consider the notes that we've retained to have equal status. And we just plain forget about those notes that we have weeded out. At least for now.

Now we'll finally go on to a key *other* than C, and it will be the **Key of G**.
We'll use the same procedure as above, laying out the Chromatic Scale starting with G, applying the formula, and then bringing down the notes that belong to the Key of G:

Chromatic Scale	G	G#	A	A#	B	C	C#	D	D#	E	F	F#	G
Formula		W		W	H		W		W		W		H
Major Scale	G		A		B	C		D		E		F#	G
Scale Degree	1		2		3	4		5		6		7	8

You probably thought we'd never get around to actually *using* one of those accidentals, but here's your first one, the F# note at the 7th degree of the G Major Scale. Of course, I picked the Key of G because I *knew* it differed from the Key of C by only one note.

As you proceed through the scale with your Whole-steps and Half-steps, it is evident that you keep hitting natural notes, just like in the Key of C, ***until** you go from the 6th to 7th degree.* The 6th degree is E, and since there is no E# note, and since you must now travel a *Whole-step,* you are forced to skip over the F note and land on F#. Then the last Half-step returns you to G, making F# the Leading Tone in the Key of G.

It turns out that in Open Position, you can play not one, but *two* octaves of G Major. The 1st octave starts on the 6th string and ends on the 3rd string, and the 2nd octave starts on the 3rd string and ends on the 1st string. Play through both octaves:

Here's a pop quiz: What would happen if you played this scale with an ***F-natural*** instead of an F-sharp? Answer: You'd just be playing a C Major Scale starting on the "wrong" note! In the determination of key, the Starting Note of the scale doesn't matter; all that matters is ***which accidental notes** you happen to find in the scale.* If it's all natural, it's got to be C. If F# is your only accidental, then you must be playing in the Key of G.

On the following worksheet, I'd like you to get some experience counting out the intervals in order to generate the Major Scales for the five *C-A-G-E-D* keys. Same process as above: Start with the Chromatic Scale. Draw the little brackets for the Whole-steps and Half-steps as you write out the formula and pull down the notes that belong to the Major Scale. I've even scratched in the first Whole-step for you (what a guy):

Key of C

Chromatic Scale	C	C#	D	D#	E	F	F#	G	G#	A	A#	B	C
Formula		W											
Major Scale	C	---	D	---	---	---	---	---	---	---	---	---	---
Scale Degree	1st		2nd										

Key of G

Chromatic Scale	G	G#	A	A#	B	C	C#	D	D#	E	F	F#	G
Formula													
Major Scale	---	---	---	---	---	---	---	---	---	---	---	---	---
Scale Degree													

Key of D

Chromatic Scale	D	D#	E	F	F#	G	G#	A	A#	B	C	C#	D
Formula													
Major Scale	---	---	---	---	---	---	---	---	---	---	---	---	---
Scale Degree													

Key of A

Chromatic Scale	A	A#	B	C	C#	D	D#	E	F	F#	G	G#	A
Formula													
Major Scale	---	---	---	---	---	---	---	---	---	---	---	---	---
Scale Degree													

Key of E

Chromatic Scale	E	F	F#	G	G#	A	A#	B	C	C#	D	D#	E
Formula													
Major Scale	---	---	---	---	---	---	---	---	---	---	---	---	---
Scale Degree													

I hope you ran through the exercise on the previous page, because nothing will convince you that I'm not just pulling your leg quite as effectively as doing the scale mechanics yourself.

Now, why did I pick that particular sequence of keys? Why "**C** -- **G** -- **D** -- **A** -- **E**"? We've already said that these keys are the most commonly played keys on the guitar. But there is something special about ***this particular sequence***.

As I have mentioned before, the number **5** is very important in music. Look at the following sequence of notes taken from several octaves of the C Major Scale:

C - D - E - F - **G** - A - B - C - **D** - E - F - G - **A** - B - C - D - **E**.....

The **C** note is our starting point. The Key of C has no sharps or flats.
From C, travel to the **5th** degree and find **G**. The Key of G has 1 sharp.
From G, travel to the **5th** degree and find **D**. The Key of D has 2 sharps.
From D, travel to the **5th** degree and find **A**. The Key of A has 3 sharps.
From A, travel to the **5th** degree and find **E**. The Key of E has 4 sharps.

Each time, we are traveling an interval of a **Fifth** (or **5th**.) There are other useful intervals, like **2nds**, **3rds**, **4ths**, **6ths** and **7ths**, but the **octave** and the **5th** are the most important.

Also important: If you want to count up a **Fifth** by yourself, with no music professional to guide you, just remember to treat the starting note as "1" and then count to "5" from there.

*A **Fifth** measures 3-and-a-half Whole-steps, which is equal to **7 Half-steps**.*

Let's dig a little deeper, still referring to the results of the previous page:

The Key of C, as I keep saying over and over, has no sharps or flats.

The Key of G has 1 sharp, F#, at the 7th degree, or Leading Tone, of the G Major Scale.

The Key of D has 2 sharps: F# again, and now C#, which is the new Leading Tone.

The Key of A has 3 sharps: F# and C# again, and now G#, which is the Leading Tone.

The Key of E has 4 sharps: F#, C# and G# again, and now D#, which is the Leading Tone.

I think there's a pattern here, eh? Starting with the Key of C, every time you go up a **Fifth**, you add 1 sharp to the new key. The sharps from each key are retained in the next key, and the new sharp is always added at the 7th degree (Leading Tone) of the scale. The next page shows all the answers for the exercise on the previous page.

Major Scales for the Guitar

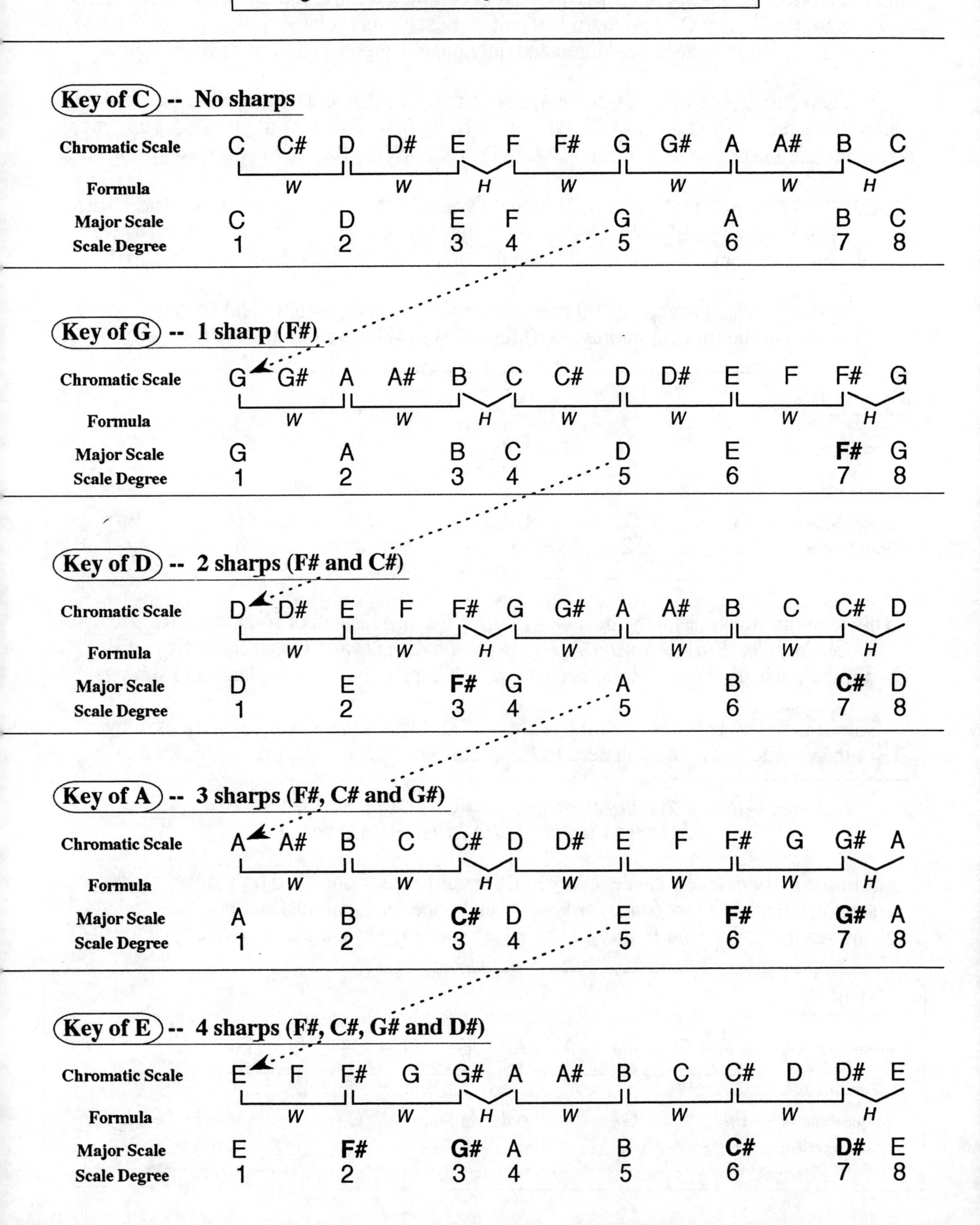

So the farther away you travel by **Fifths** from the Key of C, the more sharps you add. This means that those keys have less and less in common with, and are therefore less closely ***related*** to, the Key of C. The sharp key that is most closely related to the Key of C is the Key of G, with 6 notes in common and only one difference, namely F# instead of F.

We could continue with this process, going up by a **Fifth** and adding sharps to each successive key. After the Key of E comes the Key of B---count it out yourself---use your fingers like I do. The Key of B adds A#. Then comes the Key of F# which adds E#.....

"Now, hold on a minute," you say, "I thought you said there was no E-sharp. And what's this Key of F-*sharp* stuff? What happened to the Key of F-*natural?* And as long as we're asking questions, what about all those ***flat*** notes and keys you keep bringing up?"

Okay, okay. Let's start with the questions concerning F-sharp and E-sharp. Lay out the (not commonly used) Key of B in Whole-steps and Half-steps:

Key of B

							↓						
Chromatic Scale	B	C	C#	D	D#	E	F	F#	G	G#	A	A#	B
Formula		W		W		H		W		W		W	H
Major Scale	B		**C#**		**D#**	E		(**F#**)		**G#**		**A#**	B
Scale Degree	1		2		3	4		5		6		7	8

This diagram illustrates why the next key up is F-sharp instead of F-natural. Regardless of the key, *the **Fifth** is always 7 Half-steps above the **Root**.* Up until the Key of B, this rule has produced natural notes at the 5th degree, but now we land on F-*sharp*.

So our next key is F-sharp, with 6 sharps. We'll lay out the Key of F-sharp as above. But there's one more rule you need to know concerning the "spelling" of Major Scales:

Each degree of a Major Scale must be occupied by a ***different letter*** *of the Musical Alphabet.*

So, in the F-sharp Major Scale, every letter should appear once and only once; however, we see the letter "F" *twice* (once for F-sharp and once for F-natural) and no letter "E" at all. *So we need to create the **E-sharp** note, which is really the same as F, to satisfy the rule.*

Key of F#

Chromatic Scale	F#	G	G#	A	A#	B	C	C#	D	D#	E	F	F#
Formula		W		W		H		W		W		W	H
Major Scale	**F#**		**G#**		**A#**	B		**C#**		**D#**		(**F**)	(**F#**)
Scale Degree	1		2		3	4		5		6		7	8
												→**E#**←	

Now let's take a brief look at why we need those flat notes and flat keys.
What if we were to travel ***backward*** or ***downward*** by a **Fifth** from the C note?
Well, it would help if we had been taught to recite the alphabet *backward* in school,
but here goes: **C** - B - A# - A - G# - G - F# - **F** (7 Half-steps or 3 1/2 Whole-steps).
This is where the Key of F-*natural* comes into play. Here's the layout for the Key of F,
using the Chromatic Scale expressed in natural notes and sharps, as we've been doing:

Key of F

Chromatic Scale	F	F#	G	G#	A	A#	B	C	C#	D	D#	E	F
Formula		W		W		H		W		W		W	H
Major Scale	F		G		(A)	(A#)		C		D		E	F
Scale Degree	1		2		3	4		5		6		7	8
						→ B♭ ←							

Even a casual inspection of the above diagram reveals a conflict with our new rule:
Every letter should appear once and only once in the Major Scale; however, we see
the letter "A" *twice* (once for A-natural and once for A-sharp) and no letter "B" at all.
Since A-sharp is the same note as B-flat, we need to go with B-flat to satisfy the rule.

The Key of F contains all natural notes ***except for 1 flat.*** So the Key of F is just as closely
related to the Key of C as the Key of G is, which has all natural notes ***except for 1 sharp.***
But the Key of G and the Key of F differ *from each other* by 2 accidentals, F versus F# and
B versus B♭. This means that each of them is more closely related to the Key of C than they
are to *each other,* even though F and G sit right next to each other in the Musical Alphabet!

Let's do one more flat key. Let's do the key that has 2 flats, which happens to be
the Key of B-flat. And from your most recent experiences, you might have guessed
that the B-flat note is a ***Fifth below F.*** This time we'll lay out the Chromatic Scale using
natural notes and **flats**, as we *should* have done for the F Major Scale in the diagram above:

Key of B♭

Chromatic Scale	B♭	B	C	D♭	D	E♭	E	F	G♭	G	A♭	A	B♭
Formula		W		W		H		W		W		W	H
Major Scale	B♭		C		D	E♭		F		G		A	B♭
Scale Degree	1		2		3	4		5		6		7	8

For the Key of B-flat, we keep the B-flat note that we got from the Key of F,
and add one more flat, E-flat, at the **4th** degree. (Note the required 7 Half-steps
of a **5th** between B-flat and F.) As a rule, for the flat keys, the **4th** degree of the
scale you happen to be looking at indicates the next key that is down a **Fifth**.
So from B-flat, the subsequent keys are E-flat, A-flat, D-flat and G-flat.

As I've said before, the flat keys don't particularly interest the average guitar player, since we would need to play lots of hard barre chords. But you might be wondering *exactly why* the flat keys require the extensive use of barre chords. Well, I'll tell you. It's because the ***open strings*** of the guitar are tuned to E - A - D - G - B - E.

Now, if a Root Note of a chord is on an open string, you don't need to use up a finger in order to play that note; you've got it for free. And the 5 open-string notes (EADGB) figure prominently in the five *C-A-G-E-D* keys, which give us those nice, simple chords. The flat keys just don't give us as many opportunities to use open strings, and we grumble.

In other words, if the guitar were tuned E♭ - A♭ - D♭ - G♭ - B♭ - E♭, (which is a Half-step lower than Standard Tuning), we'd prefer the *flat* keys, because then we could take advantage of the open flat-noted strings.

But we still need to understand flat keys, since piano and horn players like them because those instruments are set up to play flat keys more easily. And if you ever play with these folks, you'll keep smacking right into them. The flats, I mean.

Guitarists have several options for playing in flat keys. One option is to bite the bullet and learn how to finger barre chords. You will be amazed at the vast array of chord qualities you'll have at your fingertips when you can play barre chords. The other option is to strategically place a capo where you can play simple chord shapes instead of needing to barre. More on this process in ***Volume Two.***

By the way, it turns out that the sharp Keys of B and F-sharp contain lots of barre chords, too, so we aren't just picking on the flat keys. But even within the keys we like, the more sharps you have in the key, the more barre chords show up. Look at C, G, D, A and E:

The Key of C has one *potential* barre chord, F, but we can play a decent simpler version.

The Key of G has one barre chord, **Bm**. This is the **3m chord** in the Key of G, so it doesn't appear too often anyway.

The Key of D has 2 barre chords: Bm and now **F#m**, which is also the **3m chord** in this key.

The Key of A has 3 barre chords: Bm, F#m and now **C#m**, which is, again, the **3m chord** in this key.

The Key of E has 4 barre chords: Bm, F#m, C#m, and now **G#m**, which is, yet again, the **3m chord**.

By the way, in the interests of trying to help you learn the order of the keys (by **Fifths**) from C all the way to F#, I present the following memory aid:

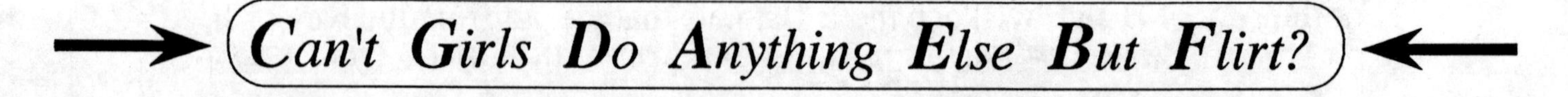

If you are female, substitute the word **G**uys. I thought of that all by myself.

Here are the C, G, D, A and E Major Scales for both fretboard and keyboard.
I took piano lessons as a tyke, and I still visualize how Major Scales look on the keyboard.

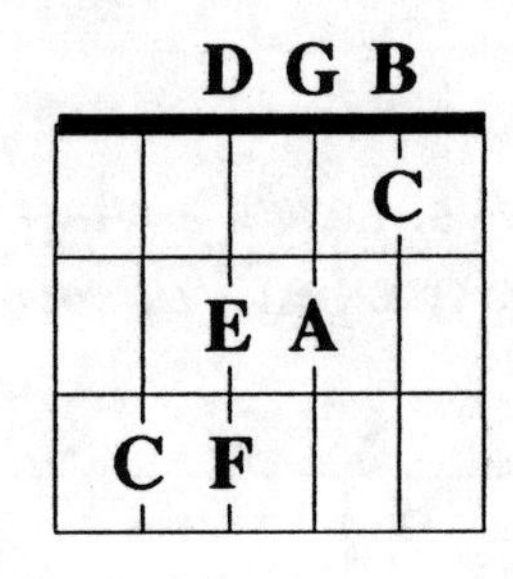

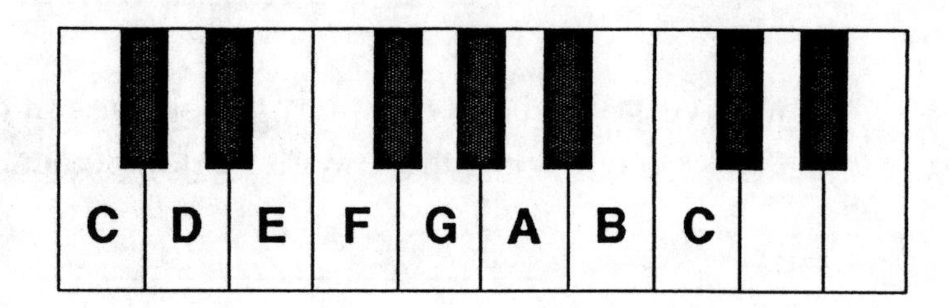

Two octaves

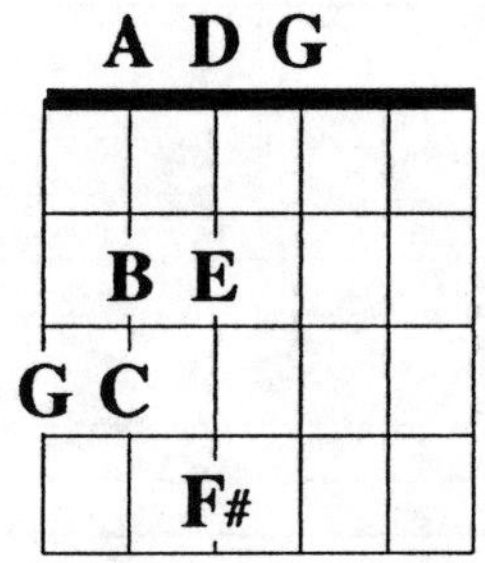

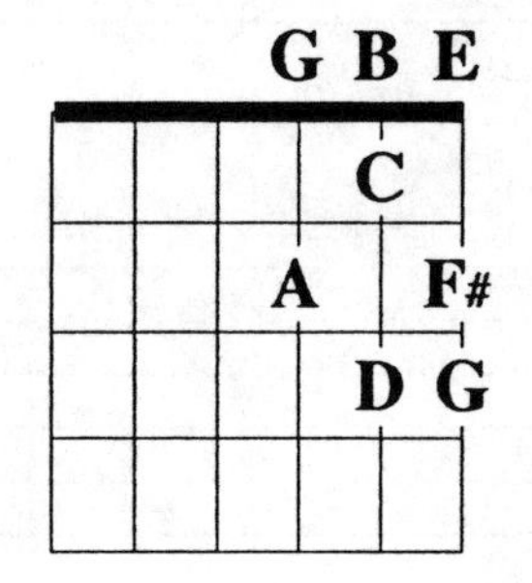

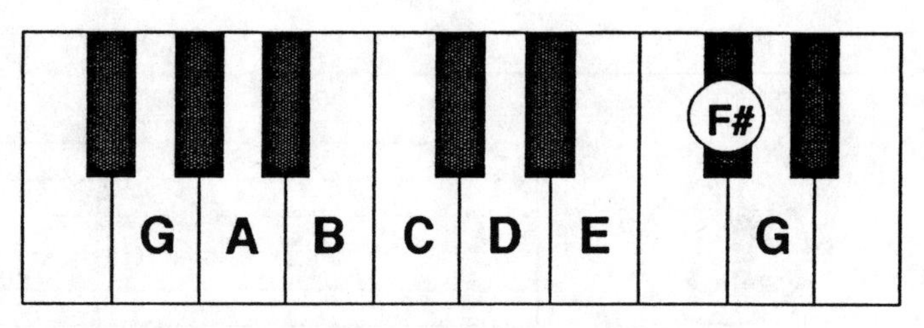

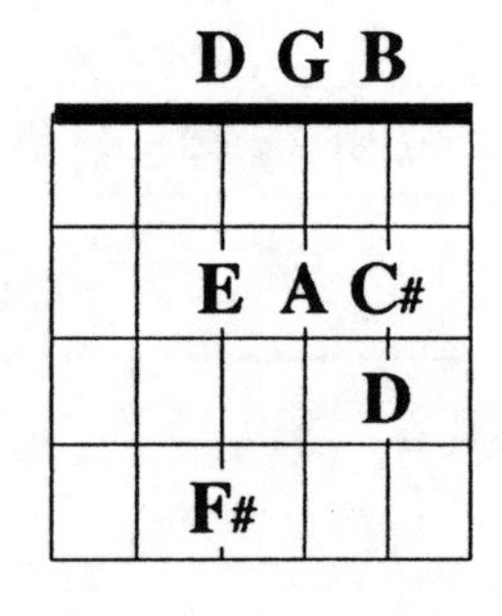

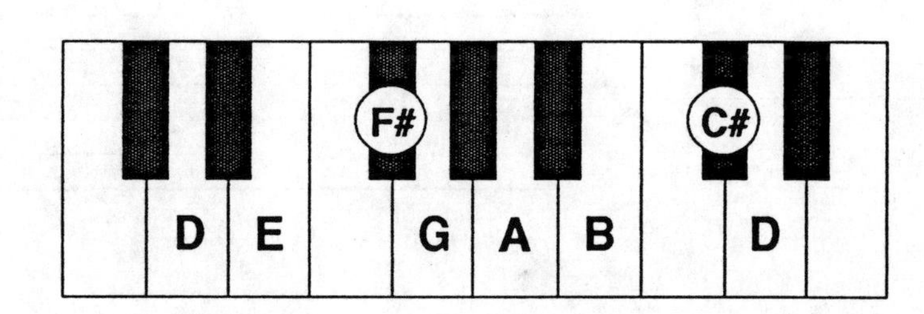

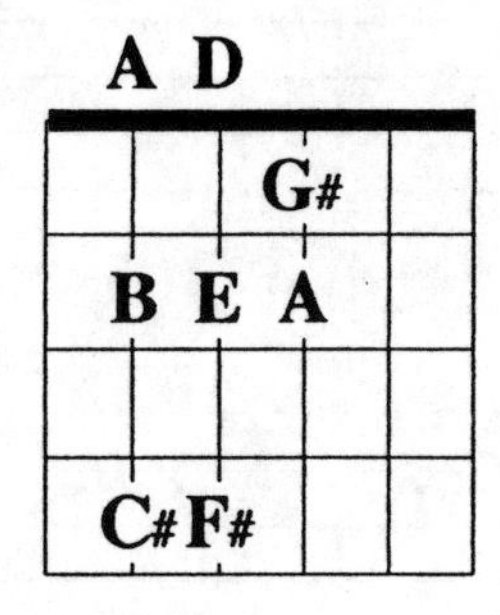

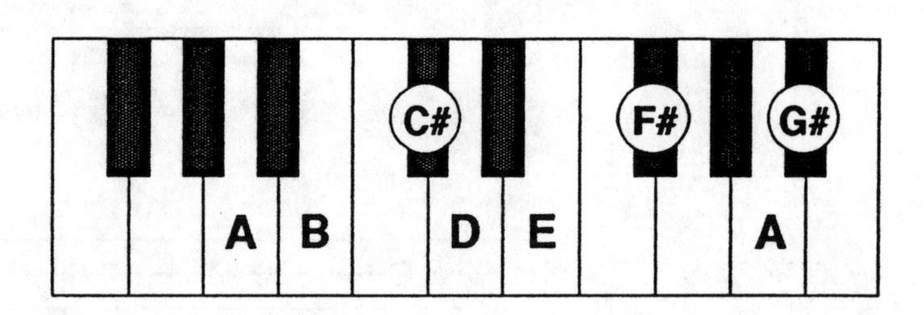

Two octaves

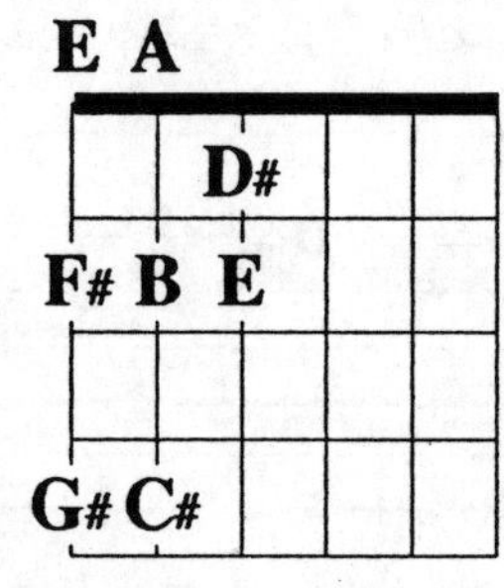

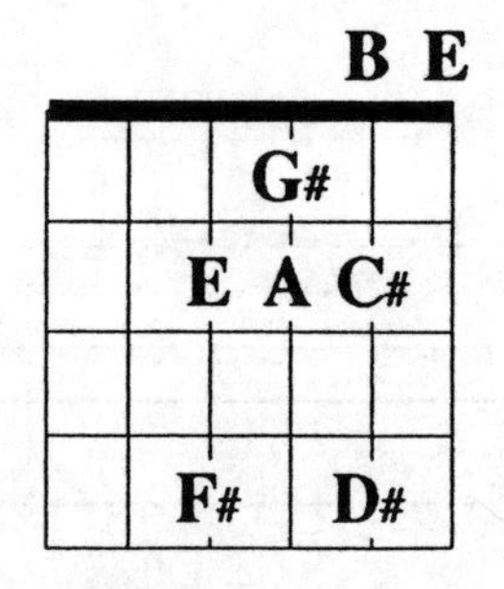

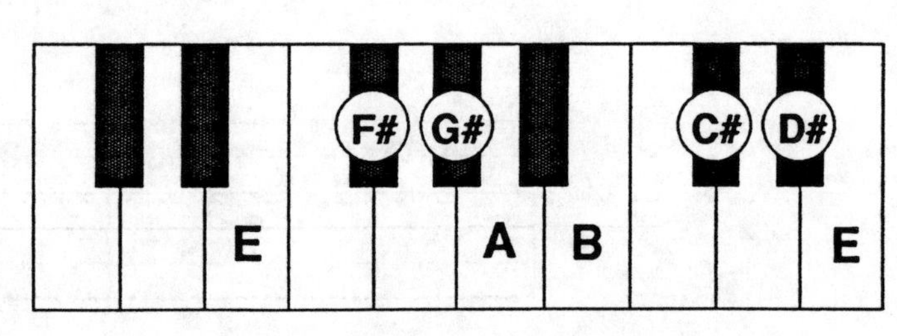

Major Scale Exercises

Just to give you a taste of playing melodies in different keys, here's a Major Scale exercise. We'll work more with Major Scales all over the neck in ***Volume Two.***

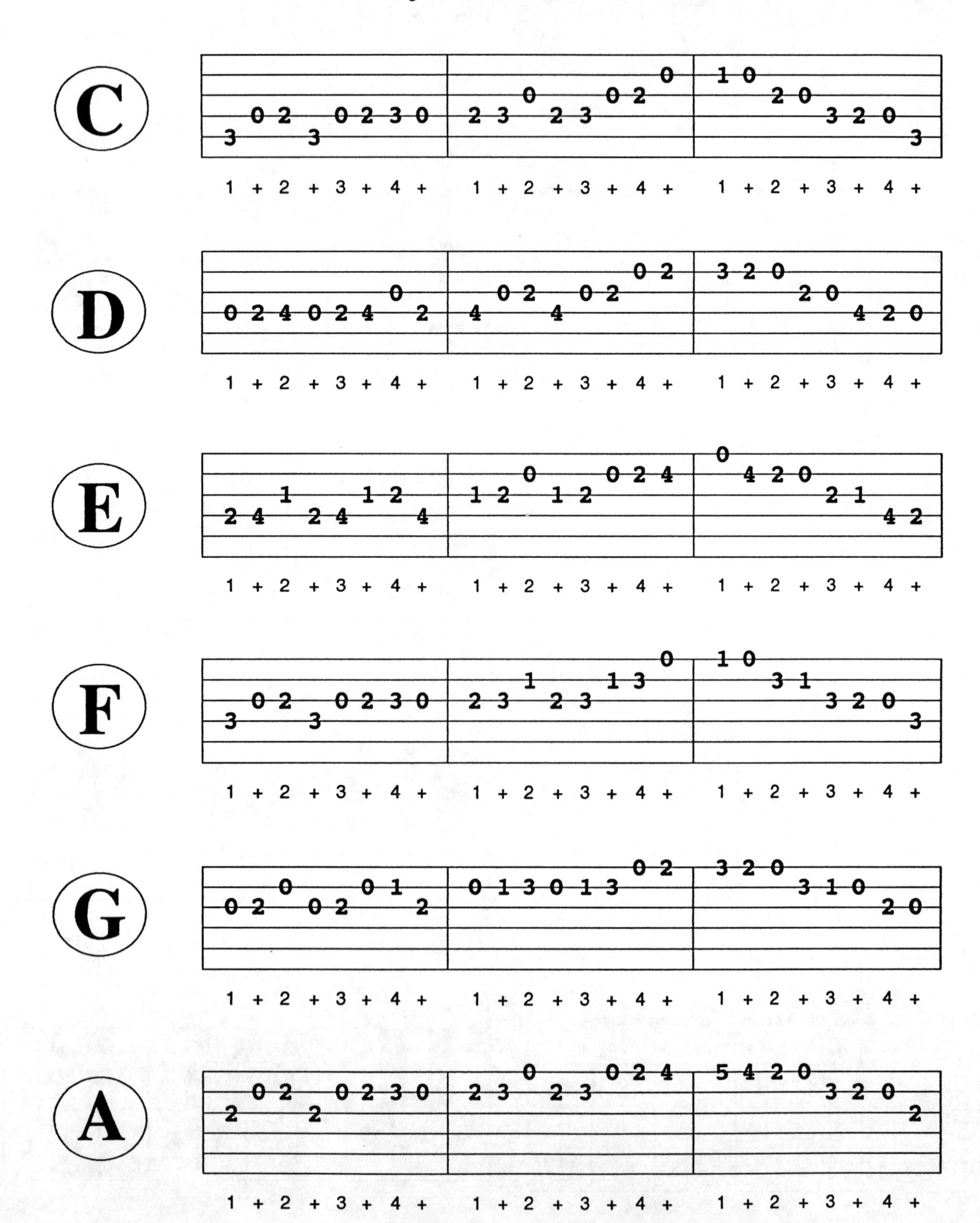

Back to Chord Families

Now that you have a pretty good grasp of how Major Scales are generated from the raw material of the Musical Alphabet, it's time to return to the world of **chords** and find out how Chord Families are themselves generated from the Major Scale. Some of this will be a rehash, but if you're like me, you don't mind hearing the same thing several times over if it helps to reinforce what I *think* I understand.

The simplest kind of chord is known as a **triad**, because it contains 3 ("tri") different notes. A chord like an E chord may have all 6 strings ringing, but you are hearing various octaves of only ***3 different notes*** (three E notes, two B notes and a G#).

There is a rule for constructing these triads from Major Scales; in a nutshell, it's "**1 - 3 - 5**" (not to be confused with "**1 - 4 - 5**"). You can take any note in the scale and call it the **Triad Root** (not necessarily the Root Note, or keynote, of the scale itself). Proceeding up the scale (to the right), skip the 2nd note, take the ***3rd*** one, skip the 4th one and take the ***5th*** one. That's a triad: **1 - 3 - 5**.

Let's generate the Chord Family for our old friend, the Key of C. We'll begin, as always, with the C Major Scale and show the scale degrees:

C	D	E	F	G	A	B
1	2	3	4	5	6	7

The C note is the **1st** degree of the C Major Scale. When the C note is the Triad Root, then the C triad will be "**C** - (skip D) - **E** - (skip F) - **G**," or just "**C - E - G.**" This is the **1 chord**.

The D note is the **2nd** degree of the C Major Scale. When the D note is the Triad Root, then the D triad will be "**D** - (skip E) - **F** - (skip G) - **A**," or just "**D - F - A.**" This is the **2 chord**.

The E note is the **3rd** degree of the C Major Scale. When the E note is the Triad Root, then the E triad will be "**E** - (skip F) - **G** - (skip A) - **B**," or just "**E - G - B.**" This is the **3 chord**.

Well, you get the idea. This process continues all the way through the **7th** degree, and the resulting group of 7 chords constitutes the C Chord Family. The whole thing is worked out for you on the next page.

You may remember from before that the **1**, **4** and **5 chords** have Major chord qualities; the **2**, **3** and **6 chords** have Minor chord qualities; and the **7 chord** has a Diminished quality. Over the next several pages, I'll explain *exactly* what the structural differences are between these 3 types of chords, beyond just saying that they are "happy" or "sad" or something. And we'll use our new tools, Whole-steps and Half-steps, to get the job done.

There is a more technical expression for the Chord Family. In classical music theory, it is called the **Harmonized Diatonic Scale.** We take a *diatonic* scale, one that is composed of Whole-steps and Half-steps, and we *harmonize* each note in the scale by adding other notes according to the formula: **1 - 3 - 5.**
Here, then, is the C Harmonized Diatonic Scale:

C - E - G is **C Major.**
It has a **1st**-degree
Triad Root.

C - D - **E** - F - **G** - A - B - C - D - E - F
1 3 5

D - F - A is **D Minor.**
It has a **2nd**-degree
Triad Root.

C - **D** - E - **F** - G - **A** - B - C - D - E - F
1 3 5

E - G - B is **E Minor.**
It has a **3rd**-degree
Triad Root.

C - D - **E** - F - **G** - A - **B** - C - D - E - F
1 3 5

F - A - C is **F Major.**
It has a **4th**-degree
Triad Root.

C - D - E - **F** - G - **A** - B - **C** - D - E - F
1 3 5

G - B - D is **G Major.**
It has a **5th**-degree
Triad Root.

C - D - E - F - **G** - A - **B** - C - **D** - E - F
1 3 5

A - C - E is **A Minor.**
It has a **6th**-degree
Triad Root.

C - D - E - F - G - **A** - B - **C** - D - **E** - F
1 3 5

B - D - F is **B Diminished.**
It has a **7th**-degree
Triad Root.

C - D - E - F - G - A - **B** - C - **D** - E - **F**
1 3 5

Here are fretboard diagrams, tabs and staves for the chords in the C Chord Family. I wanted to put the notes in each triad on ***3 different strings*** so you could hear the notes all ringing together. Problem is, there are some awkward fingerings here.

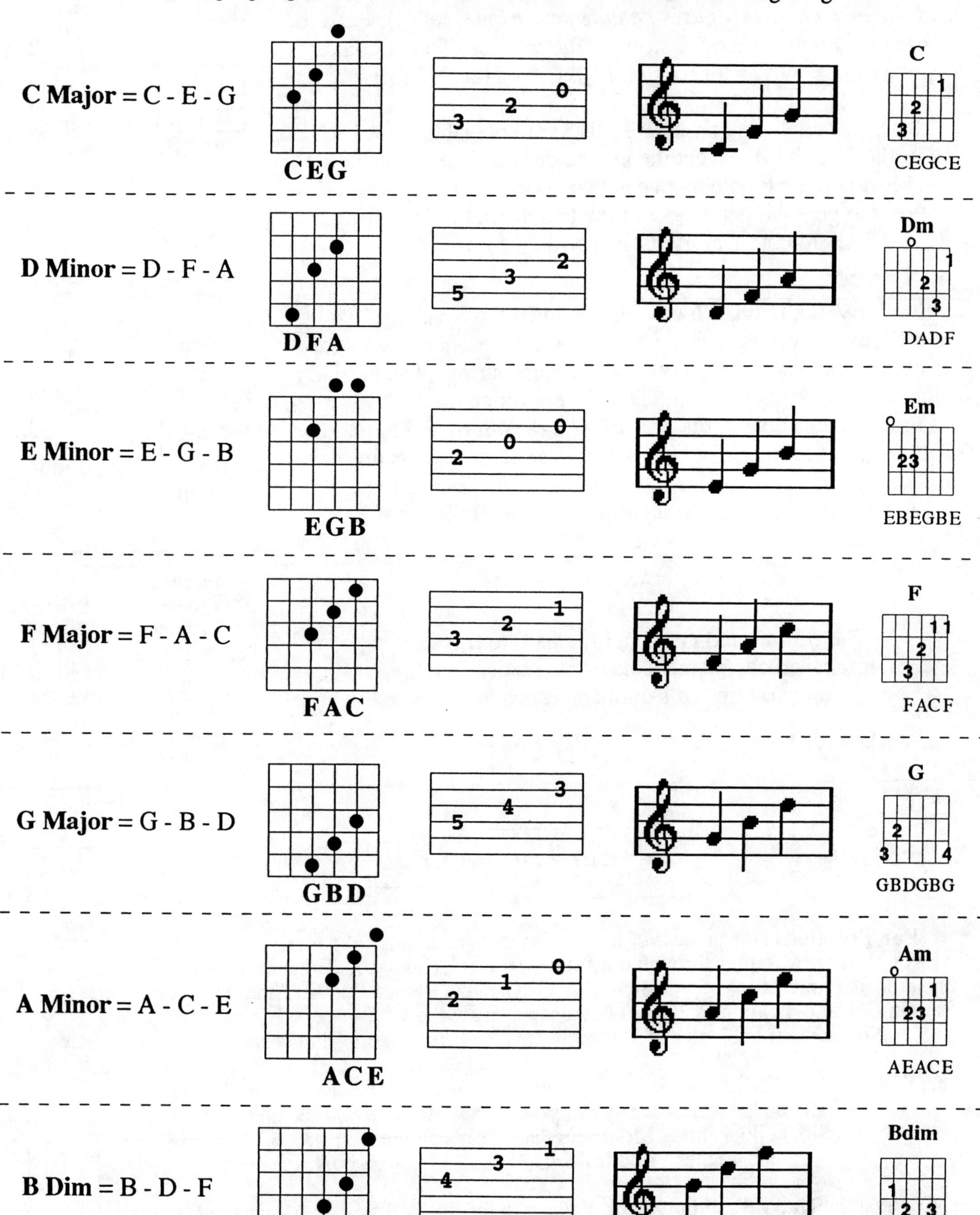

Why does the **Dm triad** look the way it does? My goal was to get all 3 notes on separate strings. The Dm triad is spelled D-F-A. Well, the 4th string contains both the D and the F note, *and since you can only play one note per string* (really!), I had to use the D note on the *5th* string at the *5th* fret. Then I could play the F on the 4th string (and the A on the 3rd string).

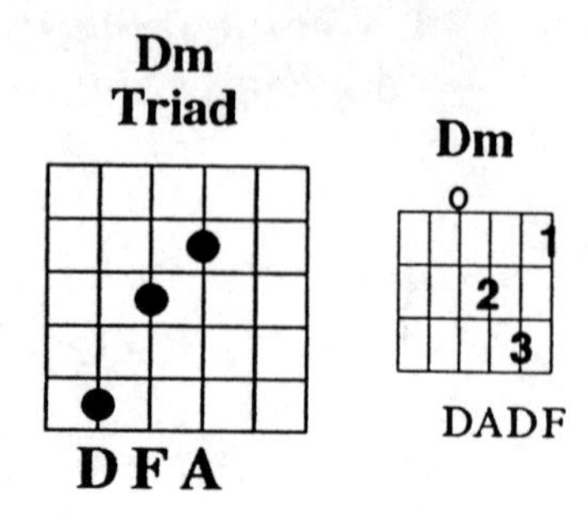

Sorry about that stretch. In the more playable form of the Dm chord, we get the D note on the open 4th string, and just pop the F note up one octave to the 1st string, 1st fret. We also get a higher octave of the D note on the 2nd string. They're both Dm triads, just arranged differently.

Similarly, the **G triad** looks funny. In fact, it looks just like the F triad moved up 2 frets. I had the same problem here that I had with Dm: There are 2 notes on the same string. The G triad is spelled G-B-D. Both the B and D notes are found on the 2nd string, so I moved the B note to the 3rd string at the 4th fret. Ah, but then I had another problem. The G note that I needed *also* occupies the 3rd string (the open note), so I had to move the G over to the 4th string at the 5th fret. Good thing we have all these strings.

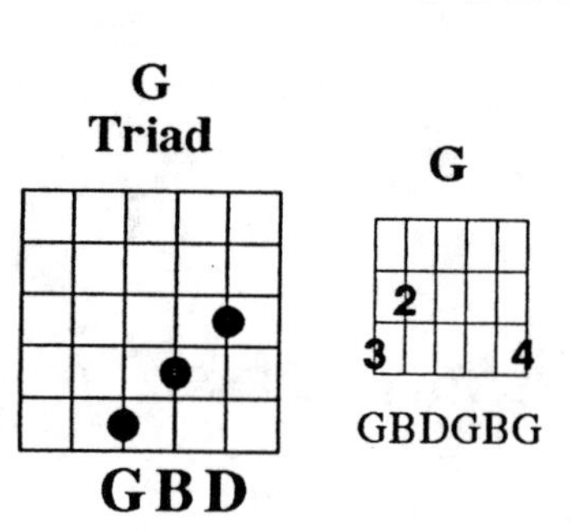

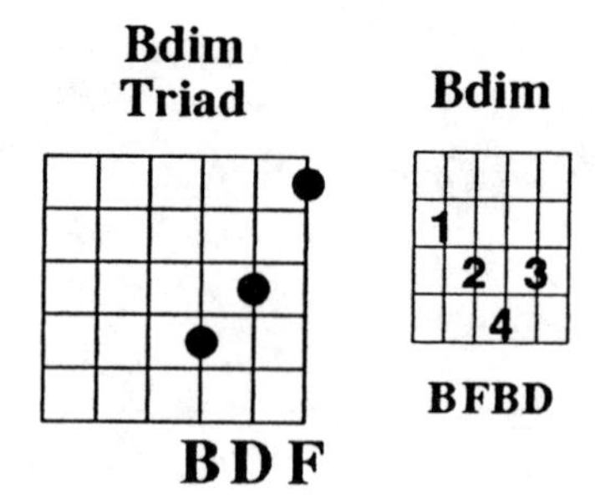

The **Bdim triad** is also a little hard to finger. Diminished chords have that same restless quality that you find in Dominant 7th chords.

Ear Training Tip

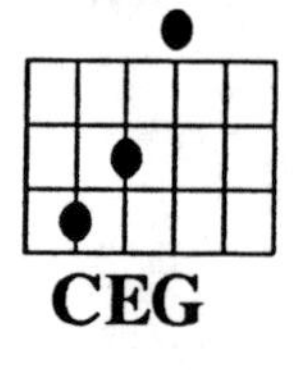

Ear Training is the process of learning to recognize musical patterns by ear. I would like you to play through the Major triads (C, F and G), shown here again, one note at a time. **1 - 3 - 5**. C-E-G. F-A-C. G-B-D. Remember the Three Stooges singing, "Hello, hello, hello!"? Well, those notes are the **1 - 3 - 5** of a Major triad. So are the first 3 notes of "Morning Has Broken:" "Morn - ing has..."

FAC

There's also a **1 - 3 - 5** Major triad embedded in the first line of our National Anthem. It falls on the words "...say can you..." "Oh, *say can you* see..." "Hello, hello, hello.....Morn - ing has.....say can you.....**1 - 3 - 5**." Same 3 notes. And it works for all 3 Major chords.

Contrast the **1 - 3 - 5's** of the Major triads with the **1 - 3 - 5's** of the Minor triads. The Minor chords sound more like "Goodbye, goodbye, goodbye." Melancholy.

GBD

Major Chords Versus Minor Chords

Skip It, sorta

Skip It, sorta

So, what exactly distinguishes a Major chord from a Minor chord, and where did this *Diminished* chord come from?

You know that a triad has a **1 - 3 - 5** structure that comes from a Major Scale. These 3 scale degrees are also known as the **Root**, the **3rd** and the **5th**. We can divide the **1 - 3 - 5** structure into two intervals, the **1 - 3** interval and the **3 - 5** interval. The **1 - 3** interval is considered to be the *lower* interval of the two, in terms of pitch. The **1 - 3** interval sits on the "bottom" of the triad and the **3 - 5** interval sits on "top."

The interval between the **Root** and the **3rd** is called a **Third** (counted 1-2-3, or C-D-E). And the interval between the **3rd** and the **5th** is *also* a **Third** (counted 3-4-5, or E-F-G).

The jargon is getting a bit confusing, but it does fit our rule for naming intervals: For each interval, think of the first note as "1," then count up 2 more notes to make "3." So both the **1 - 3** interval (1-2-3) and the **3 - 5** interval (3-4-5) are counted out as **Thirds.**

But here's the kicker: *Those **Thirds** are not the same size.*

Okay, let's back up and use the C Chromatic and Major Scales in some examples. First we'll look at the size of the **Fifth**, then we'll look at the the sizes of the two **Thirds.** Here's the Chromatic Scale from C, which is the **Root**, to G, which is the **5th degree.** I've highlighted the notes that are also in the Major Scale:

C - C# - **D** - D# - **E** - **F** - F# - **G**

The interval is called a **Fifth**. Count the notes in the *Major Scale:* C-D-E-F-G. But the interval measures **7 Half-steps**. Count the number of ***spaces*** between all the notes in the *Chromatic Scale* (or the hyphens, if you like).

Do you see the distinction between these two ways of counting? One is for ***calculating the size,*** or width, of an interval and the other is for ***naming*** the interval. Look at it this way:

*The **size** of an interval is based on the **distances** between the notes measured in the **Chromatic** Scale. For a **Fifth**, that's 7 Half-steps.*

*But the **name** of the interval is based on the **number** of notes counted in the **Major** Scale. For a **Fifth**, that's 5.*

The good news is that an interval of a **Fifth** always equals 7 Half-steps.
But look at the **1 - 3** interval versus the **3 - 5** interval, both of which we call **Thirds**:

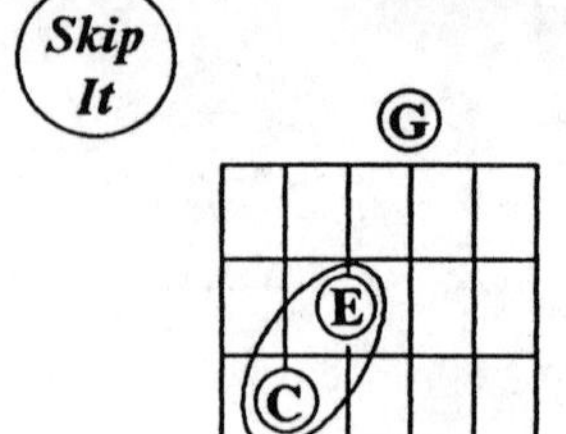

Bottom Third

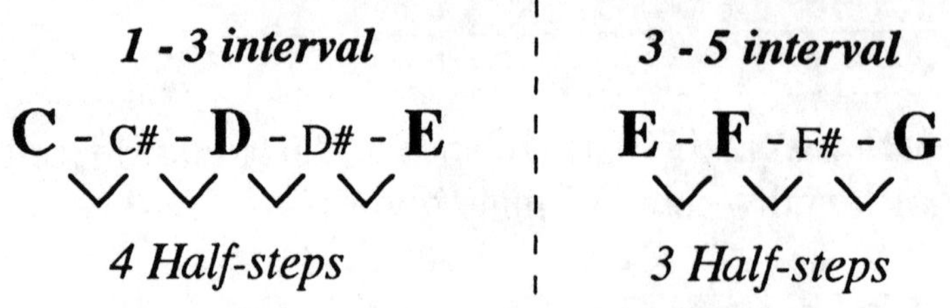

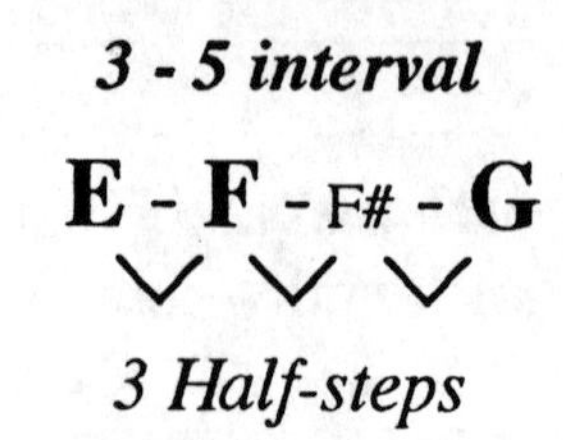

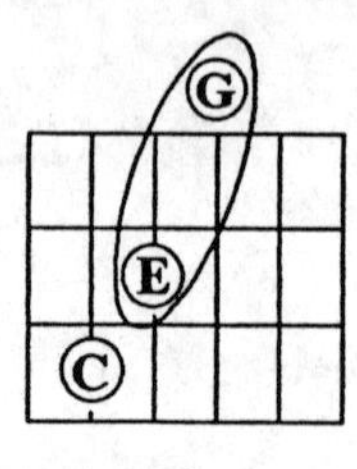

Top Third

The two intervals differ by one Half-step.
So we need to further distinguish between types of **Thirds**:

> An interval of ***4 Half-steps*** is called a **Major Third**.
> An interval of ***3 Half-steps*** is called a **Minor Third**.
>
> *So a **C Major triad** consists of a **Major Third** (C to E) on the bottom plus a **Minor Third** (E to G) on the top.*

Of course, the interval from C straight to G is a **Fifth**, which seems to imply that "***3 + 3 = 5,***" that is, a **Third** (C-D-E) plus a **Third** (E-F-G) equals a **Fifth** (C-D-E-F-G). But when adding the two **Thirds** together, you only count the overlapping E note ***once.***

Let's take a side-trip here. Behold the structure of a ***C Minor triad (Cm).***
We haven't talked about Cm before, but bear with me for a few minutes.

> *To construct a C Minor triad, lay out the Chromatic Scale and put the **Minor Third** on the **bottom** and the **Major Third** on the **top**.*

It's just the reverse of a Major triad. Here's how it works out:

C - C# - D - **E♭** - E - F - F# - **G**

3 Half-steps *4 Half-steps*

We just reverse the order of the 2 intervals and use E-flat instead of D-sharp (our rule).
By the way, does the Cm chord belong to the Key of C? Nope, no flats allowed.

> To summarize: In distinguishing between Major and Minor triads, we focus on the **1 - 3** interval, which is the bottom **Third** of the triad:
>
> *If the **1 - 3** interval of a triad is a **Major Third**, the chord quality is **Major**.*
> *If the **1 - 3** interval of a triad is a **Minor Third**, the chord quality is **Minor**.*

Skip It

I would like you to play the **1 - 3** intervals on your guitar for the 6 Major and Minor chords in the C Chord Family. So I've given you 6 fretboard diagrams so you can both *hear* and *see* the Major Thirds and Minor Thirds that determine chord quality.

Skip It

I've located the notes belonging to each of the **1 - 3** intervals on the same string, so you can more easily count the number of Half-steps. For the C chord, for example, the **1 - 3** interval is "C-E," and those notes are to be found on the 3rd and 7th frets, respectively, of the 5th string. That's a 4-fret difference. For the Dm chord, the **1 - 3** interval is "D-F," found on the open and 3rd frets of the 4th string. That's a 3-fret difference. I've used an arrow to indicate where a playable unison note is found, so that you can actually get both notes in the interval ringing at the same time on two separate strings. Listen for "Happy" and "Sad."

C chord

C to E = 4 Half-steps
= **Major Third**

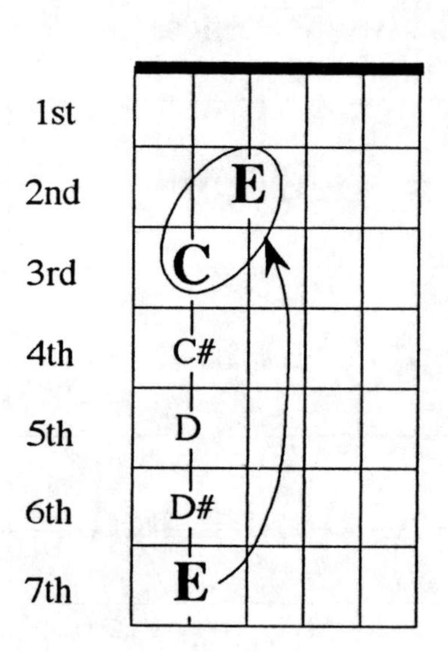

Dm chord

D to F = 3 Half-steps
= **Minor Third**

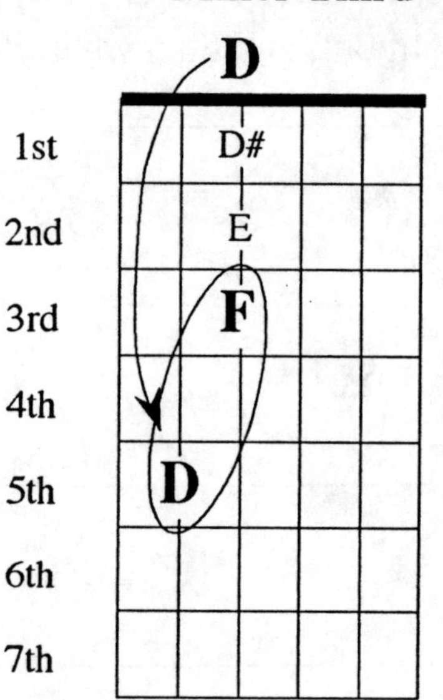

Em chord

E to G = 3 Half-steps
= **Minor Third**

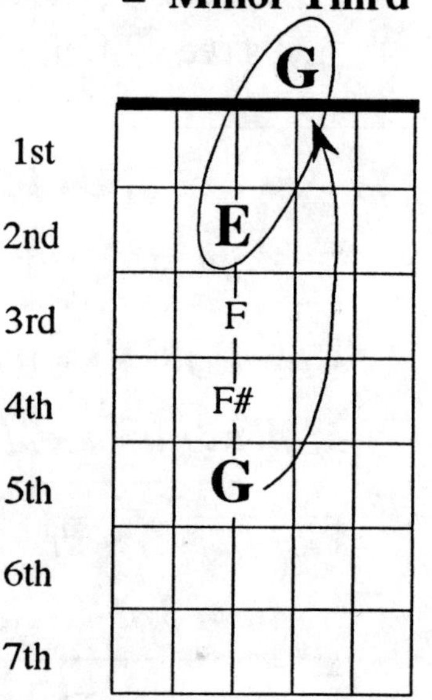

F chord

F to A = 4 Half-steps
= **Major Third**

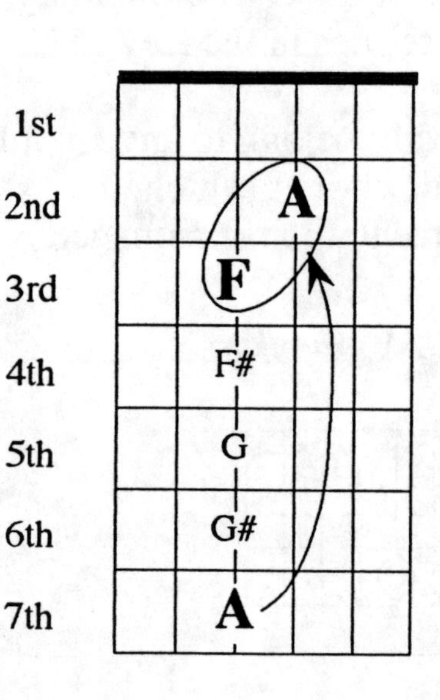

G chord

G to B = 4 Half-steps
= **Major Third**

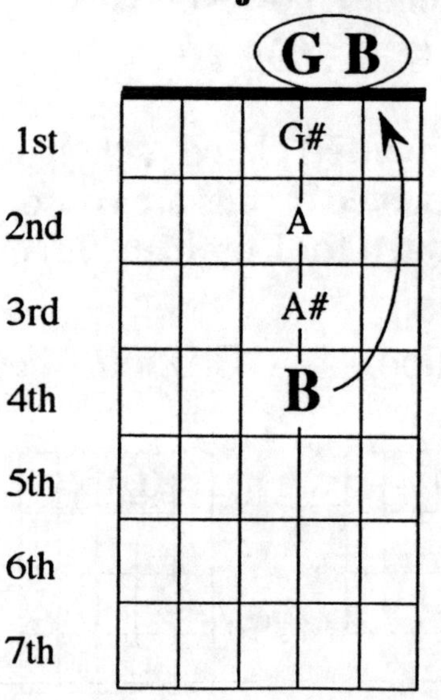

Am chord

A to C = 3 Half-steps
= **Minor Third**

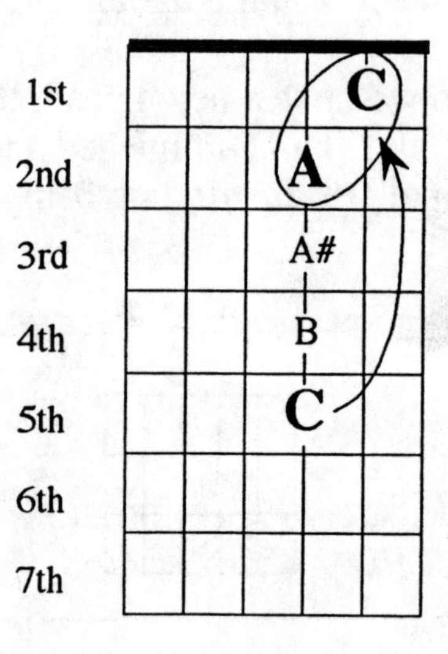

Four Combinations of Thirds

I intend to continue talking about the Chord Family System very shortly, but I want to devote one more page to this issue of **Minor** and **Major Thirds.**

We've seen that there's really no mystery to the distinction between Major and Minor. For a ***Major*** chord, you start off with a **Major Third** and then add a **Minor Third.** For a ***Minor*** chord, you do the opposite: Start with the **Minor** and add the **Major.**

But you might have realized that there are two other possible ways to add these intervals, two other combinations of **Thirds** besides **Major plus Minor** and **Minor plus Major:** *We also have **Minor plus Minor** and **Major plus Major.*** Oh boy. Let's see all four of them laid out, and then we'll identify the two new ones:

C - C# - D - D# - **E** - F - F# - **G** ***Major 3rd*** + ***Minor 3rd***	**C - E - G = C Major**
C - D♭ - D - **E♭** - E - F - G♭ - **G** ***Minor 3rd*** + ***Major 3rd***	**C - E♭ - G = C Minor**
C - D♭ - D - **E♭** - E - F - **G♭** ***Minor 3rd*** + ***Minor 3rd***	**C - E♭ - G♭ = C Diminished**
C - C# - D - D# - **E** - F - F# - G - **G#** ***Major 3rd*** + ***Major 3rd***	**C - E - G# = C Augmented**

Aha, we finally come to the **Diminished chord**, which is comprised of 2 **Minor Thirds,** one on top of the other. The Cdim chord, however, is not a member of the C Chord Family, since it contains 2 flats. Rather, it is the ***Bdim chord*** (B-D-F) that resides in the Key of C.

And we have a new friend, the **Augmented chord**, which doesn't really belong to any Chord Family. The Diminished and Augmented chords are sort of renegade chords, which, if used at all, often wind up being substituted for Dominant 7th chords, due to their dissonance.

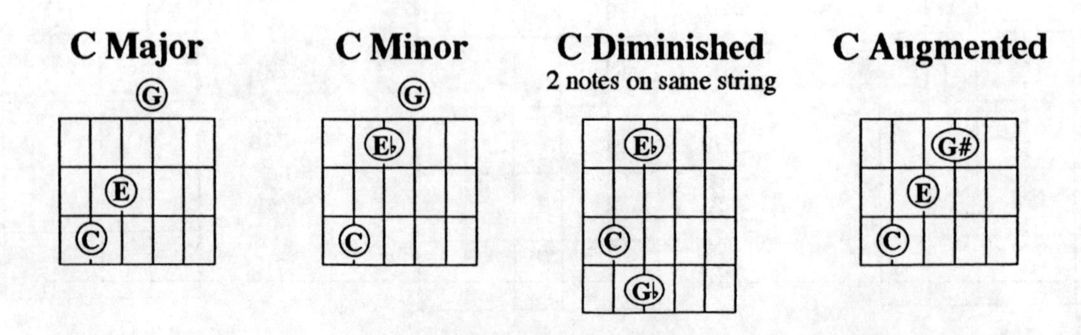

Other Chord Families

Now that we've worked through the specific case of the Key of C, let's generalize to all keys. As you may recall from before, this means using **scale degrees** rather than letter names. So instead of talking about the C, Dm, Em, F, G, Am and Bdim chords, we'll use the ***number*** of the scale degree of the **Root Note** of each chord.

The Major chords are the C, F and G chords, which happen to be the **1, 4** and **5 chords**. The Minor chords are the Dm, Em and Am chords, which are the **2, 3** and **6 chords**. The Diminished chord is Bdim, which is the **7 chord**.

(As I said earlier, I'm supposed to be using Roman numerals here, but I find them to be less readable than the usual Arabic numerals.)

Regardless of what key you are in:

The **1**, **4** and **5 chords** are always Major;
the **2**, **3** and **6 chords** are always Minor;
and the **7 chord** is always Diminished.

This brings us back to where we started in the **First Approach** to Chord Families. Here is a chart that shows the five *C-A-G-E-D* Chord Families organized by scale degree:

Degree / Key	1	2m	3m	4	5	6m	7dim
C	C	Dm	Em	F	G	Am	Bdim
G	G	Am	Bm	C	D	Em	F#dim
D	D	Em	F#m	G	A	Bm	C#dim
A	A	Bm	C#m	D	E	F#m	G#dim
E	E	F#m	G#m	A	B	C#m	D#dim

Below is a regrouping of the members of the five Chord Families into Major and Minor chords. The Minor chords are listed in the order of their importance to the Chord Family. Major chords appear more often than Minor chords in most music.

Let's recap what was said about the various Chord Family members earlier in the book: The **1 chord** is the most important Major chord, then comes the **5 chord**, then the **4 chord**. The **1 chord** is strong and stable; the **5 chord** is pushy and, with a 7th chord quality, restless and unstable; and the **4 chord** is friendly, everybody's buddy, content to be played or not.

Among the Minor chords, the **6m** is the most common and is even given special status: It is the **Relative Minor** chord of the Chord Family (strongly *related* to the **Tonic**). The **2m chord** is a close second in popularity, and the **3m** runs a distant third. The **7dim** isn't even in the running. It is the black sheep of the Chord Family.

	Major Chords			Minor Chords		
Degree / Key	1	4	5	6m	2m	3m
C	C	F	G	Am	Dm	Em
G	G	C	D	Em	Am	Bm
D	D	G	A	Bm	Em	F#m
A	A	D	E	F#m	Bm	C#m
E	E	A	B	C#m	F#m	G#m

As I implied before, people tend to confuse the **1 - 4 - 5** business with the **1 - 3 - 5** business, and the distinction is critical. Apples versus ball-peen hammers, you might say.

"1 - 3 - 5" refers to the underlying structure of the triad, or the notes that make up a chord. So it is a reference to ***notes within a chord.*** All triads have a **1 - 3 - 5** structure.

"1 - 4 - 5" is shorthand for a group of triads that have *already been constructed,* namely, the 3 Major chords. In other words, it is a reference to ***chords within a key.***

In *other* other words, each of the **1 - 4 - 5's** is comprised of a **1 - 3 - 5.** Heavy.

The next 5 pages are worksheets that you can use to practice generating the *C-A-G-E-D* Chord Families. The 6th page is the summary and answer sheet.

As I've said before, the only way to really get a feel for this material is to force yourself to write it out on your own, so I hope you will try it. The answers are on p. 82.

Key of C
Chord Family Worksheet

Chromatic Scale:

↓

A A# B (C) C# (D) D# (E)(F) F# (G) G# (A) A# (B)(C) C# D D# E F F# G G# A

Find the key note above, then lay out the other notes that are in the Major Scale, using the formula: **2 Whole-steps, 1 Half-step, 3 Whole-steps, 1 Half-step.** (I did it for you this first time.) Bring these notes down to the next line:

Major Scale:

Beginning of Second Octave

C	D	E	F	G	A	B	C	D	E	F
1	2	3	4	5	6	7	8 / 1	2	3	4

Now generate the Chord Family for this key.
Start with each of the 7 degrees of the scale, create triads (**1 - 3 - 5**), and fill in the Chord Quality for each chord (Major, Minor or Diminished):

Scale Degree	**Triad** 1	3	5		**Chord Name and Quality**
1	C	E	G	=	C Major
2	___	___	___	=	___
3	___	___	___	=	___
4	___	___	___	=	___
5	___	___	___	=	___
6	___	___	___	=	___
7	___	___	___	=	___

Key of G
Chord Family Worksheet

Chromatic Scale:

A A# B C C# D D# E F F# G G# A A# B C C# D D# E F F# G G# A

Find the key note above, then lay out the other notes that are in the Major Scale, using the formula: **2 Whole-steps, 1 Half-step, 3 Whole-steps, 1 Half-step.** Bring these notes down to the next line:

Major Scale:

Beginning of Second Octave

___	___	___	___	___	___	___	___	___	___	___
1	2	3	4	5	6	7	8 / 1	2	3	4

Now generate the Chord Family for this key. Start with each of the 7 degrees of the scale, create triads (**1 - 3 - 5**), and fill in the Chord Quality for each chord (Major, Minor or Diminished):

Scale Degree	Triad 1	3	5		Chord Name and Quality
1	___	___	___	=	______________
2	___	___	___	=	______________
3	___	___	___	=	______________
4	___	___	___	=	______________
5	___	___	___	=	______________
6	___	___	___	=	______________
7	___	___	___	=	______________

Key of D
Chord Family Worksheet

Chromatic Scale:

A A# B C C# D D# E F F# G G# A A# B C C# D D# E F F# G G# A

Find the key note above, then lay out the other notes that are in the Major Scale, using the formula: **2 Whole-steps, 1 Half-step, 3 Whole-steps, 1 Half-step.** Bring these notes down to the next line:

Major Scale:

Beginning of Second Octave

___	___	___	___	___	___	___	___	___	___	___
1	2	3	4	5	6	7	8 / 1	2	3	4

Now generate the Chord Family for this key. Start with each of the 7 degrees of the scale, create triads **(1 - 3 - 5)**, and fill in the Chord Quality for each chord (Major, Minor or Diminished):

Scale Degree	Triad 1	3	5		Chord Name and Quality
1	___	___	___	=	___________
2	___	___	___	=	___________
3	___	___	___	=	___________
4	___	___	___	=	___________
5	___	___	___	=	___________
6	___	___	___	=	___________
7	___	___	___	=	___________

Key of A
Chord Family Worksheet

Chromatic Scale:

A A# B C C# D D# E F F# G G# A A# B C C# D D# E F F# G G# A

Find the key note above, then lay out the other notes that are in the Major Scale, using the formula: **2 Whole-steps, 1 Half-step, 3 Whole-steps, 1 Half-step.** Bring these notes down to the next line:

Major Scale:

Beginning of Second Octave

___	___	___	___	___	___	___	___	___	___	___
1	2	3	4	5	6	7	8 / 1	2	3	4

Now generate the Chord Family for this key. Start with each of the 7 degrees of the scale, create triads **(1 - 3 - 5)**, and fill in the Chord Quality for each chord (Major, Minor or Diminished):

Scale Degree	**Triad** 1	3	5		**Chord Name and Quality**
1	___	___	___	=	__________
2	___	___	___	=	__________
3	___	___	___	=	__________
4	___	___	___	=	__________
5	___	___	___	=	__________
6	___	___	___	=	__________
7	___	___	___	=	__________

Key of E
Chord Family Worksheet

Chromatic Scale:

A A# B C C# D D# E F F# G G# A A# B C C# D D# E F F# G G# A

Find the key note above, then lay out the other notes that are in the Major Scale, using the formula: **2 Whole-steps, 1 Half-step, 3 Whole-steps, 1 Half-step.**
Bring these notes down to the next line:

Major Scale:

Beginning of Second Octave

___	___	___	___	___	___	___	___	___	___	___
1	2	3	4	5	6	7	8 / 1	2	3	4

Now generate the Chord Family for this key.
Start with each of the 7 degrees of the scale, create triads **(1 - 3 - 5)**,
and fill in the Chord Quality for each chord (Major, Minor or Diminished):

Scale Degree	Triad 1	3	5		Chord Name and Quality
1	___	___	___	=	______________
2	___	___	___	=	______________
3	___	___	___	=	______________
4	___	___	___	=	______________
5	___	___	___	=	______________
6	___	___	___	=	______________
7	___	___	___	=	______________

Summary of the C-A-G-E-D Chord Families

Key of C -- No sharps

C D E F G A B C D E F

1	C	E	G	=	**C** major
2	D	F	A	=	**D** minor
3	E	G	B	=	**E** minor
4	F	A	C	=	**F** major
5	G	B	D	=	**G** major
6	A	C	E	=	**A** minor
7	B	D	F	=	**B** dim

Key of G -- 1# -- F#

G A B C D E F# G A B C

1	G	B	D	=	**G** major
2	A	C	E	=	**A** minor
3	B	D	F#	=	**B** minor
4	C	E	G	=	**C** major
5	D	F#	A	=	**D** major
6	E	G	B	=	**E** minor
7	F#	A	C	=	**F#** dim

Key of D -- 2#'s -- F#, C#

D E F# G A B C# D E F# G

1	D	F#	A	=	**D** major
2	E	G	B	=	**E** minor
3	F#	A	C#	=	**F#** minor
4	G	B	D	=	**G** major
5	A	C#	E	=	**A** major
6	B	D	F#	=	**B** minor
7	C#	E	G	=	**C#** dim

Key of A -- 3#'s -- F#, C#, G#

A B C# D E F# G# A B C# D

1	A	C#	E	=	**A** major
2	B	D	F#	=	**B** minor
3	C#	E	G#	=	**C#** minor
4	D	F#	A	=	**D** major
5	E	G#	B	=	**E** major
6	F#	A	C#	=	**F#** minor
7	G#	B	D	=	**G#** dim

Key of E -- 4#'s -- F#, C#, G#, D#

E F# G# A B C# D# E F# G# A

1	E	G#	B	=	**E** major
2	F#	A	C#	=	**F#** minor
3	G#	B	D#	=	**G#** minor
4	A	C#	E	=	**A** major
5	B	D#	F#	=	**B** major
6	C#	E	G#	=	**C#** minor
7	D#	F#	A	=	**D#** dim

Play through each of the *C-A-G-E-D* Chord Families in order from **1** to **6m**.
(Notice how a new barre chord comes along with each key change.)

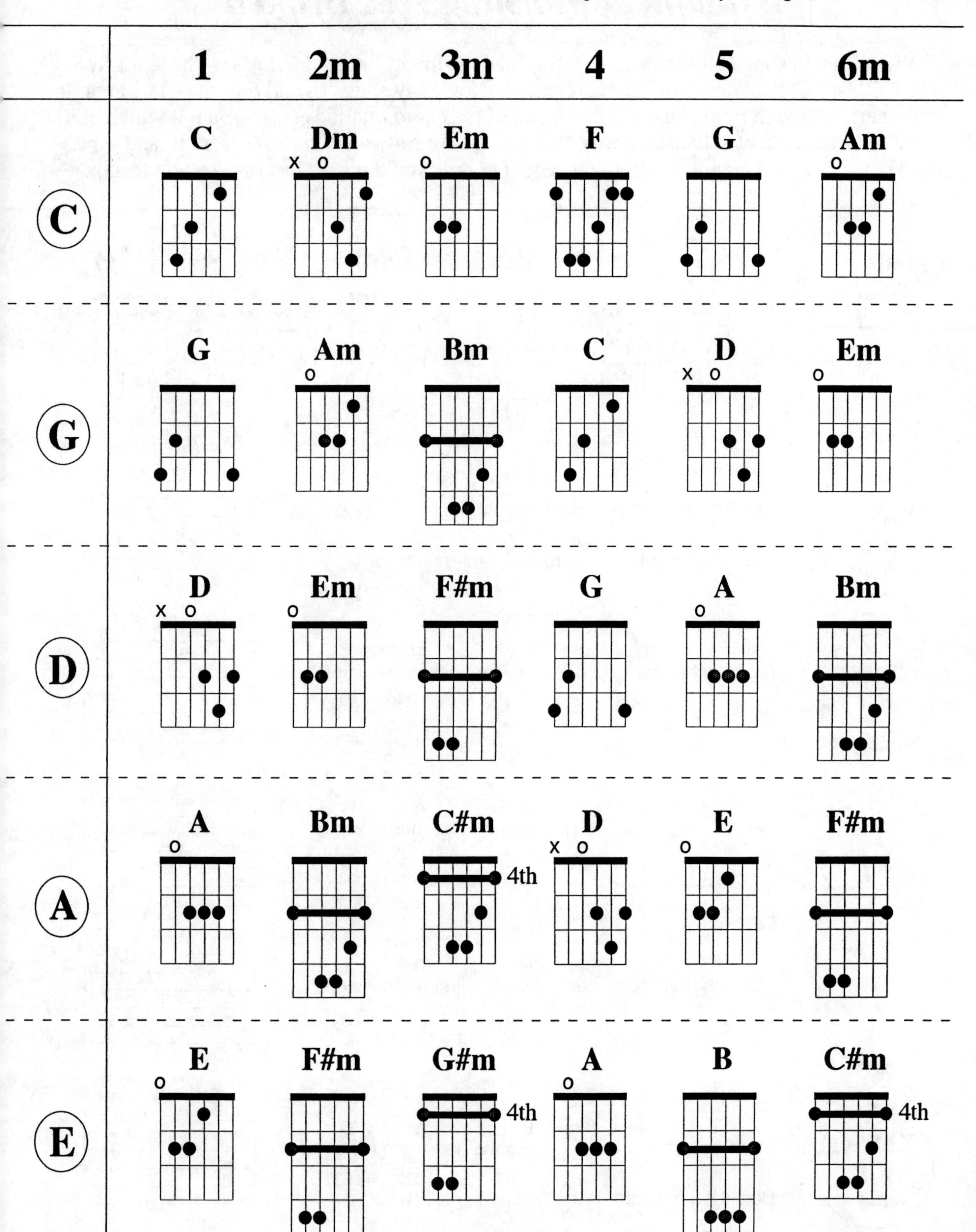

Example: "Morning Has Broken"

We used this song before when we talked about Minor Chords, but here we have all five of the *C-A-G-E-D* Chord Families represented. Not many songs use all 6 of the Chord Family members, although I did cheat a little on one of the chord qualities. Can you tell which one? (By the way, I cheated the same way the last time we saw this song. We'll fix it next time.) There are chord diagrams for all the Minor chords you'll need. Just in case you forgot.

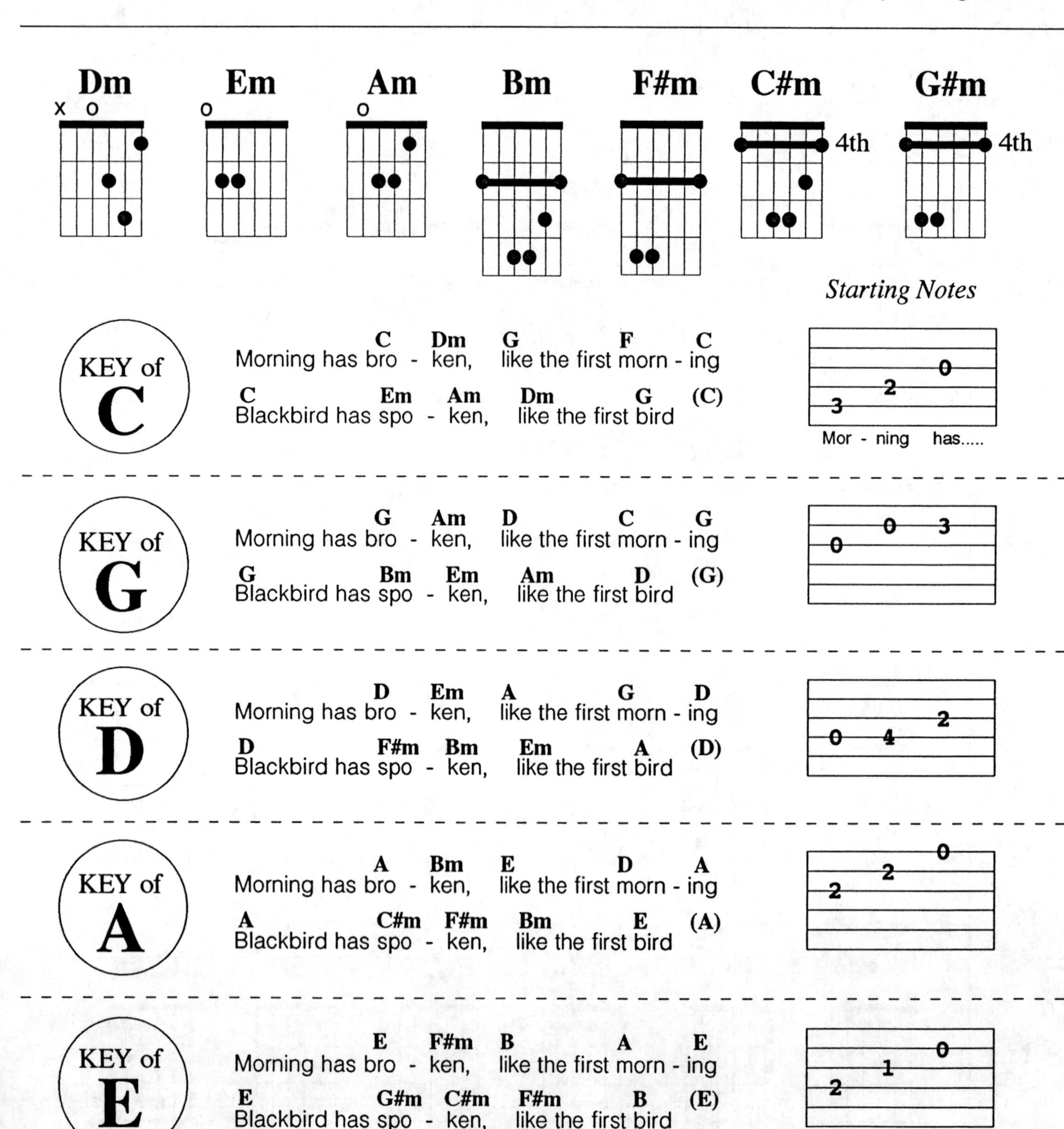

For all 12 keys, here is the

Chord Family Summary

Sharp keys are up top and flat keys are down below:

Key	1	2m	3m	4	5	6m	7dim
C (no #)	C	Dm	Em	F	G	Am	Bdim
G (1#)	G	Am	Bm	C	D	Em	F#dim
D (2#)	D	Em	F#m	G	A	Bm	C#dim
A (3#)	A	Bm	C#m	D	E	F#m	G#dim
E (4#)	E	F#m	G#m	A	B	C#m	D#dim
B (5#)	B	C#m	D#m	E	F#	G#m	A#dim
F# (6#)	F#	G#m	A#m	B	C#	D#m	E#dim
C (no♭)	C	Dm	Em	F	G	Am	Bdim
F (1♭)	F	Gm	Am	B♭	C	Dm	Edim
B♭ (2♭)	B♭	Cm	Dm	E♭	F	Gm	Adim
E♭ (3♭)	E♭	Fm	Gm	A♭	B♭	Cm	Ddim
A♭ (4♭)	A♭	B♭m	Cm	D♭	E♭	Fm	Gdim
D♭ (5♭)	D♭	E♭m	Fm	G♭	A♭	B♭m	Cdim
G♭ (6♭)	G♭	A♭m	B♭m	C♭	D♭	E♭m	Fdim

The Keys of F-sharp and G-flat share ***the very same notes***, just expressed as sharps in one and flats in the other.

There are also, technically, two other keys: **C-flat** and **C-sharp**. C-flat contains all 7 flat notes and C-sharp contains all 7 sharp notes. Pretty useless, huh? Well, the Key of C-flat is really the same as the Key of B, which has only 5 *sharps,* which is less trouble. And the Key of C-sharp is really the same as the Key of D-flat, which only has 5 flats, so I *guess* D-flat is better. Anyway, you'll rarely see any of these keys.

Skip It

Transposition Chart

Skip It

This is an alphabetical listing of the 12 chord families, with the extra keys left out. This chart is useful if you want to switch a song (**transpose**) from one key to another. You'll often see songs in music books expressed in such hideous keys as A-flat and E-flat, and I'm not sure who really likes these keys (maybe keyboard players), but we hate 'em.

Let's say you want to transpose a song from the evil Key of A-flat to the kindly Key of C. Just take the chords in A-flat and read down ***4 rows*** to the corresponding chords in C. The A-flat chord becomes C, the B-flat Minor chord becomes D Minor, and so forth. Just keep the chord qualities the same, and don't change columns on the way down!

Key	1	2m	3m	4	5	6m	7dim
A♭	A♭	B♭m	Cm	D♭	E♭	Fm	Gdim
A	A	Bm	C#m	D	E	F#m	G#dim
B♭	B♭	Cm	Dm	E♭	F	Gm	Adim
B	B	C#m	D#m	E	F#	G#m	A#dim
C	C	Dm	Em	F	G	Am	Bdim
D♭	D♭	E♭m	Fm	G♭	A♭	B♭m	Cdim
D	D	Em	F#m	G	A	Bm	C#dim
E♭	E♭	Fm	Gm	A♭	B♭	Cm	Ddim
E	E	F#m	G#m	A	B	C#m	D#dim
F	F	Gm	Am	B♭	C	Dm	Edim
F#	F#	G#m	A#m	B	C#	D#m	E#dim
G	G	Am	Bm	C	D	Em	F#dim

Details of the 1 - 4 - 5 Relationship

Let's conduct a brief review of Chord Family dynamics, and also take the opportunity to fill in some details, now that you know more about the notes that make up the chords.

So, the **Tonic** chord, or the **1 chord**, is the boss. It is restful and stable.
The **Subdominant** chord, or the **4 chord**, is cordial and non-threatening.
The **Dominant** chord, or the **5 chord**, creates tension and is rather pushy.

The Dominant chord has a very strong tendency to resolve to the Tonic chord.
This **5 - 1** resolution is known in classical music theory as a **Perfect Cadence**.

And there is a musical principle that supports and explains the Perfect Cadence, and it is known as ***Root Movement Downward By a Fifth.***

We've mentioned the power of the number **5** in music several times before.
In the Key of C, for example, the Root Note of the **5 chord**, which is G, wants to travel downward by a **Fifth**, which is 7 Half-steps in the Chromatic Scale, or 5 scale degrees in the Major Scale, to come to rest on the Root Note of the **1 chord**, which is C.
Here's the **1 - 5 - 1** chord progression in the Key of C:

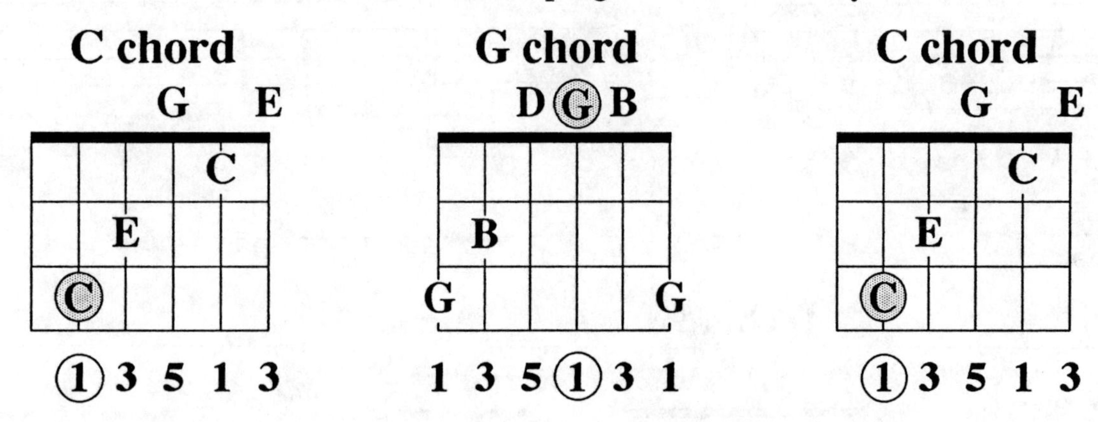

In the above diagrams, you see the notes in the C chord (C-E-G) and the G chord (G-B-D).
Beneath each diagram, you see the **1 - 3 - 5's** corresponding to the actual notes in the triad.
Of course, as we've mentioned before, you can see several *octaves* of most of the notes.
Play each chord, then just ***the circled Root Notes,*** G and C, which are a **Fifth** apart.
Think of the song "Twinkle, Twinkle, Little Star." That's "C-C-G-G" on the words, "Twin - kle, Twin - kle," which is an interval of a **Fifth**. Ear training, you know.

Listen to all 5 notes in the interval, in a C Major Scale run (1 - 2 - 3 - 4 - **5** - 4 - 3 - 2 - 1).
There is a distinct pull downward at the end, with a certain conviction and sense of finality:

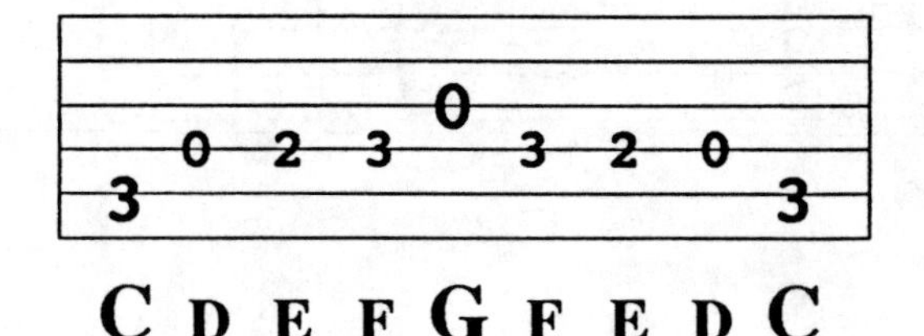

Let's do a similar analysis for the **1 chords** and the **5 chords** in our 4 other *C-A-G-E-D* keys. For each pair of chords, play the **1 chord**, the **5 chord**, then end on the **1 chord**, emphasizing the Root Note that I've labeled in each one. I also give you the **1** - 2 - 3 - 4 - **5** - 4 - 3 - 2 - **1**. If you have ever sung in a choir, you may recognize this scale segment as a warm-up exercise. Try playing it and singing it. And try "Twinkle, Twinkle" for each key: **1 - 1 - 5 - 5**. Remember, these examples are here to improve your musical ear.

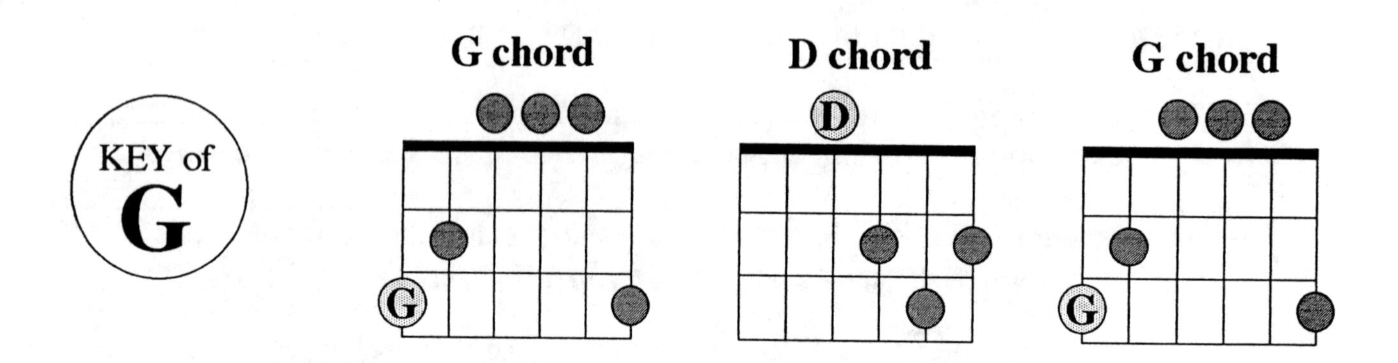

Twinkle, Twinkle = G - G - D - D

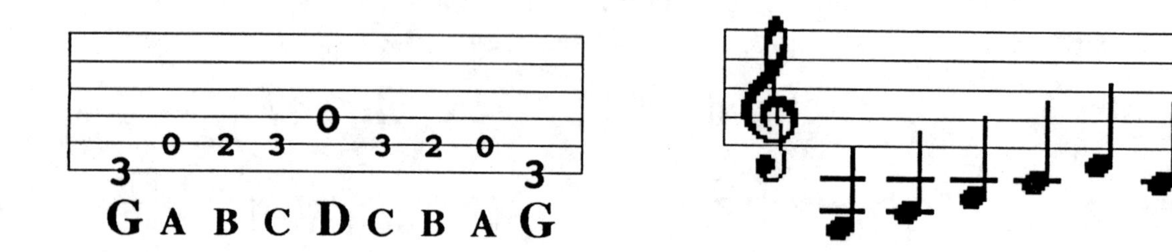

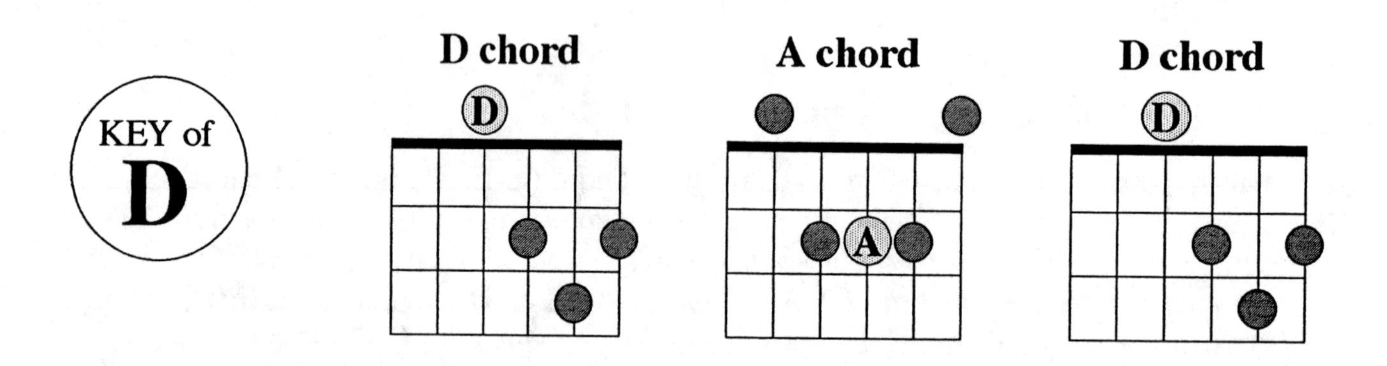

Twinkle, Twinkle = D - D - A - A

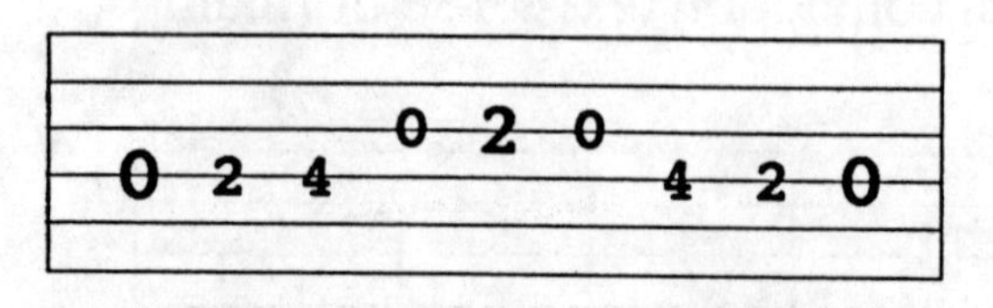

D E F# G **A** G F# E **D**

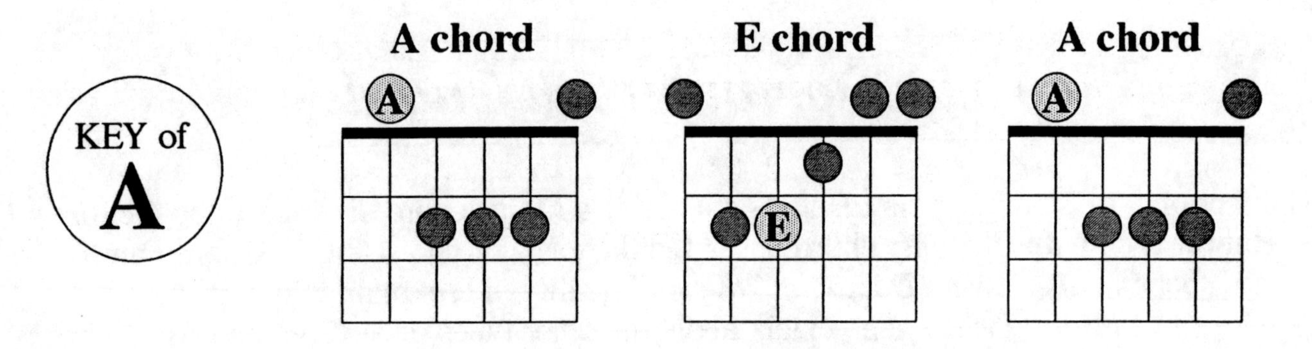

Twinkle, Twinkle = A - A - E - E

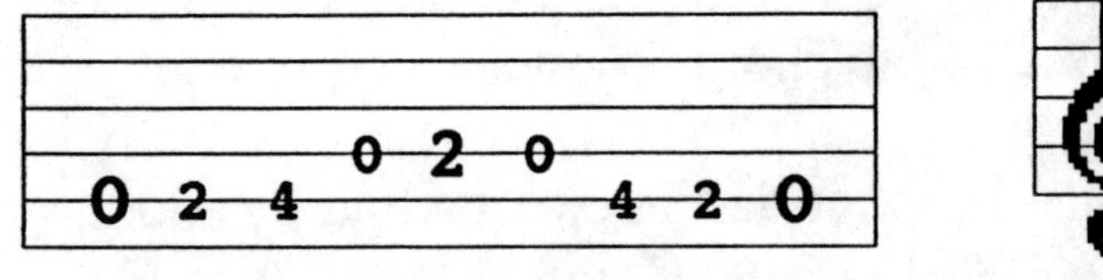

A B C#D E D C#B A

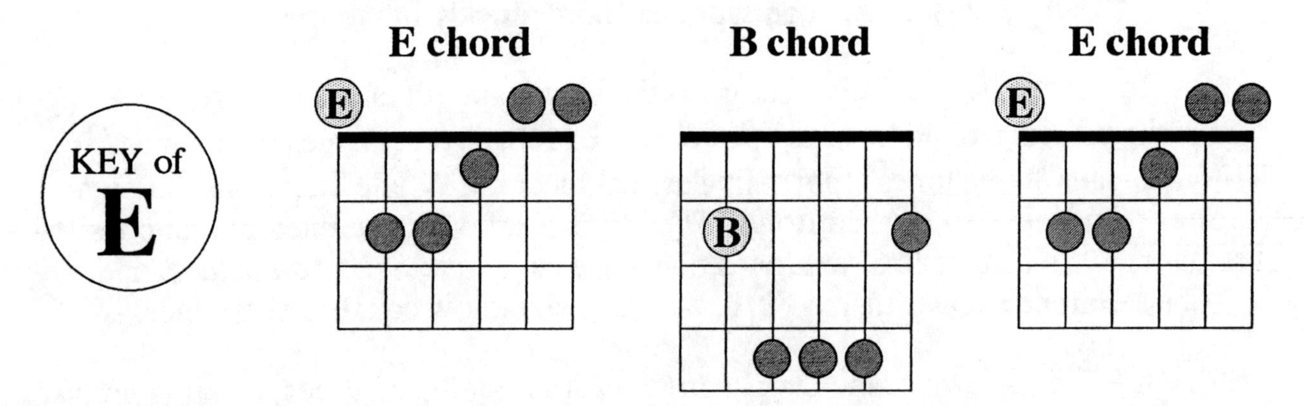

Twinkle, Twinkle = E - E - B - B

I know that when you play each pair of chords back and forth, you hear quite a jumble of notes, and it's hard to pick out and distinguish the effects of certain *individual* notes. Perhaps for now, you'll just need to trust me on this **Root Movement Downward By a Fifth** business. It really is the driving force behind the Perfect Cadence.

And notice: *The Root Note of the* ***5 chord*** *actually* ***belongs*** *to the* ***1 chord*** *as well.* And it is the only note that the two chords have in common. For the Key of C, the **1 chord** is spelled "C-E-**G**" and the **5 chord** is spelled "**G**-B-D." This is a strong link between these two chords and helps to explain why **Root Movement Downward By a Fifth** works.

The Dominant 7th Chord

The **5 chord**, or Dominant chord, starts out life as a Major chord, like the **1** and **4 chords**. But the **5 chord** is the ***only*** chord out of the three Major chords in the Chord Family that can ***also*** have a *Dominant 7th* chord quality. I'll explain why this is so in ***Volume Two,*** when we talk about the other types of Seventh chords, like the Major 7th, Minor 7th, and Diminished 7th chords.

Let's focus on just the Dominant 7th chord for now. We've talked about chords with 3 notes, known as triads, but the Dominant 7th chord is a 4-note chord, known as a **quadrad**.

In the Key of C, the G chord, spelled "G-B-D," can be **extended** into a quadrad by adding the next odd-numbered note in the sequence, yielding **1 - 3 - 5 - 7**, which is "G-B-D-**F**." So while the Dominant 7th chord is based on a Major chord, it has one additional note that changes it from a happy, almost bland chord into a pushy, restless chord. A catalyst.....an aggressor.....a chord already in motion.

But what is it, precisely, that gives the Dominant 7th chord its edge? It is the presence of an interval known as a **Tritone** that creates the tension. Tritone means "three tones" (no!). In classical theory, a Whole-step is also known as a **tone** and a Half-step is a **semitone**. Therefore, a Tritone is an interval that consists of 3 tones, which equals 6 semitones. This is exactly *one-half of an octave,* and one semitone smaller than a **Fifth**, which as you know equals 7 semitones.

The Tritone has been known as the ***Devil's Interval*** since medieval times, and it is *precisely* the element that makes the Dominant 7th chord sound so restless and dissonant, almost jarring. Apparently, this interval sounded slightly evil to early Christian music makers, but they felt compelled to use it anyway, for the sake of the energy and drive that it imparts.

The Tritone is found between the **3rd** and **7th** degrees of the Dominant 7th chord; for G7, this is the interval from B to F. Count the 3 Whole-steps yourself:

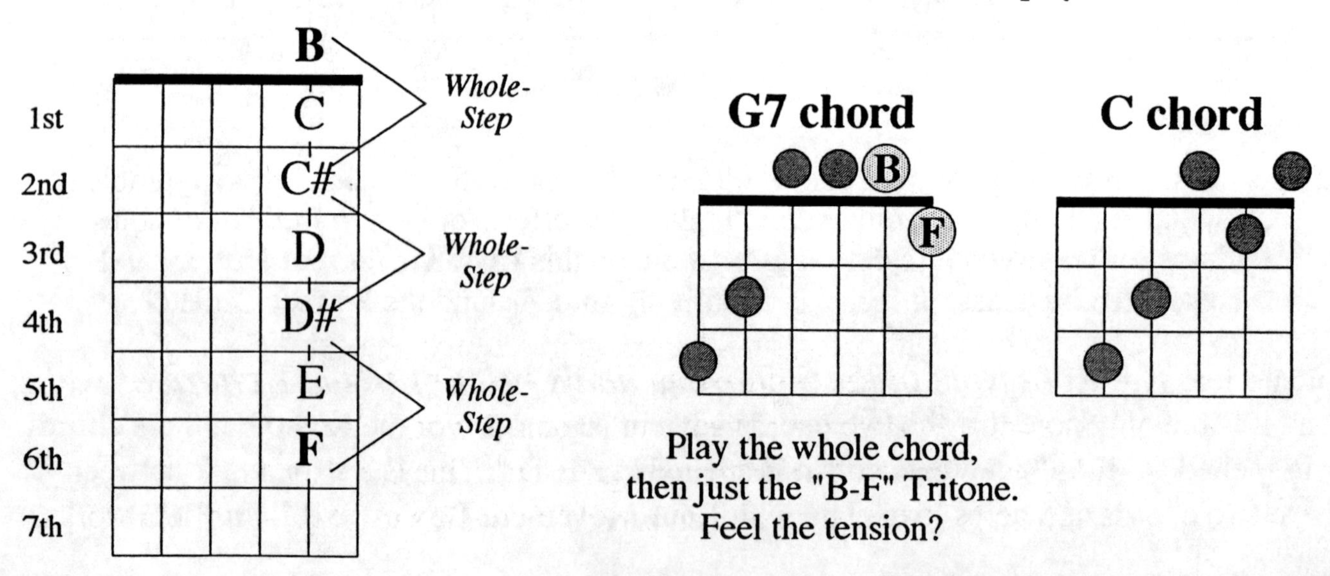

Play the whole chord, then just the "B-F" Tritone. Feel the tension?

Here are the Dominant 7th chords for the other *C-A-G-E-D* keys.
I've labeled the two notes in the Tritone, the **3rd** and **7th**, with the letter "T."
Play each of these **5 chords**, then resolve them to their corresponding **1 chords**.

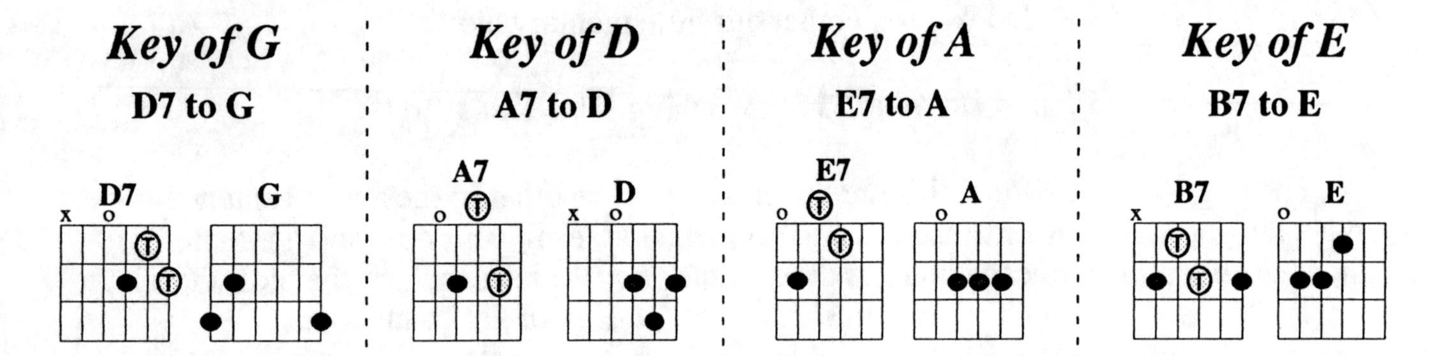

Most Dominant 7th-type chords have Tritones that fall on adjacent strings.
And, as you can infer from the above diagrams, the shape of the interval on the guitar is always a diagonal from upper left to lower right, sometimes separated by one fret.
By the way, you know the first few bars of Hendrix's "Purple Haze?" All Tritones.

To summarize,

There are 2 elements at work in the Tonic / Dominant relationship:

1. There is a tendency for **Root Movement Downward By a Fifth.** That's G moving to C in the Key of C.

2. In the Dominant 7th chord, there is the **Tritone**, which gives extra propulsion back to the Tonic chord.

And there is one additional influence here. Again, take the Key of C.
Let's say that the **5 chord**, G, is simply a Major chord, so that there is no Tritone.
Nevertheless, there is a ***B note*** in the G chord (G-**B**-D), and the B note happens to be *the* ***Leading Tone*** *for the C Major Scale,* or the **7th** degree of the scale. That individual B note in the G chord is *dying* to go one Half-step upward to resolve to that C note in the C chord. The fact that the B note just happens to belong to the G chord has little bearing on the situation. This is *melodic (scale) tension* at work rather than *harmonic (chord tension),* as it was with the Tritone.

A Reminder:

We've been talking a lot about the **5 chord** having a *"seventh chord quality."*
It's easy to confuse this terminology with the **"7 chord,"** which is a different member of the Chord Family altogether (the Diminished chord.)
We just mean the **5 chord** having a Seven***th*** chord quality.
There is also a "seven-seven chord," as you'll see later.

Overlapping Chord Families

Do you remember our little memory aid:

Can't **G**uys/Girls **D**o **A**nything **E**lse **B**ut **F**lirt?

The keys (capital letters) that are the closest to each other in the above sentence have the greatest number of natural and accidental notes in common, and are therefore most closely related to each other. For example, the two keys that are the most closely related to the Key of A (3 sharps) are the Key of D (2 sharps) and the Key of E (4 sharps). **D**o **A**nything **E**lse.

page 60

And the two keys that are the farthest apart are the Key of C (no accidentals) and the Key of F# (6 sharps). **C**an't.....**F**lirt? In fact, the Keys of C and F# have only one note, the B note, in common.

But right now, the most interesting and important question is:

How much do different Chord Families ***overlap*** *with each other?*

Or, ***how closely related*** are they? This is important because, the more two keys have in common, *the greater the potential for borrowing chords from each other.* Let's compare and contrast the ***Key of C*** with the ***Key of G.***

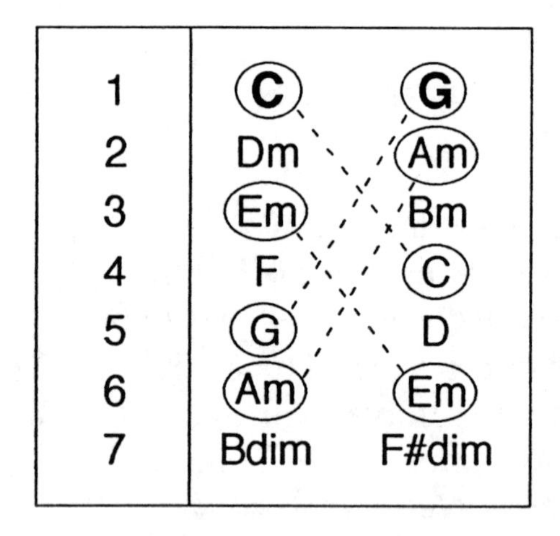

Here are the C and G Chord Families. If you scan the two columns, you'll see that there are ***4 chords in common: C, Em, G and Am.***

Notice that they occupy different positions in the respective Chord Families: C is the **1 chord** in the Key of C and the **4 chord** in the Key of G; Em is the **3m chord** in the Key of C and the **6m chord** in the Key of G; and so forth.

Meanwhile, there are 3 chords that belong to C and not G, and 3 chords that belong to G and not C.

Now, remember, the Keys of C and G differ by *only one note:* The Key of C has an F, while the Key of G has an F#. So it may seem odd that a difference of only 1 note out of 7, namely F versus F#, should result in a difference of *3 chords* out of 7.

But it makes sense. In the Key of C, the F note belongs to 3 different triads: "F-A-C," where it is the **1st** degree; "D-F-A," where it is the **3rd** degree; and "B-D-F," where it is the **5th** degree. Wherever the F note appears, it helps create a chord that just ***cannot*** belong to G Chord Family because *the F note does not belong to the G Major Scale.*

Here's an approach that might help you digest all of this. The Key of G is nothing more than the Key of C where the F note is changed to F#, and all the chords are rotated around until the G chord assumes the position of the **1 chord**. In other words, this is a way that the C Chord Family can be transformed into the G Chord Family.

You see the C Chord Family, with the triads spelled out, in column (1). Now, wherever you see an F note, change it to F#, as in column (2):

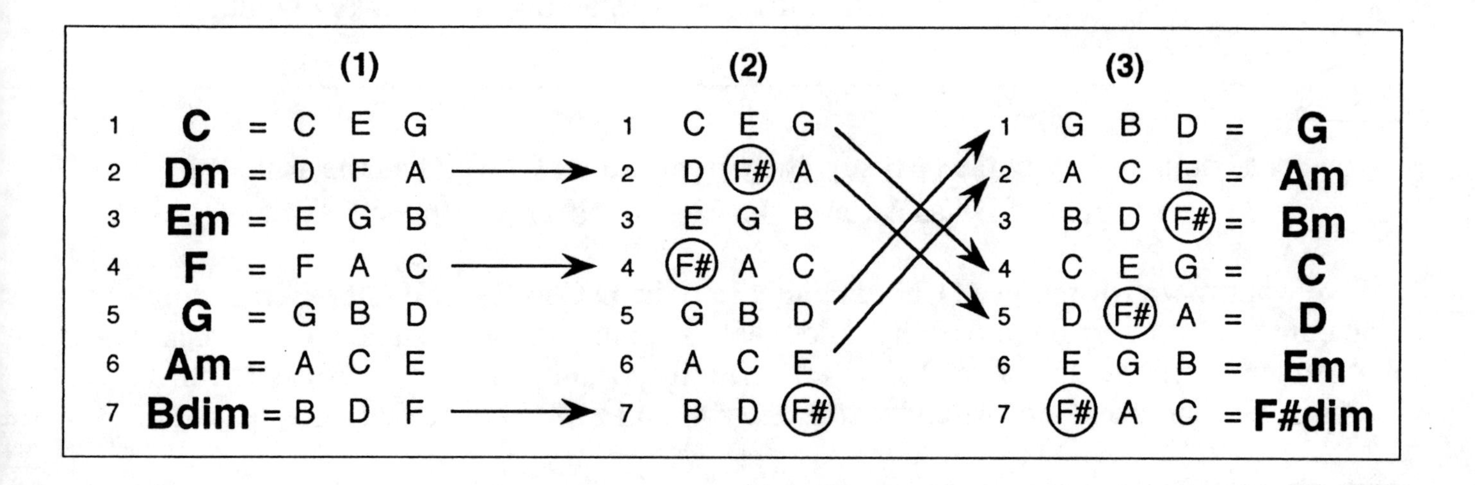

D-F-A becomes D-**F#**-A. So, the **Dm** chord becomes **D**.
F-A-C becomes **F#**-A-C. So, the **F** chord becomes **F#dim**.
B-D-F becomes B-D-**F#**. So, the **Bdim** chord becomes **Bm**.

Then, scroll the triads in column (2) around so that the G chord,G-B-D, lands in the 1st position, where it assumes its new role as the Tonic chord in the Key of G. This is shown in column (3). Likewise, the Am chord, which used to be the **6m chord** in the Key of C, becomes the **2m chord** in the Key of G. The C chord experiences a loss of status, as it goes from being the top dog in the Key of C to being the **4 chord** in the Key of G. Dm becomes D, and takes over as the Dominant chord. And so forth.

In summary, when you change the Key of C into the Key of G by changing the F note to F#, the **F, Dm** and **Bdim** chords are transformed into new **chord qualities**, while the **C, Em, G** and **Am** chords are not affected by the key change. Those 4 chords remain the same (Major stays Major and Minor stays Minor), since none of them contains either the F note or the F# note. All 7 chords assume new positions in the new key, but the triads stay in alphabetical order as they are rotated around.

Since Diminished chords don't concern us much, the practical result of all this is that (1) **Dm** becomes **D**, (2) **F** disappears and (3) **Bm** appears.

	C Chord Family	G Chord Family
C	**1**	**4**
Em	**3m**	**6m**
G	**5**	**1**
Am	**6m**	**2m**

Here again are the 4 chords that the 2 keys share. Pop quiz: If I were playing these 4 chords in random order as you walked into the room, would you be able to tell me exactly which key I was using, C or G? Answer: Sorry, no.

You could narrow it down to C or G, but you would need to hear me play a chord containing either an F note or an F# note before you could pinpoint it. If I slipped in a D chord, containing an F# note, the key would be G. If I chose Dm, containing an F, the key would be C.

Now let's compare C with the next key away from C after G, which is the **Key of D** (Can't Guys **D**o). The Key of D has 2 sharps: F# (which it shares with the Key of G) and **C#**.

If we want to transform the C Chord Family into the D Chord Family, then every triad that contains either the F note or the C note will be transformed into a new chord quality when we substitute the F# and C# notes. After the switch, ***only 2 chords are left*** that have no sharps and are shared by both keys: **G** and **Em**. See the diagrams below:

	Key of C	Key of D
1	C E G	D **F#** A
2	D F A	(E G B)
3	(E G B)	**F#** A **C#**
4	F A C	(G B D)
5	(G B D)	A **C#** E
6	A C E	B D **F#**
7	B D F	**C#** E G

→

1	C	D
2	Dm	**Em**
3	**Em**	F#m
4	F	**G**
5	**G**	A
6	Am	Bm
7	Bdim	C#dim

(I suppose if you walked into the room while I played G and Em back and forth, you could only narrow it down to 3 different possible keys: either C, G or D.)

If we proceed to the **Key of A**, which has F#, C# and now **G#**, even the **Em** and **G** are transformed by that new G#, so that there is *no chord overlap at all* between the C and A Chord Families. Now, certainly there are 4 other ***notes,*** namely A, B, D and E, that are shared by the C and A Major Scales. But every triad in the A Chord Family contains at least one sharp (some even have 2 sharps), *excluding them all from the Key of C.*

So the take-home message is that the farther away two keys are in their number of accidentals, the fewer chords they share, and the less strongly they are related.

Here's another little worksheet. Let's take the Key of D, with 2 sharps. I've laid out the Chord Families that are within 3 accidentals on either side of the Key of D, even going so far as the Key of F in the "flat" direction, as in "**F**udge! **C**an't **G**irls **D**o **A**nything **E**lse **B**ut....."

Circle the chords shared by D and each one of those six other keys. I've gone and done G and Bm for you:

Keys / Scale Degrees	F	C	G	D	A	E	B
	1♭	0	1#	2#	3#	4#	5#
1	F	C	(G)	***D***	A	E	B
2	Gm	Dm	Am	***Em***	Bm	F#m	C#m
3	Am	Em	(Bm)	***F#m***	C#m	G#m	D#m
4	B♭	F	C	***G***	D	A	E
5	C	G	D	***A***	E	B	F#
6	Dm	Am	Em	***Bm***	F#m	C#m	G#m
7	Edim	Bdim	F#dim	***C#dim***	G#dim	D#dim	A#dim
Chords in common with Key of D	0	2	4		4	2	0

I know this isn't much of a challenge, but I think it helps to scan through the keys and add them up yourself.

The Key of D has 2 sharps. The most strongly related Keys are G, with 1 sharp, and A, with 3 sharps. Next out comes C, with no sharps, and E, with 4 sharps. The Keys of F, with 1 flat, and B, with 5 sharps, are so far away that they share no chords at all with the Key of D, nor do any of the other 5 keys not shown above, namely, B-flat, E-flat, A-flat, D-flat, and F-sharp.

Chord Substitutions

Here's an interesting little sidelight: Chords that have at least half of their notes in common can be substituted for each other on occasion. This will be true for triads whose Roots are

2 scale degrees away from each other, up or down.

This means that for every triad, there are 2 other triads, one that has a Root Note two steps higher and one that has a Root Note two steps lower, that can be substituted. Let's take a look at the C chord in the C Chord Family. I put the C chord in the middle so you can see better:

5	6m	7dim	1	2m	3m	4
G	**Am**	**Bdim**	**C**	**Dm**	**Em**	**F**
G-B-D	**A-C-E**	**B-D-F**	**C-E-G**	**D-F-A**	**E-G-B**	**F-A-C**

The C chord is spelled "C-E-G". The Em chord, which is 2 steps above C and is spelled "E-G-B," has two out of three notes in common with C, namely E and G. The Am chord, which is 2 steps *below* C and is spelled "A-C-E", also has two out of three notes in common with C, namely C and E. All 3 chords contain E:

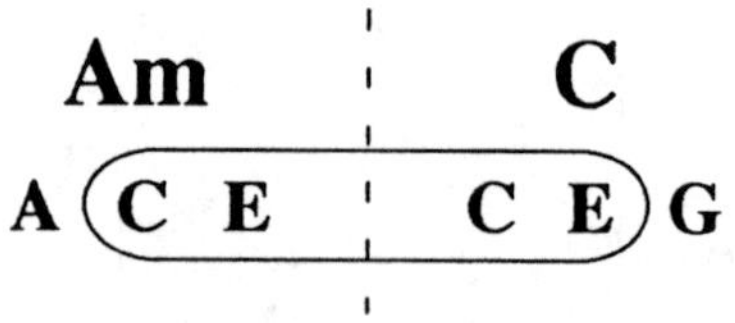

Am | **C**
A (C E | C E) G

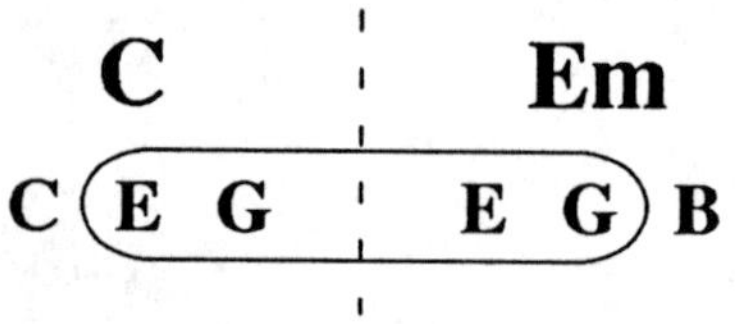

C | **Em**
C (E G | E G) B

So, under certain conditions, either Em or Am can be substituted for C. What conditions? Well, I don't know, try it and see. When you would normally play a C chord in some song, try substituting either Am or Em. *Notice that Am and Em would **not** easily substitute for **each other**, since there is only 1 out of 3 notes, namely E, in common.*

Both Am and Dm can substitute for F. And G and Em can stand in for each other. By the way, chords that are *right next to each other* in the Chord Family can**not** substitute for each other, because they have no notes in common at all.

Take special notice of the G and the Bdim chords, which can substitute for each other:

G | **Bdim**
G (B D | B D) F

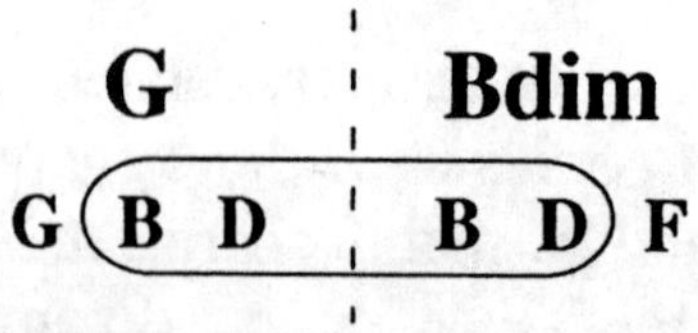

There are 2 notes in common, B and D. But if we substitute in the ***G7*** chord, spelled "G-B-D-F," we find that the ***entire*** Bdim chord, "B-D-F," is *embedded* in G7. In fact, you could say that the Bdim chord is simply a G7 chord that lacks the G Root Note. *This is the main reason that we don't talk much about the **7dim chord**. We can just use the **57 chord** instead.*

Triad Spellings

This next section is designed to give you practice in figuring out the Triad Spelling for any chord in any key. The approach I want to use is not specific to the guitar. I once took a music theory course in which the instructor delighted in going around the class, asking the students to spell out every conceivable kind of chord known to humanity. It really sharpens your musical skills. Besides, elements of our discussion so far suggest certain ***shortcuts*** we can take.

You know those Triad Spellings, like C-E-G and D-F-A?
Well, maybe I should point out that:

There are only 7 different Triad Spellings in the world!
*The only difference is the number and location of the **accidentals**.*

All you need to do is to memorize the 7 different Triad Spellings, and keep track of which accidentals belong to which keys.
Here are all the Triad Spellings you need to know:

A - C - E
B - D - F
C - E - G
D - F - A
E - G - B
F - A - C
G - B - D

Let's try an easy one: Spell the **4 chord** in the Key of A. First of all, you know that the **4 chord** will be a Major chord, since **1**, **4**, and **5 chords** are always Major. Next, count up 4 notes from the A note (and you needn't keep track of the accidentals): **A** - B - C - **D**. So you conjure up from memory the Triad Spelling: **D**-F-A. But you also know that the Key of A has 3 sharps, one of which is F#, so the final answer is D-F#-A, the D Major chord. Piece of cake.

How about the **6 chord** in the Key of E? This one must be a Minor chord, since the **2**, **3**, and **6 chords** are always Minor. Count to 6: **E** - F - G - A - B - **C**, then come up with **C**-E-G as your Triad Spelling. But the Key of E has 4 sharps, and C and G happen to be 2 of them. So the final answer is C#-E-G#, which is the C# Minor chord. Easy as pie.

If you care to develop this particular skill, I've given you a worksheet on the next page involving the five *C-A-G-E-D* Chord Families. The 7 Triad Spellings and numbers of sharps for each Chord Family are listed on the left side, and the answers appear on the right side.

Skip It

Worksheet on Triad Spellings

Skip It

Triad Spellings

A-C-E
B-D-F
C-E-G
D-F-A
E-G-B
F-A-C
G-B-D

Key of C: no sharps

Key of G: F#

Key of D: F# C#

Key of A: F# C# G#

Key of E: F# C# G# D#

(Cover the answers with a sheet of paper you can move down.)

		Answers
The 1 chord in the key of G:	___ ___ ___ = ____	G - B - D = G
The 1 chord in the key of D:	___ ___ ___ = ____	D - F# - A = D
The 3 chord in the key of C:	___ ___ ___ = ____	E - G - B = Em
The 4 chord in the key of A:	___ ___ ___ = ____	D - F# - A = D
The 6 chord in the key of D:	___ ___ ___ = ____	B - D - F# = Bm
The 4 chord in the key of C:	___ ___ ___ = ____	F - A - C = F
The 2 chord in the key of A:	___ ___ ___ = ____	B - D - F# = Bm
The 5 chord in the key of E:	___ ___ ___ = ____	B - D# - F# = B
The 6 chord in the key of G:	___ ___ ___ = ____	E - G - B = Em
The 1 chord in the key of C:	___ ___ ___ = ____	C - E - G = C
The 4 chord in the key of D:	___ ___ ___ = ____	G - B - D = G
The 6 chord in the key of A:	___ ___ ___ = ____	F# - A - C# = F#m
The 5 chord in the key of G:	___ ___ ___ = ____	D - F# - A = D
The 3 chord in the key of A:	___ ___ ___ = ____	C# - E - G# = C#m
The 2 chord in the key of D:	___ ___ ___ = ____	E - G - B = Em
The 4 chord in the key of G:	___ ___ ___ = ____	C - E - G = C
The 1 chord in the key of E:	___ ___ ___ = ____	E - G# - B = E
The 6 chord in the key of C:	___ ___ ___ = ____	A - C - E = Am
The 4 chord in the key of E:	___ ___ ___ = ____	A - C# - E = A
The 2 chord in the key of C:	___ ___ ___ = ____	D - F - A = Dm
The 5 chord in the key of D:	___ ___ ___ = ____	A - C# - E = A
The 3 chord in the key of G:	___ ___ ___ = ____	B - D - F# - Bm
The 1 chord in the key of A:	___ ___ ___ = ____	A - C# - E = A
The 6 chord in the key of E:	___ ___ ___ = ____	C# - E - G# = C#m
The 2 chord in the key of G:	___ ___ ___ = ____	A - C - E = Am
The 5 chord in the key of C:	___ ___ ___ = ____	G - B - D = G
The 3 chord in the key of D:	___ ___ ___ = ____	F# - A - C# = F#m
The 2 chord in the key of E:	___ ___ ___ = ____	F# - A - C# = F#m
The 5 chord in the key of A:	___ ___ ___ = ____	E - G# - B = E
The 3 chord in the key of E:	___ ___ ___ = ____	G# - B - D# = G#m

I would like to announce that on the next page, I'll be presenting the **Circle of Fifths**, also known as the Cycle of Fifths. It is a diagramatic way to summarize all of this **1 - 4 - 5 chord** stuff in a condensed format that I know you'll love.

But this seems like a good time to talk about ***myself*** for awhile, so you can skip the rest of this page if you like. Often, when I read a book or hear a recording, I want to know a little more about the person behind the work. So here's a little bit about the *real* Bruce Emery, beyond the usual glamor, media hype, and pop star deification.

My earliest musical memories are of singing with my mom in the car on long trips; since she loved to harmonize, she'd get me to provide the melody. She also played a baritone ukelele and would accompany my grandmother's mandolin playing. (Grandma played for dances as a teenager growing up in Sweden.)

I played piano and organ for a year or so, moved on to the uke at age 9, and finally got started on the guitar at about 12. I guess I had a few gigs in my early period: playing for Christmas parties at school, performing old Smothers Brothers routines with a buddy, and singing "A Boy Named Sue" at a square dance retreat. The sky was the limit!

At 15, I started studying classical guitar technique, and I found my thrill in the fingerpicking style. While I loved some of those Villa-Lobos Etudes and Preludes, I realized that I was more attuned to popular and folk music, and I discovered the likes of James Taylor, Chet Atkins, Jerry Reed, Leo Kottke and Pierre Bensusan (still my favs). I played at dormitory steak dinners, at a gin mill in Bly, Oregon, even on an *international* television production (well, actually, it was Dick Stacey's Country Music Jamboree, in Bangor, Maine, and the folks in the maritime provinces of Canada saw it, too.)

After pursuing a career in forestry for ten *long* years, I decided to try my hand at guitar instruction, and it seems to be working out. I've been teaching out of my home studio in Raleigh, North Carolina, since 1986, with one day of the week at Hoffman Stringed Instruments and Repair. I try to keep between 40 and 45 regular students. And I give a workshop and sell teaching materials every year at the Chet Atkins Appreciation Society convention in Nashville, TN.

I performed regularly at the Irregardless Cafe in Raleigh for 6 years, until a car wreck forced me to take a break, and then I just never got back into the habit. Recently I've played at weddings, luncheons, Christmas parties and nursing homes, and I might just start playing out more extensively again soon. But teaching is my bread and butter.

My teaching approach is simple: I give them a lot of what they want, and some of what they need. When I was a nipper, I was charmed by the *sound* of music. I just wanted to sing it, play it and enjoy it. The actual study of music should begin after the heart of the student has been *playfully engaged.* Maybe this approach won't produce many child virtuosi, but who cares? I know it will produce ardent lovers of music.

The Circle of Fifths

The **Circle of Fifths** is, without a doubt, the most useful musical roadmap ever devised by humankind. Just look over this diagram for a few moments. Parts of it should look familiar. We'll devote the next several pages (really the rest of our lives) to studying it.

You'll find this diagram repeated on the inside back cover for easy reference.

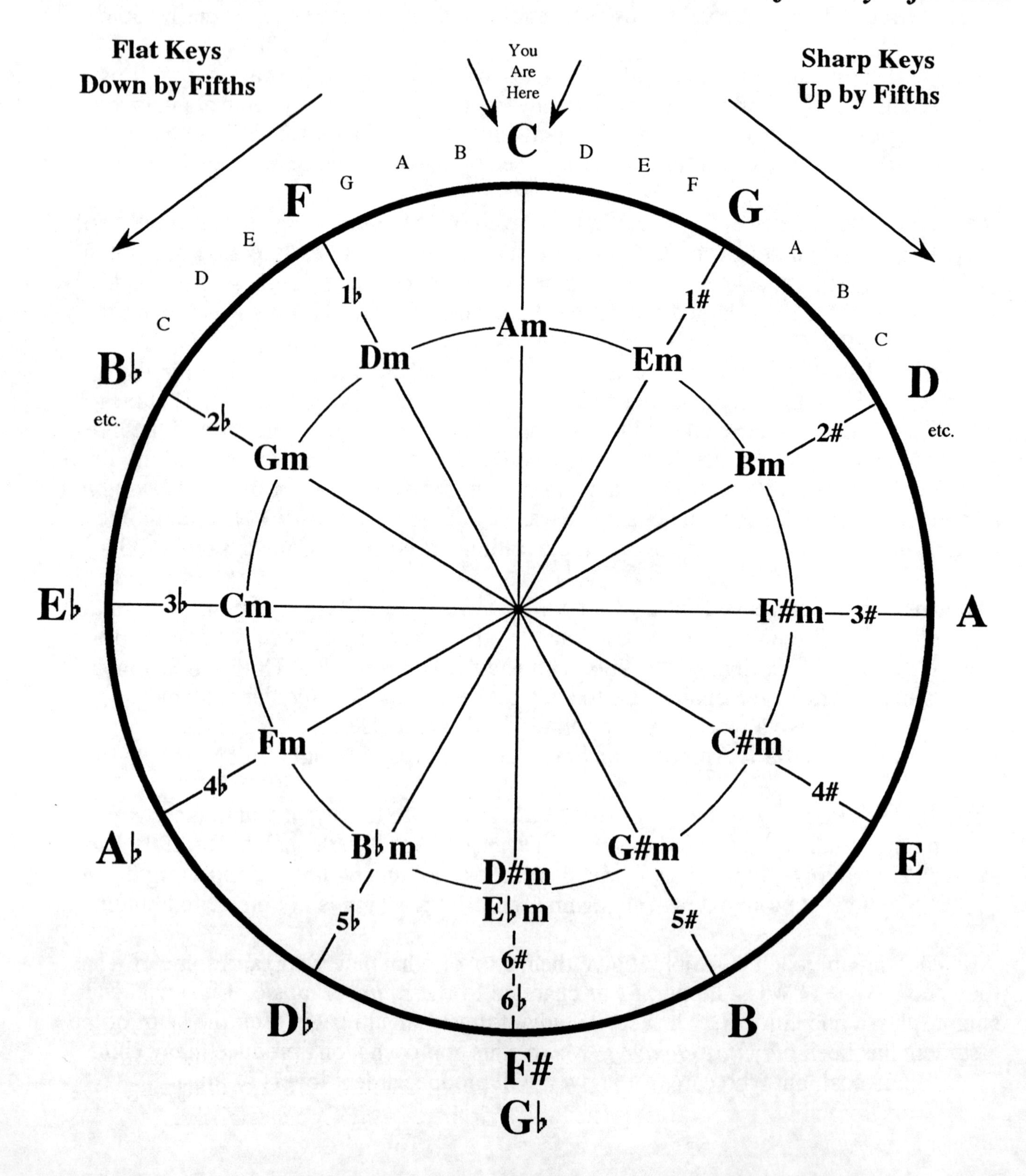

The **Circle of Fifths** is really a bird's-eye view of the totality of the study of music. It is the cosmic nutshell of the entire musical universe. It serves 2 main functions:

(1) It is a clear illustration of the relationships among the 12 keys based on the numbers of natural and accidental notes found in each key. Keys that are closer to each other on the Circle are more strongly related.

(2) If you consider the letters on the Outer Circle to be Major *chords* instead of keys, and if you include their *Relative Minor* chords on the Inner Circle, ***you can see the members of every Chord Family at a glance.***

Don'tcha think that's pretty neat? Let's look at the Outer Circle first. The 12 keys are positioned on the Circle like the hours on a clockface, and they are laid out, of course, by intervals of a **Fifth**.

Start with the Key of C at 12 o'clock and move ***clockwise.***
Count up a **5th** from C and find G at 1 o'clock. G has 1 sharp.
Count up a **5th** from G and find D at 2 o'clock. D has 2 sharps.
Count up a **5th** from D and find A at 3 o'clock. A has 3 sharps.
Count up a **5th** from A and find E at 4 o'clock. E has 4 sharps.
Count up a **5th** from E and find B at 5 o'clock. B has 5 sharps.
Count up a **5th** from B and find F# at 6 o'clock. F# has 6 sharps.

"**C**an't **G**uys **D**o **A**nything **E**lse **B**ut **F**lirt?"

(C) D E F **(G)** A B C **(D)** E F# G **(A)** B C# D **(E)** F# G# A **(B)** C# D# E **(F#)**

Now start at C and move ***counterclockwise (down by Fifths)*** for the flat keys.

Count down a **5th** from C and find F at 11 o'clock. F has 1 flat.
Count down a **5th** from F and find B♭ at 10 o'clock. B♭ has 2 flats.
Count down a **5th** from B♭ and find E♭ at 9 o'clock. E♭ has 3 flats.
Count down a **5th** from E♭ and find A♭ at 8 o'clock. A♭ has 4 flats.
Count down a **5th** from A♭ and find D♭ at 7 o'clock. D♭ has 5 flats.
Count down a **5th** from D♭ and find G♭ at 6 o'clock. G♭ has 6 flats.

All of this counting down by a **5th** each time makes my brain hurt. Again, since we're not used to reciting the alphabet backward, I'm using a trick:
Counting down by a 5th is equivalent to counting up by a 4th:

So in the flat direction, we have "C-F," then the word "BEAD," then G. And so it goes, around the circle, either clockwise or counterclockwise, either adding or subtracting an accidental, always moving by a **5th**, and seeing Chord Families overlapping and evolving from one to the next. It's all there in the Circle of Fifths.

Now let's isolate some Chord Families. Below, I've pulled out five *overlapping* sections from the Circle of Fifths that center around each of our five *C-A-G-E-D* keys.

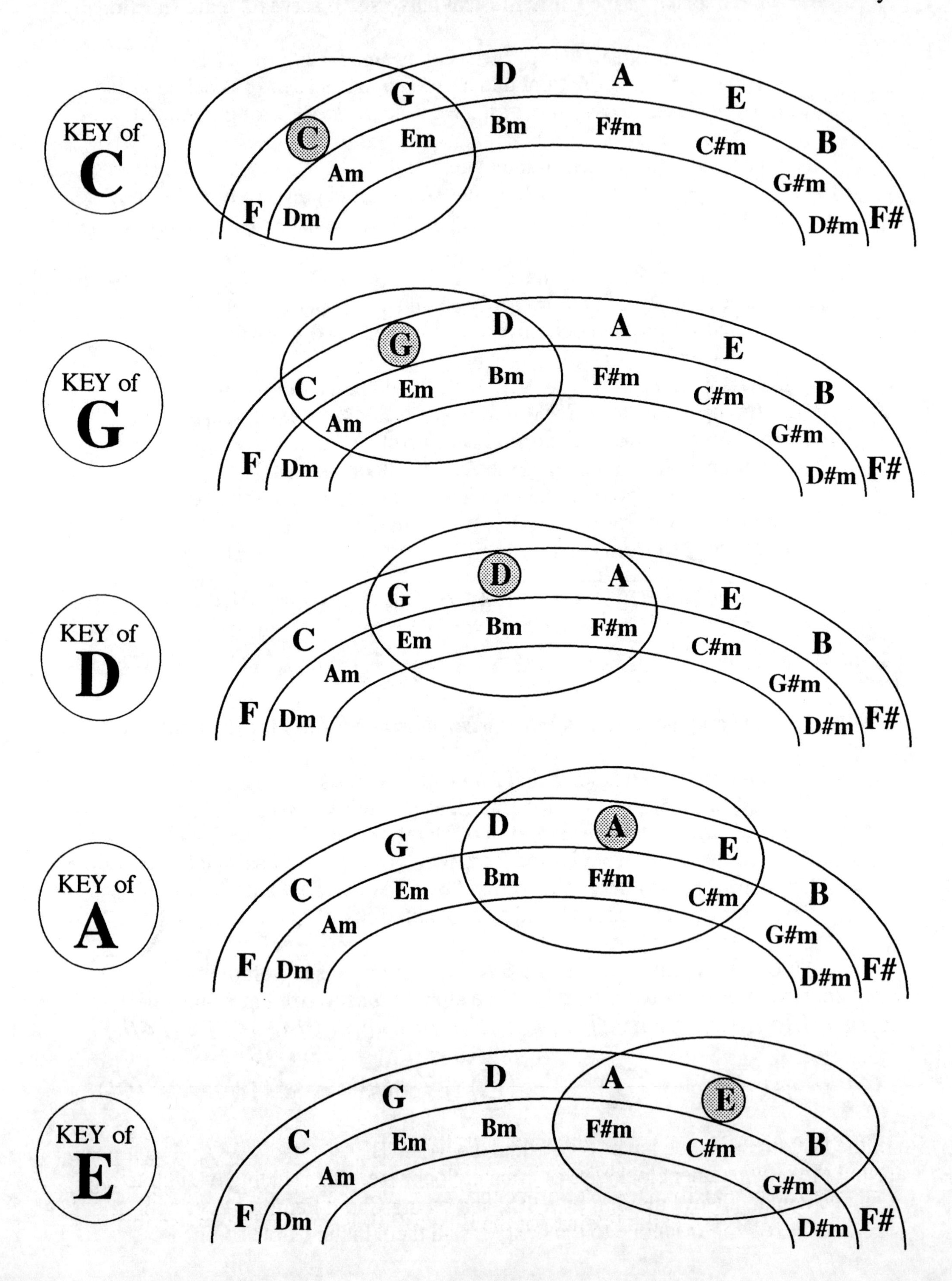

For each **Tonic** chord, you can find the **Dominant** chord for the Chord Family one position around in the ***clockwise*** direction, and you can find the **Subdominant** chord one position around in the ***counterclockwise*** direction. For the Key of C, that's up to G and down to F.

Incidentally, the reason that the **4 chord** is called the "Subdominant" chord is ***not*** that the number "4" is a step below ("sub") the number "5," which denotes the Dominant chord. It is because the Subdominant chord is considered to be a sort of "dominant" chord itself, which is located ***down a Fifth*** *from the Tonic chord.* Actually, the Subdominant chord should be called the "**Minus-5 chord.**" In the Key of C, the F chord, which is called the **4 chord** because we count up "4" to find it, is also located down a **Fifth** from C, or one notch around the Circle in the counterclockwise direction.

Next, notice that on the Inner Circle in every diagram, you see the Minor chord that is the **Relative Minor (6m) chord** to the corresponding Major chord on the Outer Circle. Remember, to find the Relative Minor, you count up 6 notes from the Tonic chord:

For the Key of C, the **6m chord** is A Minor (C-D-E-F-G-**A**).
For the Key of F, the **6m chord** is D Minor (F-G-A-B-C-**D**).
For the Key of G, the **6m chord** is E Minor (G-A-B-C-D-**E**).
For the Key of D, the **6m chord** is B Minor (D-E-F#-G-A-**B**).
And so on.

But the more interesting and useful thing to notice is the following:

Pick a Key. The ***Relative Minors*** *for the Dominant and Subdominant chords also happen to be the* ***2m*** *and* ***3m chords*** *in the Chord Family you picked!*

So, for the Key of C, the Relative Minor is simply Am, which is the **6m chord**.
The Relative Minor (**6m**) of F is Dm, which is the **2m chord** in the Key of C.
The Relative Minor (**6m**) of G is Em, which is the **3m chord** in the Key of C.
Confusing? A little. Useful? You bet!

Let's try the Key of G, where G is the Tonic chord and Em is the Relative Minor.
The Relative Minor of the **4 chord**, C, is Am, which is the **2m chord** in the Key of G.
The Relative Minor of the **5 chord**, D, is Bm, which is the **3m chord** in the Key of G.

Using the diagrams on the previous page, pick a key, find the Tonic chord, add the Dominant and Subdominant chords on either side of it, and take the 3 corresponding Relative Minor chords, and that's the Chord Family.

If you are a hardcore musician who cares deeply about the **7dim chord**, you can go to the letter name that is *one more notch* around the Inner Circle in the clockwise direction from the Chord Family, and that will be the **7dim**. For the Key of C, it is the Bdim; for the Key of G, it is the F#dim; for the Key of D, it is the C#dim; and so forth.

More on Secondary Dominant Chords

I hope you're beginning to get an idea of what the **Circle of Fifths** can do for you. We've spent some time to learn how to use the Circle to identify the 7 chords belonging to each of the 12 Chord Families in music. But now let's go exploring *beyond* the Chord Family (whose boundaries begin to seem less and less rigidly defined).

And this brings us back to **Secondary Dominant Chords**, and our old friend, the Key of C. As we said earlier, we can go up a **5th** from the C Major chord to find the G Major chord, which is the Dominant chord in the Key of C. Now just for a moment, let's pretend that ***we're in the Key of G,*** and go up another **5th** from the G chord to find ***its*** Dominant, the **D** chord, which is at the 2 o'clock position in the original Circle of Fifths:

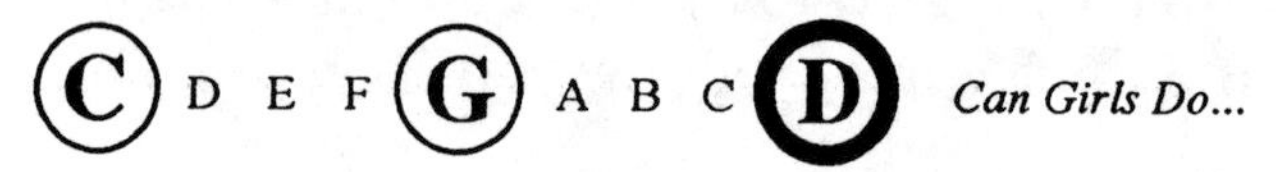

page 31

The D chord is known as the **Fifth of the Fifth (5/5)** with regard to the Key of C, or as a **Secondary Dominant.** Since Major chords are fairly inert and resistant to change, we usually give these Secondary Dominant chords a *Dominant 7th* chord quality, to make them edgier, less stable and more likely to resolve to another chord.

Play the following Secondary Dominant chord progression in the Key of C, **1 - 5/5 - 5 - 1.** The strings bearing the lowest **Root Notes** in the chords are indicated with the letter "R:"

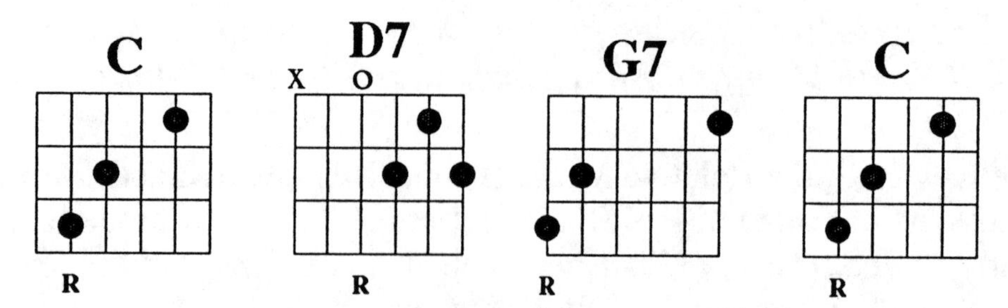

We start with C, then jump up to the **5th of the 5th**, to D7, then resolve down a **5th**, to G7, then resolve down *another* **5th** to C. *We are traveling* ***backward*** *around the Circle,* through 2 overlapping Perfect Cadences (from D down to G, then from G down to C).

Did we change keys during this progression? You bet we did, if only momentarily. Remember, the D7 chord does not belong to the C Chord Family (because of that F# note). But it *does* belong to the Key of G, where it is the **Dominant 5_7 chord**. And the Keys of G and C are quite friendly with each other since their Chord Families overlap so much.

The relationship between D7 and C is something like the relationship between *first cousins*. They're not your closest relatives, but they certainly are closer to you than randomly selected individuals from the general population.

The important lesson to learn here is that **Root Movement Downward By a Fifth** is a powerful force in music, one that will cut right across Chord Family boundaries, ***especially when the chords are destabilized with a Dominant 7th chord quality.***

Incorporating the **5th of the 5th** is only the first step. The pull of the number **5** is so strong that you can jump even farther, to the ***5th* of the 5th of the 5th**, or **5/5/5**, and still make it home in time for supper. For the Key of C, going up another **5th** from D leads to **A**, which is found at the 3 o'clock position in the Circle. *"Can't Guys Do Anything..."*
Then A7 resolves to D7, which resolves to G7, which resolves to C:

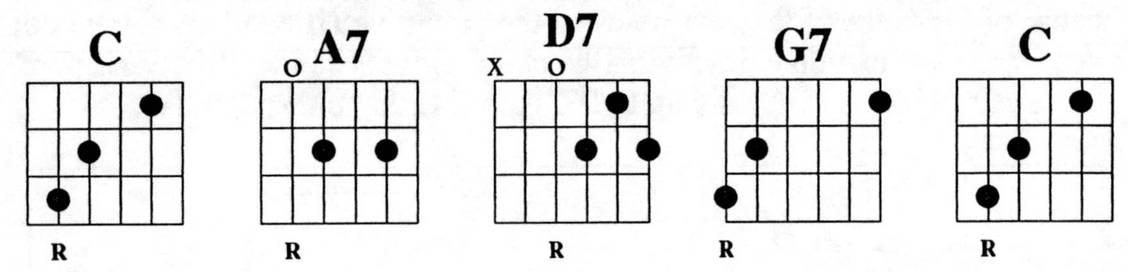

It still works, doesn't it? This very progression is used in the songs "Alice's Restaurant," "Sweet Georgia Brown," and "Salty Dog." Now, the presence of the A7 chord would be like your cousins who *themselves* have cousins on the other side of *their* family, once or twice removed from you, who you don't even *know,* but who are related to you anyway.

But why stop here? Let's go again! The 5th note up from A is **E** *("...Anything Else...")*:

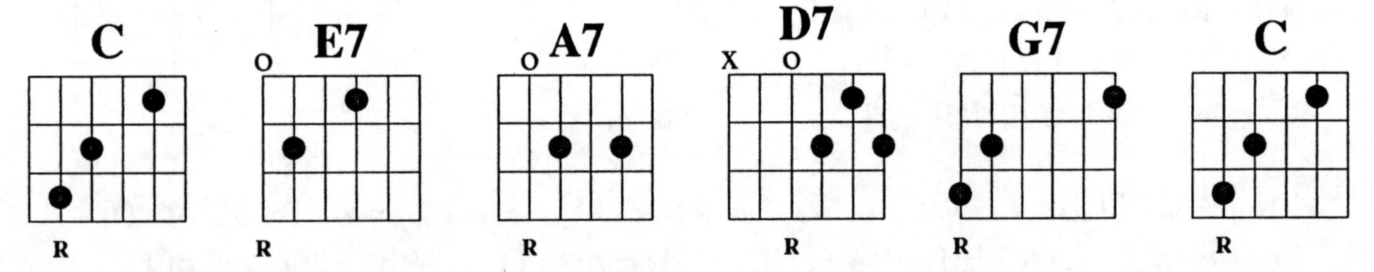

What a ride! This one's from the song, "Five Foot Two, Eyes of Blue." I guess we'd have to say that E7 is the **5th of the 5th of the 5th of the 5th** of C, or **5/5/5/5**. All you do is jump up to a particular level and just ride down through the Circle of Fifths until you hit the Tonic, *which should itself have a stable **Major** chord quality.* That's how you know it's over.

This process of running through Secondary Dominant chords is known as **Backcycling**. It's like jumping in the river and letting the current pull you downstream, or like launching a pinball and letting it roll down toward the slot. It's a **Downward Root Movement** assisted by **Seventh chords**. And I like the term **target chord** for the *first* Seventh chord you hit.

By the way, if you go up yet another **5th** to the next target chord, to **B**, and travel downstream (C-**B7**-E7-A7-D7-G7-C), you've got the chord progression to "Mr. Sandman."

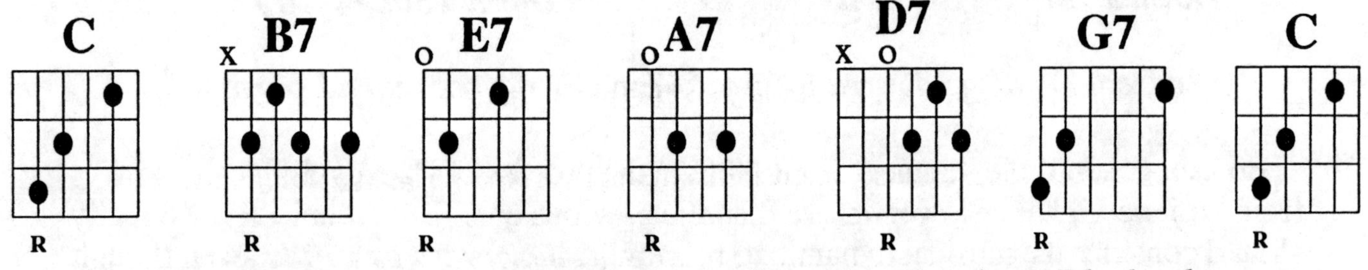

That's the longest uninterrupted string of Secondary Dominant 7th chords of which I am aware. Let me know if you find one longer.

Downward By a 5th = Upward By a 4th

I want to enlarge on something that I've mentioned before, the fact that:
*Moving **down a Fifth** is equivalent to moving **up a Fourth**.*
Because of the range of the bass notes on the guitar, you'll wind up doing both.
Consider the last example, involving the chord progression to "Mr. Sandman."
We start with C, jump way up to B7, then ride down through the **5ths**:

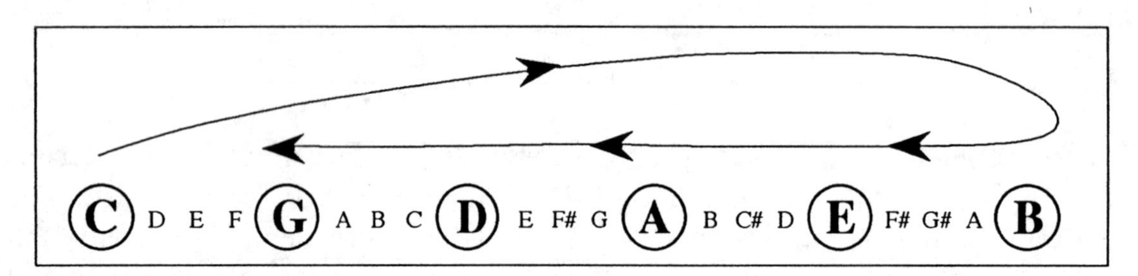

Well, from B7 to E7, you can *see* the **Root Movement *Downward* By a Fifth** from **B**, the 5th-string Root of B7, to **E**, the 6th-string Root of E7:

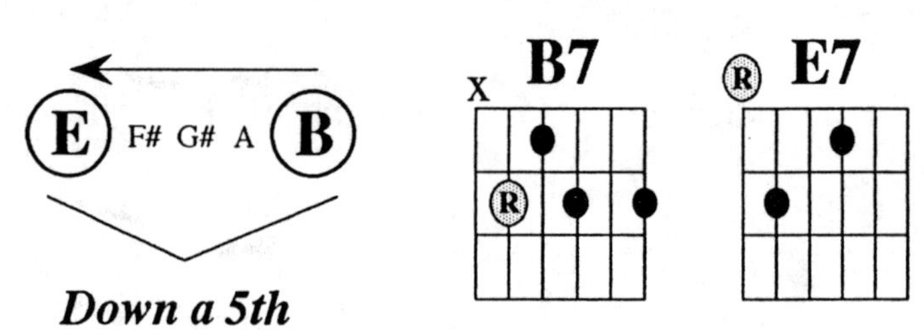

But from E7 to A7 to D7, you are seeing **Root Movement *Upward* By a Fourth** from **E** to **A**, the 5th-string Root of A7, and again to **D**, the 4th-string Root of D7.
Since E is the lowest note on the guitar, we must go upward to find A and D:

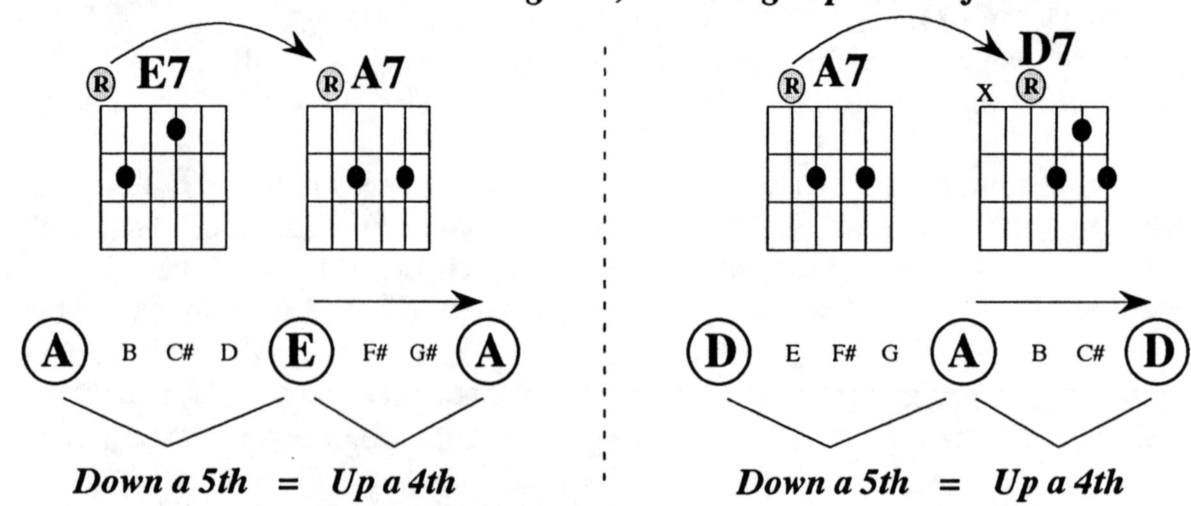

Then from **D**, we go ***down a Fifth*** to **G**, and finally back ***up a Fourth*** to **C**.

So as a general rule, the next **Root Note** in the process of Backcycling can come from either a higher or lower *octave* than the previous one. But technically, we really should consider the musical dynamic to be moving ***downward by Fifths***, even though it may be more *convenient*, alphabetically, for us to count *upward by Fourths*. Just think of it as "falling upward," and you'll be fine.

Backcycling Through All the Keys

Now, it turns out that the **Circle of Fifths** eventually Backcycles through all 12 keys. (That's what makes it a *Circle.*) If we arbitrarily start at F# and travel down by **5ths,** we get:

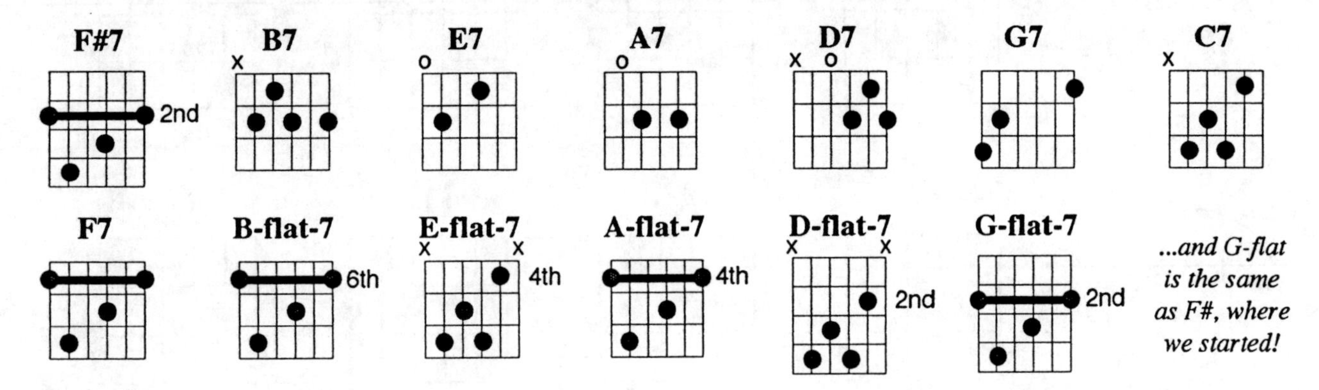

Since this sequence cuts across all chord families, it's the only one you ever need to learn. You just need to know where to jump in, and then where to jump out (not always at the Tonic). Of course, the section that we care the most about is the first half, **F# - B - E - A - D - G - C.** The second half contains the same letters, namely F-B-E-A-D-G, but these are the flat keys.

I should point out one more thing: The order of the chords from F# to C is the ***reverse order*** of *"Can Girls (Guys) Do Anything Else But Flirt?"* This makes sense. *"Can Guys Do..."* is the order of ***keys moving upward,*** while Backcycling involves ***chords moving downward.***

Perhaps we need a new memory aid. At least the most important stretch of Backcycling spells out the word "BEAD," leading to "**F - BEAD - GC.**" Or something like:

Four **B**lue **E**lephants **A**te **D**ad's **G**olf **C**art

or

Fling **B**ruce **E**mery's **A**mplifier **D**own the **G**rand **C**anyon

---

You've already seen examples of the most basic Secondary Dominants (the **5/5**). And you've seen the next song before, but here I've arranged it 4 different ways, each with a more distant target chord, and therefore an increasing number of Secondary Dominants. The Starting Note for singing is G (open 3rd string):

```
C                              G7
Camptown ladies sing this song, doo - dah, doo - dah

C                                D7       G7
Camptown ladies sing this song, doo - dah, doo - dah

C                  A7            D7       G7
Camptown ladies sing this song, doo - dah, doo - dah

C             E7   A7            D7       G7
Camptown ladies sing this song, doo - dah, doo - dah
```

But you know, after all is said and done, still the most common Secondary Dominant chord progression is 1 - 5/5 - 5 - 1. Here again is the summary for the *C-A-G-E-D* keys:

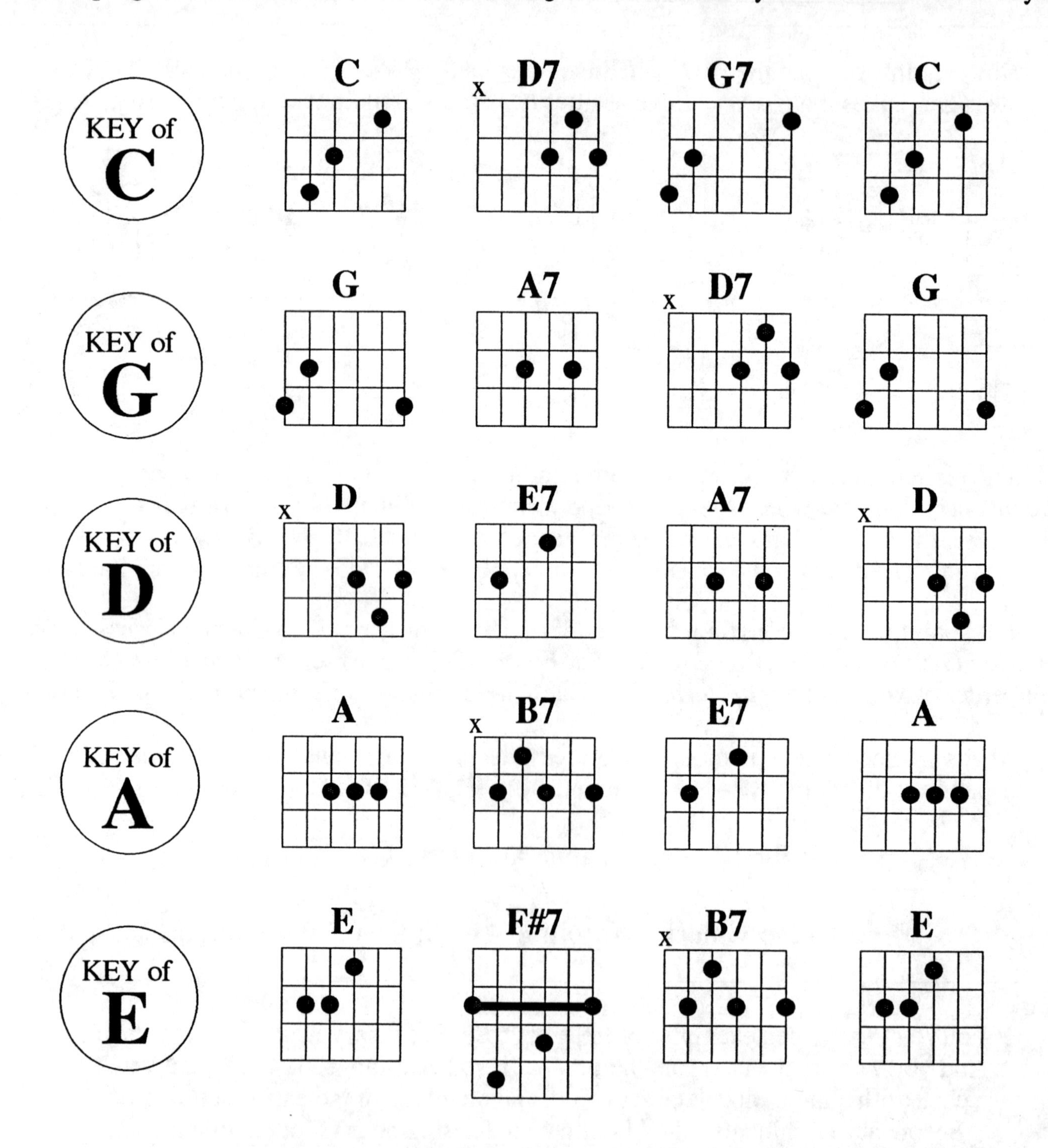

By the way................
It might be interesting to play these progressions *backward,*
just to see if they have a nice sound. Try **C - G7 - D7 - C**.
Doesn't sound so good to me. How about **G - D7 - A7 - G**?
No, they just don't sound as good played backward as they do played forward.

Maybe there *is* something to this **Root Movement Downward By a Fifth.**

And here are some clever diagrams with arrows showing the *natural flow* of chords through the Circle of Fifths. You can jump to any target chord, as long as you follow the directions indicated by the arrows.

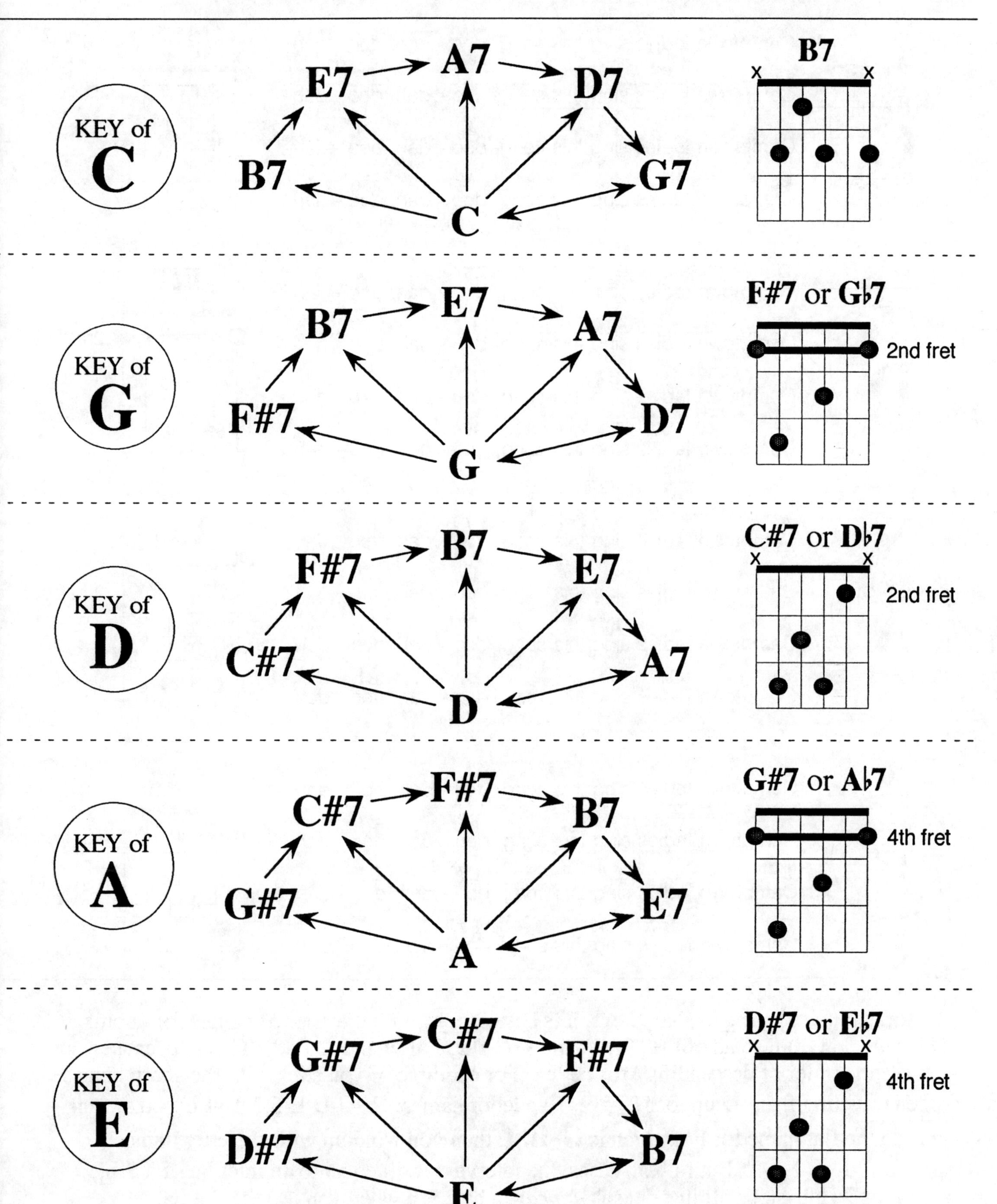

With the preceding page in mind, let's revisit "Camptown Races" from several pages back, and try the same approach for the other four *C-A-G-E-D* keys.

```
G                               D7
Camptown ladies sing this song, doo - dah, doo - dah
G                                 A7         D7
Camptown ladies sing this song, doo - dah, doo - dah
G                 E7              A7         D7
Camptown ladies sing this song, doo - dah, doo - dah
G           B7    E7              A7         D7
Camptown ladies sing this song, doo - dah, doo - dah
```

B7

KEY of
D

```
D                               A7
Camptown ladies sing this song, doo - dah, doo - dah
D                                 E7         A7
Camptown ladies sing this song, doo - dah, doo - dah
D                 B7              E7         A7
Camptown ladies sing this song, doo - dah, doo - dah
D           F#7   B7              E7         A7
Camptown ladies sing this song, doo - dah, doo - dah
```

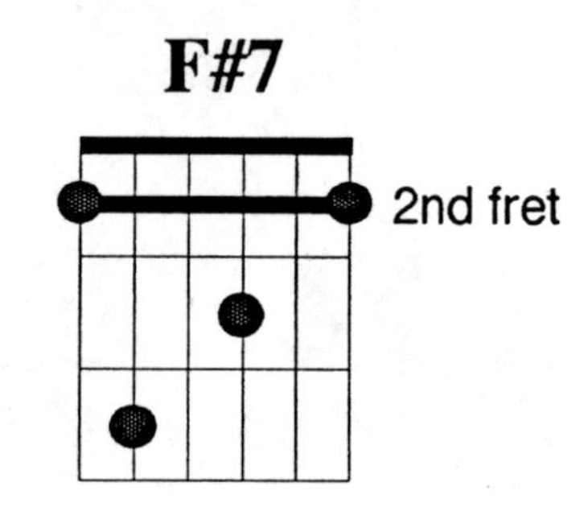

```
A                               E7
Camptown ladies sing this song, doo - dah, doo - dah
A                                 B7         E7
Camptown ladies sing this song, doo - dah, doo - dah
A                 F#7             B7         E7
Camptown ladies sing this song, doo - dah, doo - dah
A           C#7   F#7             B7         E7
Camptown ladies sing this song, doo - dah, doo - dah
```

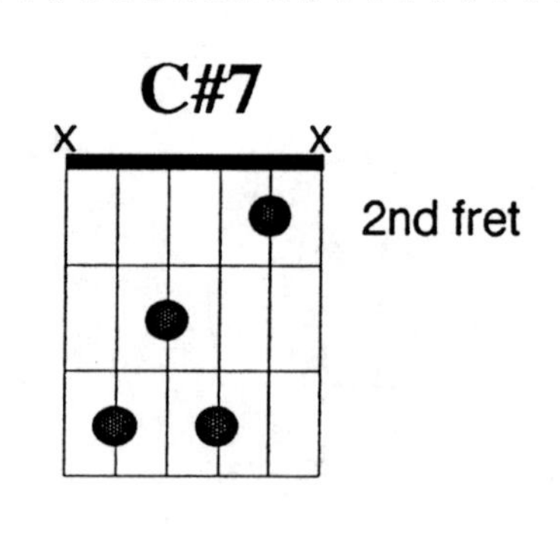

```
E                               B7
Camptown ladies sing this song, doo - dah, doo - dah
E                                 F#7        B7
Camptown ladies sing this song, doo - dah, doo - dah
E                 C#7             F#7        B7
Camptown ladies sing this song, doo - dah, doo - dah
E           G#7   C#7             F#7        B7
Camptown ladies sing this song, doo - dah, doo - dah
```

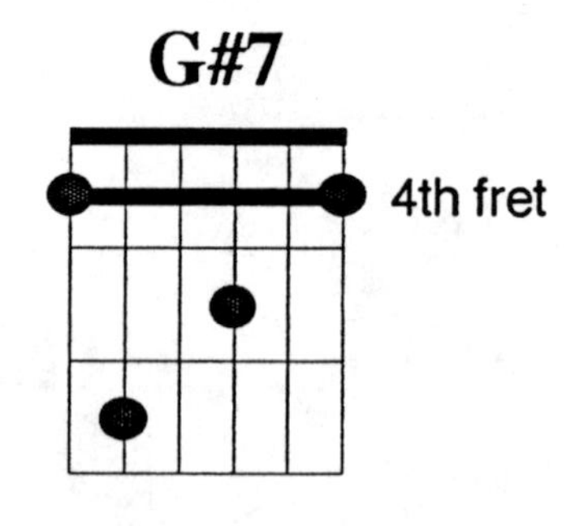

Note: When playing in sharp keys, it is customary to use the "sharp" names for chords (F#, C# and G#) instead of the "flat" names (G-flat, D-flat and A-flat). This is because you can *see* the order of descending **5ths** better. For example, if you stick with the sharp names, then traveling from **B** up to **F#** gives five letter names: "B-C-D-E-F." But if you switch to the flat name for F#, which is **G-flat**, then you wind up with *six* letter names: "B-C-D-E-F-G." But in both cases, the interval is still equal to an interval of a **5th**, or 7 Half-steps. It just doesn't ***appear*** to be a **5th** when you use the flat name.

Mixing In the Minor Chords

Now, *not all* of the chords in the Circle of Fifths need to be Seventh chords. While the actual Dominant chord (just before the Tonic) should be a Major or a 7th chord, some of the other chords in that string of descending **5ths** can be ***Minor*** chords.

Let's see what happens if we mix in several Minor chords among the Dominants:

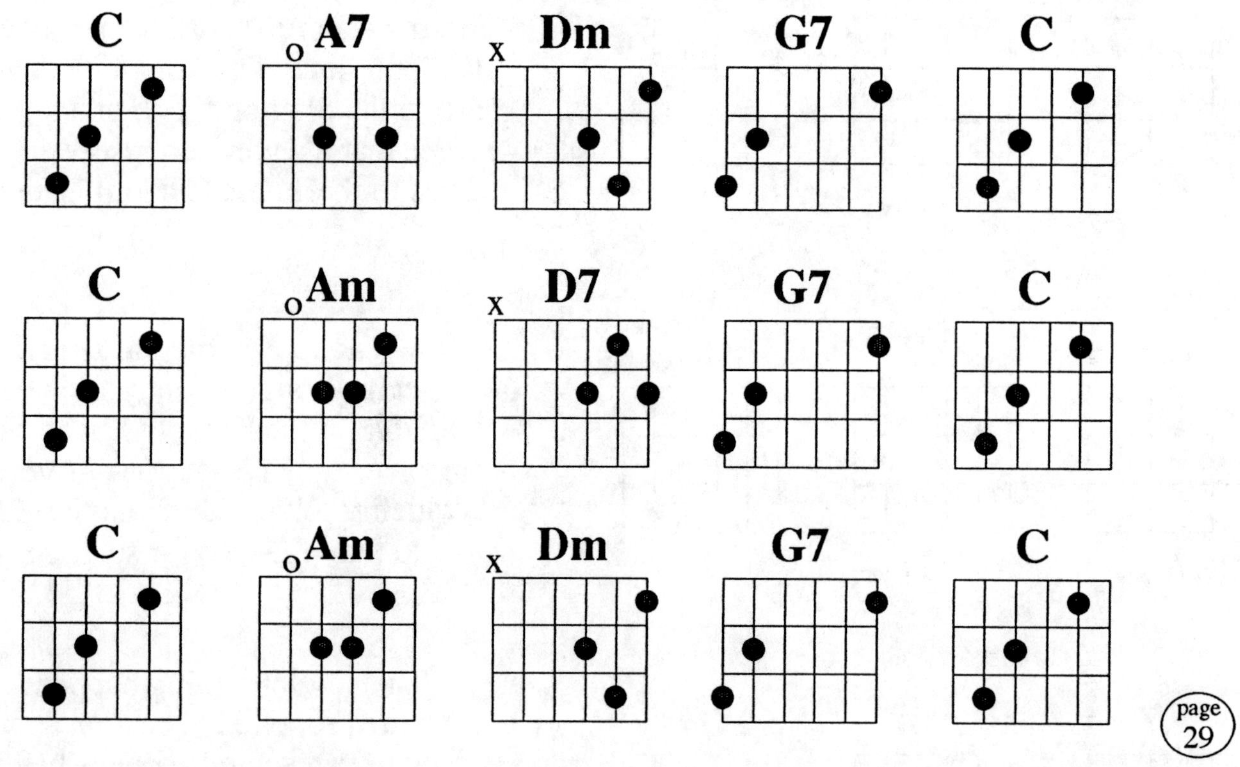

Take a look at this last one. By golly, we've seen this one before, back in the first section of the book, and we called it the **Rhythm Changes** after that song, "I've Got Rhythm." It's the famous **1 - 6m - 2m - 5**7 **- 1** progression, used in all those early rock songs.

Now, since Am and Dm are already members of the C Chord Family, we don't really *need* all of this business about Secondary Dominants and **Root Movement By a Fifth** to justify playing these chords together. But the "string of **5ths**" approach certainly gives extra weight to ***this particular sequence*** of the C, Am, Dm and G7 chords. Again, try playing the sequence in ***reverse order*** and hear how it sounds:

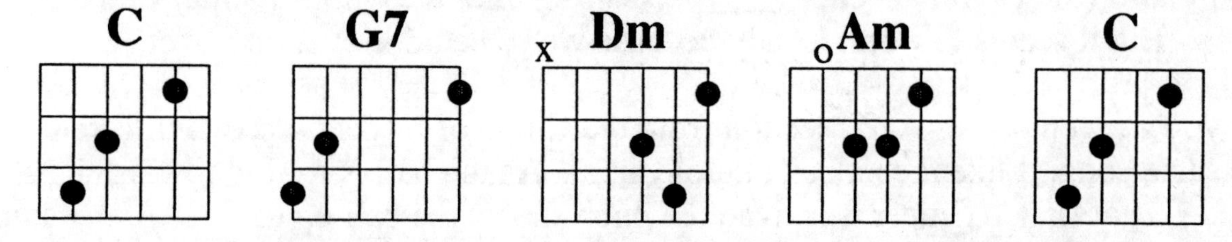

Not very satisfying, is it? A little disjointed. We really miss that **Root Movement Downward By a Fifth**, *even when we're just roaming around within the same key.*

Here's an excerpt from the 2nd Bridge section of "**Tequila Sunrise**" by the Eagles. This one is a classic, one of the best examples I know of manipulating the Circle of Fifths. I've transposed it into the Key of C; the Dm chord is the first chord of the 2nd Bridge. Don't worry if you don't know this passage; you'll still get the idea.

I've included the new Backcycling memory device, F#-BEAD-GC, so you can see where the chord progression is coming from:

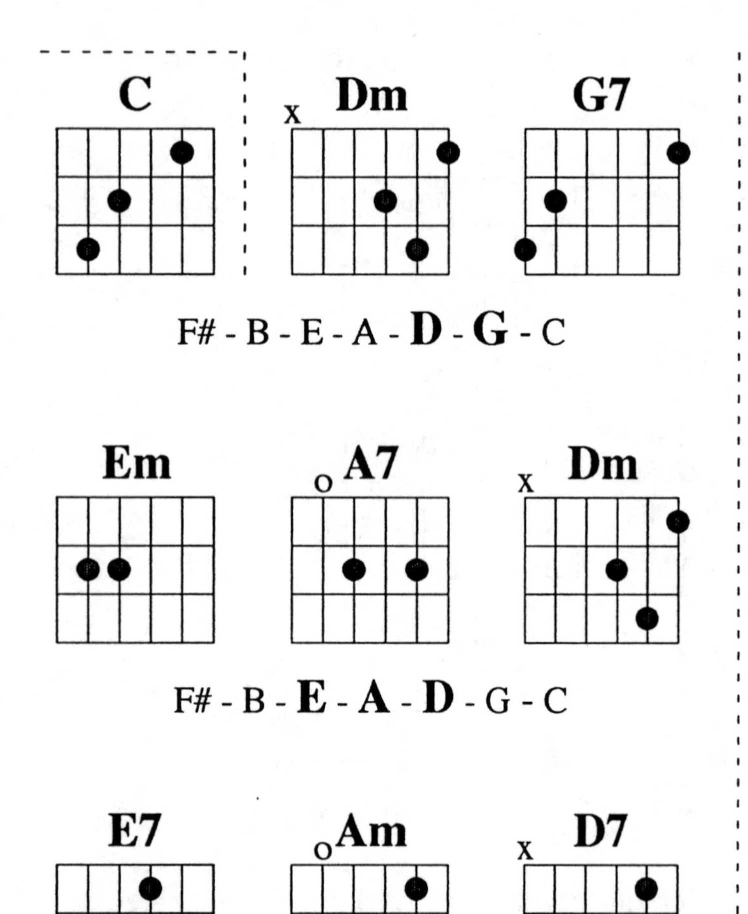

F# - B - **E** - **A** - **D** - G - C

From the **Tonic** chord, C, it moves to the **2m chord**, Dm, and then down a **5th** to the **5_7 chord**, G7, making you *think* that it's going to resolve right back to the **Tonic** C chord. But no.

We go to *Em,* the **3m chord** But more significantly, E is the **5/5/5/5** in the Key of C. The Em resolves down a **5th** to A7 (**5/5/5**), which resolves down another **5th** to Dm (**5/5**); so far so good.

Then a funny thing happens. We are propelled ***upstream*** again, back to that same E note as before, but *this* time we play an *E7* instead of an Em (again, **5/5/5/5**). Then we resolve down a **5th** to *Am* instead of A7 (**5/5/5**), then resolve down **5th** to *D7* instead of Dm (**5/5**).

Then, for some reason, we just skip right past the **5_7 chord**, G7, to the **Tonic**. Try that; play the last 3 chords, then go to the C chord. Plunk. We really miss having that G7 chord (the Dominant chord) to ease us back into the Chord Family proper. But it seems to work, if only because we've heard it over and over.

So now you've seen the "E-A-D" section from the Circle of Fifths used two different ways in the same song. I like the pinball analogy here. As the ball is rolling toward the slot (Dm to G7) at first, a flipper is activated, which shoots the ball up to Em. As it again rolls toward the slot (A7 to Dm), another flipper sends it back up, this time to E7. From here, it travels a slightly different path down (Am to D7), skips over G7 and lands in the slot, at C. Chord qualities may change, but the **5ths** go marching on.

The Jazz Turnaround

The **Jazz Turnaround** is the following chord progression: **2m - 5_7 - 1**.
"Turnaround" means getting back to the **1 chord** (and who *knows* what "jazz" means). All you need to do in jazz to establish that you are in a certain key is to play the **2 - 5 - 1** in that key; and believe me, this is very important in jazz, where they change keys ***a lot***.

As you can see, this progression is the same as the Rhythm Changes, except that there is no **6m chord** tacked onto the front. The **6m** is not required to establish the key; only the **2 - 5 - 1** is really needed. Here are just the **1 - 2 - 5 - 1's** for the *C-A-G-E-D* keys.

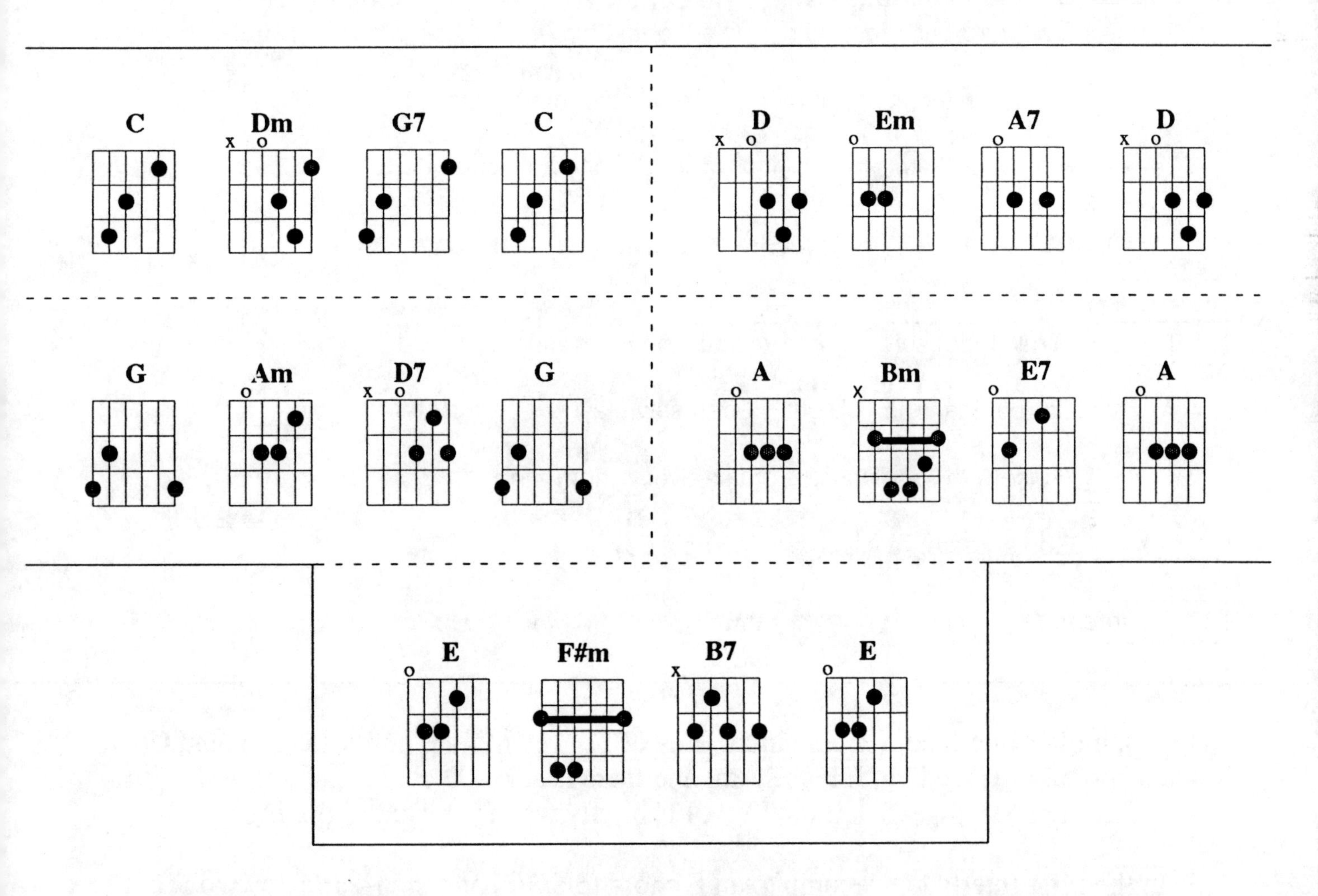

And of course, the letter names for the chords in each of these progressions can be found, in reverse sequence, on the outside ring of the **Circle of Fifths.**
Let's try our other Backcycling memory device:

***F**ling **B**ruce **E**mery's **A**mplifier **D**own the **G**rand **C**anyon*

Dm-G7-C	**Am-D7-G**	**Em-A7-D**	**Bm-E7-A**	**F#m-B7-E**
Down the Grand Canyon	*Amplifier Down the Grand*	*Emery's Amplifier Down*	*Bruce Emery's Amplifier*	*Fling Bruce Emery!*

"*Morning Has Broken*" *Again*

Let's look at a full arrangement of this popular hymn. It contains all 6 Major and Minor members of the Chord Family; Secondary Dominants; and a **modulation** (a key change) from the Key of C to the Key of D. When last we looked at this song, I said that I had cheated on one chord: Over the word "like" in the second line, the proper chord is D, as you see below, not Dm. I was shielding you from Secondary Dominants before.

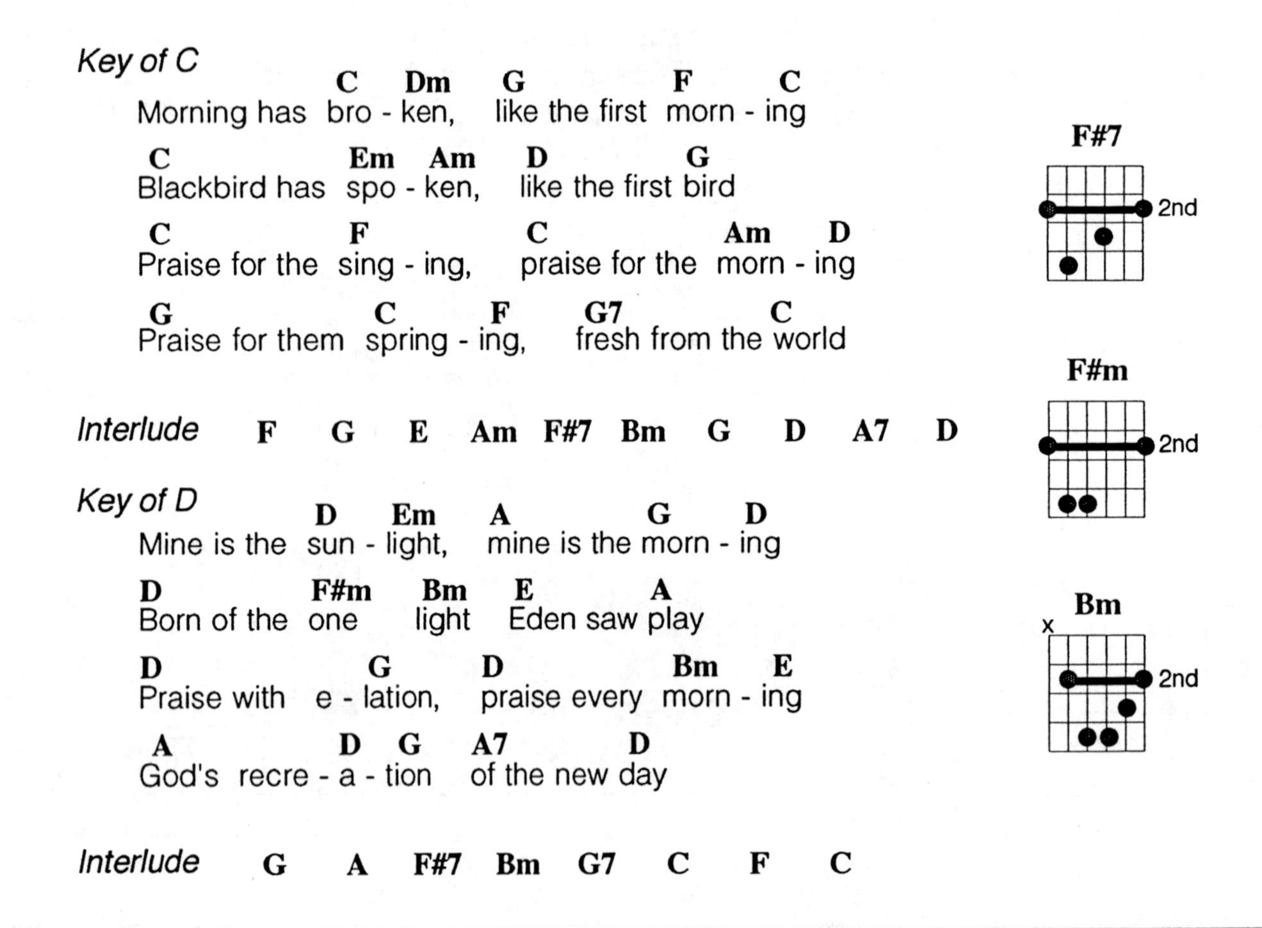

Up to the First Interlude, we play in the Key of C. The Major chords are C, F and G(7); the Minor chords are Dm, Em and Am; and there is also a D chord, the **5th** of the **5th.** (Strictly speaking, we left the Key of C briefly when we went to the D chord.)

In the First Interlude, we jump to an E chord **(5/5/5/5)** and then settle down a **5th** to an Am chord. Then very abruptly, we jump to F#7, which is far, far, away from the C Root Note. Next we move down a **5th** to a Bm chord, which in retrospect turns out to be the **6m** chord in the new Key of D. The whole second verse is in the Key of D. The Major chords are D, G and A(7); the Minor chords are Em, F#m and Bm; and the E chord is the **5th** of the **5th.**

Then in the Second Interlude, we play that unsettling progression from F#7 to Bm again, then just plop back into the Key of C when we harpoon that G7 chord. Modulation.

Yuletide Backcycling

On the following pages, you'll find several passages from some well-known Christmas carols, presented in all 5 of our favorite keys. Some degree of Backcycling, using Dominant 7ths, will occur in each song. The farther upstream you travel before hitting your target chord (that is, the farther away you move in the clockwise direction from the Tonic chord), the more *foreign* that chord will sound when you first hear it. If you need them, the Starting Notes for singing these phrases are presented on page 121.

Key of C

C G7 C D7 G7
On the fifth day of Christmas, my true love gave to me five golden rings

D7 is 5/5

C G7 C F C G7
O come all ye faithful, joyful and tri-um - phant

Am D7 G D7 G7 (C)
O come ye, O come ye to Be - ethle - hem

"Twelve Days of Christmas" is a straight **1 - 5 - 1 - 5/5 - 5** progression, where D7 is the **5/5 chord**. I love that "five golden rings" part, always have.

"O Come All Ye Faithful" starts off using **1 - 4 - 5's**. Then from the Relative Minor (Am), the Root Movement brings us down a **5th** to D7, then down a **5th** to G ***Major***. You know, at this point it almost feels like we've settled down into the *Key of G*, because in the Key of G, Am to D7 to G would be the Turnaround from the **2m** to the **57** to the **1 chord.** But after popping back upstream to D7, and then coming down to *G7* instead of G, we more definitely feel the propulsion that sends us down another **5th** to C. (Remember, the Major chord quality acts as a brake.)

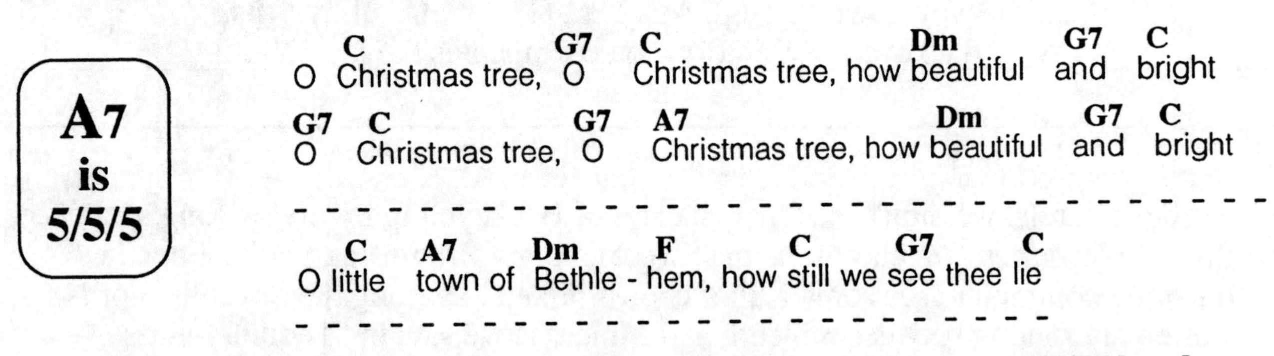

In "O Christmas Tree," we move up to the 3rd level, to A7, the **5/5/5 chord**. The first line is simple enough: **1 - 5 - 1 - 2m - 5 - 1** (a Turnaround). But in the next line, we jump upstream to the A7, then float back down by **5ths** through the same Turnaround.

"O Little Town of Bethlehem" starts right off jumping to A7, moves down a **5th** to Dm, but then steps out of the Circle of Fifths by going to an F, which is the ***Relative Major*** of Dm anyway, and finishes with a **1 - 5 - 1**. (Although we are in the Key of C, we can still talk about the Relative Major and Minor relationship between F and Dm, as if we were in the Key of F.)

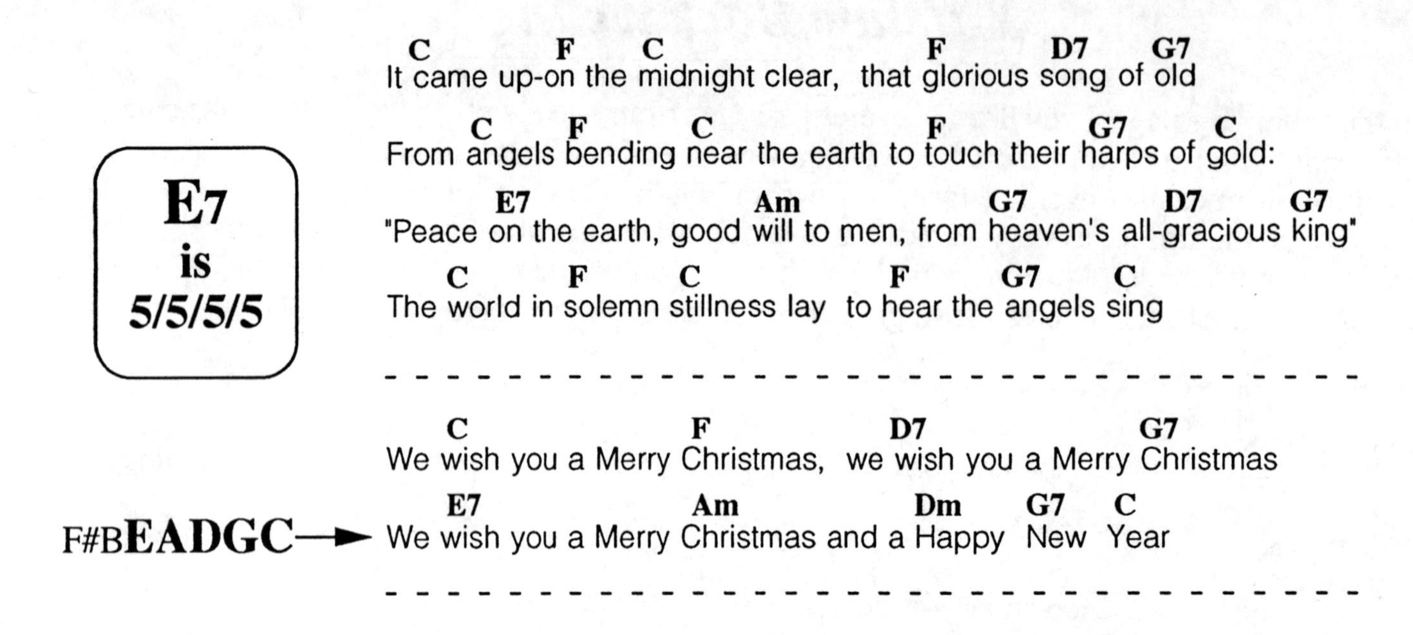

I included an entire verse of "It Came Upon the Midnight Clear" because it contains 3 different examples of Backcycling. The first one is D7, the **5/5 chord** in the 1st line. The 2nd line is normal. Then in the 3rd line, we use E7 as the target chord, which is the **5/5/5/5**, and then it's down a **5th** to Am. Okay so far.

But the next chord, G7, doesn't seem to flow naturally from the Am; in fact, from Am to G7, it's almost as if we've skipped over a chord in the Backcycling (like what happened in "Tequila Sunrise"), which could have been either Dm or D7. But then after G7, we do in fact jump back upstream to find D7, almost as if we realized we'd forgotten it and went back to get it! Then it's back down to G7 and then C. The 4th line is the same as the 2nd line.

Finally, "We Wish You a Merry Christmas" has 2 instances of Backcycling. The 1st line has: **1 - 4 - 5/5 - 5**. The 2nd line jumps up to E7, then rides all the way down through Am, Dm, G7, and C, all by **5ths**. Our Backcycling memory aid accompanies the last line.

In the above carols, we didn't see any instances of Backcycling involving long sequences of *purely Dominant 7th* chords, as in "Sweet Georgia Brown" and "Five Foot Two." It's more common to see some Minor chords mixed in among the Seventh chords, often alternating between Seventh and Minor, as we saw in "Tequila Sunrise."

To summarize what has happened here, these songs consist largely of the **1 - 4 - 5 chords** (C, F and G7), their Relative Minors (Am, Dm and Em), and the *Dominant 7th counterparts of those Minors (A7, D7, and E7),* which are also the first 3 Secondary Dominants clockwise from C.

Next, you'll find the same exercise presented for our 4 other favorite keys, G, D, A and E.

Key of G

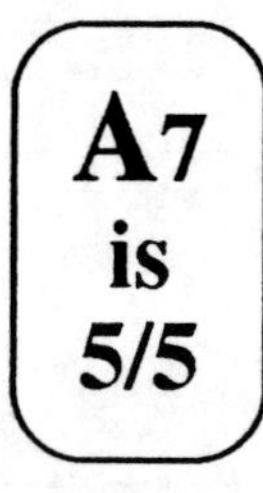

G D7 G A7 D7
On the fifth day of Christmas, my true love gave to me five golden rings

- -

G D7 G C G D7
O come all ye faithful, joyful and tri-um - phant

Em A7 D A7 D7
O come ye, O come ye to Be - ethle - hem

E7
is
5/5/5

G D7 G Am D7 G
O Christmas tree, O Christmas tree, how beautiful and bright

D7 G D7 E7 Am D7 G
O Christmas tree, O Christmas tree, how beautiful and bright

- -

G E7 Am C G D7 G
O little town of Bethle - hem, how still we see thee lie

B7
is
5/5/5/5

G C G C A7 D7
It came up-on the midnight clear, that glorious song of old

G C G C D7 G
From angels bending near the earth to touch their harps of gold:

B7 Em D7 A7 D7
"Peace on the earth, good will to men, from heaven's all-gracious king"

G C G C D7 G
The world in solemn stillness lay to hear the angels sing

- -

G C A7 D7
We wish you a Merry Christmas, we wish you a Merry Christmas

B7 Em Am D7 G
F#**BEADG**C ➤ We wish you a Merry Christmas and a Happy New Year

Key of D

E7 is 5/5

```
  D                                  A7           D       E7     A7
On the fifth  day of Christmas, my true love gave to me   five golden rings
- - - - - - - - - - - - - - - - - - - - - - - - - - - - - - - - - - -
  D            A7       D      G       D      A7
O come all ye faithful,  joyful and tri-um  -  phant
   Bm      E7      A                 E7       A7
O come   ye, O  come ye to Be - ethle - hem
```

B7 is 5/5/5

```
   D                   A7   D                         Em          A7    D
O Christmas tree,  O    Christmas tree, how beautiful   and   bright
A7    D                 A7   B7                          Em          A7    D
O     Christmas tree,  O    Christmas tree, how beautiful   and   bright
- - - - - - - - - - - - - - - - - - - - - - - - - - - - - - - - - - -
   D       B7        Em          G              D          A7          D
O little   town of  Bethle - hem, how still we see thee lie
```

F#7 is 5/5/5/5

```
  D           G        D                           G          E7       A7
It came up-on the midnight clear,  that glorious song of old
          D       G           D                        G              A7         D
From angels bending near the earth to touch their harps of gold:
        F#7                     Bm                     A7               E7          A7
"Peace on the earth, good will to men, from heaven's all-gracious king"
        D          G           D                  G          A7        D
The world in solemn stillness lay  to hear the angels sing
- - - - - - - - - - - - - - - - - - - - - - - - - - - - - - - - -
        D                       G                      E7                           A7
We wish you a Merry Christmas,  we wish you a Merry Christmas
            F#7                 Bm                       Em       A7     D
We wish you a Merry Christmas and a Happy  New  Year
```

F#BEADGC ⟶ (points to "We wish you a Merry Christmas and a Happy New Year")

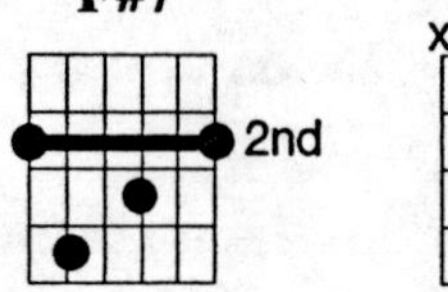

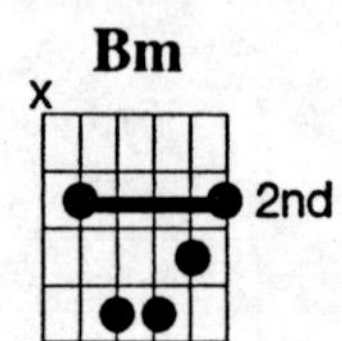

Skip It

If you've had enough Christmas cheer, you can skip the Keys of A and E. But if you'd like some more practice playing barre chords, then carry on:

Skip It

Key of A

B7 is 5/5

```
              A                                         E7                  A              B7     E7
On the fifth  day of Christmas, my true love gave to me   five golden rings
- - - - - - - - - - - - - - - - - - - - - - - - - - - - - - - - - - - - - - -
   A                  E7           A          D           A          E7
O come all ye faithful,  joyful and tri-um  -  phant
   F#m      B7       E                      B7         E7
O come    ye, O  come ye to Be - ethle - hem
```

F#7 is 5/5/5

```
   A                        E7    A                              Bm            E7      A
O Christmas tree,  O    Christmas tree, how beautiful   and   bright
E7     A                       E7   F#7                               Bm            E7      A
O     Christmas tree,  O    Christmas tree, how beautiful   and   bright
- - - - - - - - - - - - - - - - - - - - - - - - - - - - - - - - - - - - - - -
   A         F#7         Bm         D                  A          E7          A
O little   town of  Bethle - hem, how still we see thee lie
```

C#7 is 5/5/5/5

```
  A              D        A                                 D              B7          E7
It came up-on the midnight clear,  that glorious song of old
       A           D           A                            D                E7           A
From angels bending near the earth to touch their harps of gold:
           C#7                          F#m                       E7                     B7          E7
"Peace on the earth, good will to men, from heaven's all-gracious king"
     A             D           A                          D           E7          A
The world in solemn stillness lay  to hear the angels sing
- - - - - - - - - - - - - - - - - - - - - - - - - - - - - - - - - - - - - - -
     A                                   D                               B7                           E7
We wish you a Merry Christmas,  we wish you a Merry Christmas
        C#7                           F#m                          Bm       E7      A
We wish you a Merry Christmas and a Happy  New  Year
```

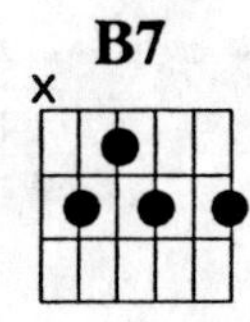

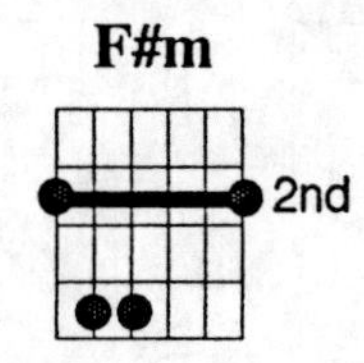

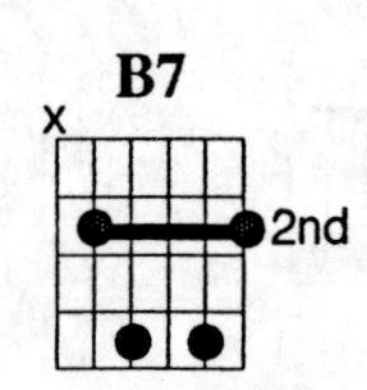

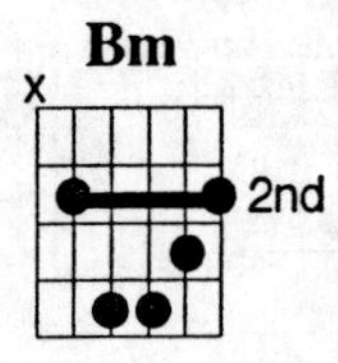

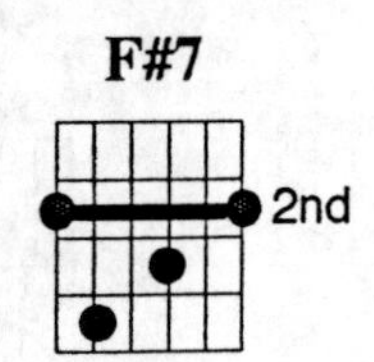

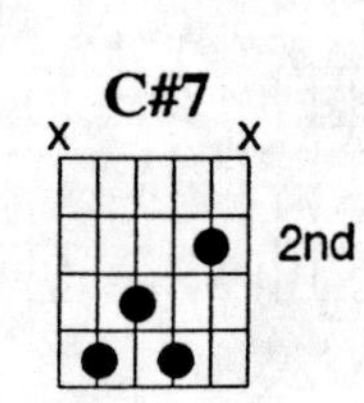

Skip It

Key of E

Skip It

F#7 is 5/5

E **B7** **E** **F#7** **B7**
On the fifth day of Christmas, my true love gave to me five golden rings

\- -

E **B7** **E** **A** **E** **B7**
O come all ye faithful, joyful and tri-um - phant

C#m **F#7** **B** **F#7** **B7**
O come ye, O come ye to Be - ethle - hem

C#7 is 5/5/5

E **B7** **E** **F#m** **B7** **E**
O Christmas tree, O Christmas tree, how beautiful and bright

B7 **E** **B7** **C#7** **F#m** **B7** **E**
O Christmas tree, O Christmas tree, how beautiful and bright

\- -

E **C#7** **F#m** **A** **E** **B7** **E**
O little town of Bethle - hem, how still we see thee lie

G#7 is 5/5/5/5

E **A** **E** **A** **F#7** **B7**
It came up-on the midnight clear, that glorious song of old

E **A** **E** **A** **B7** **E**
From angels bending near the earth to touch their harps of gold:

G#7 **C#m** **B7** **F#7** **B7**
"Peace on the earth, good will to men, from heaven's all-gracious king"

E **A** **E** **A** **B7** **E**
The world in solemn stillness lay, to hear the angels sing

\- -

E **A** **F#7** **B7**
We wish you a Merry Christmas, we wish you a Merry Christmas

G#7 **C#m** **F#m** **B7** **E**
We wish you a Merry Christmas and a Happy New Year

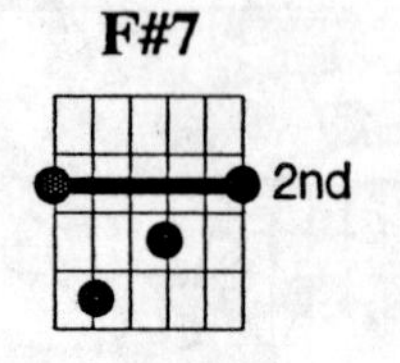

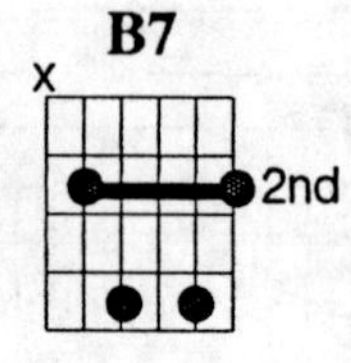

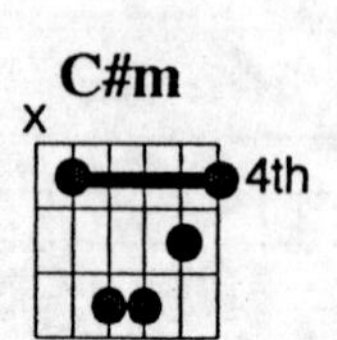

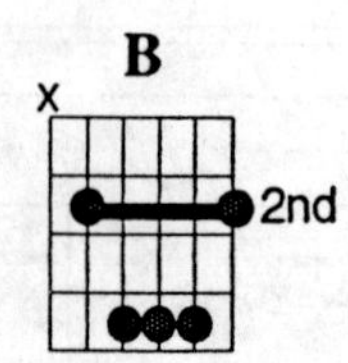

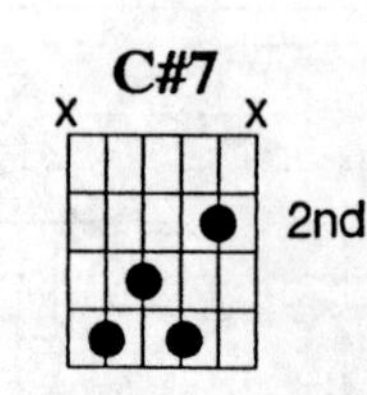

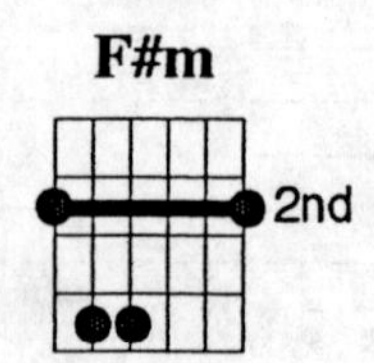

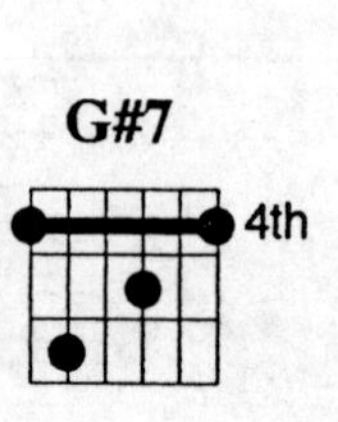

Starting Notes for Singing the Carols

Key of C

```
0 0 0 1 | 1 1 0 1 | 0 1 1 1 | 0 0 0 4 0 | 0 0 | 0 1 1
```

On the 5th day... O come all ye... O Christmas tree... O little town of... It came... We wish you...

Key of G

```
0 0 0 0 | 0 0 0 0 | 0 0 0 0 | 0 0 0 3 0 | 0 0 | 0 0 0
```

On the 5th day... O come all ye... O Christmas tree... O little town of... It came... We wish you...

Key of D

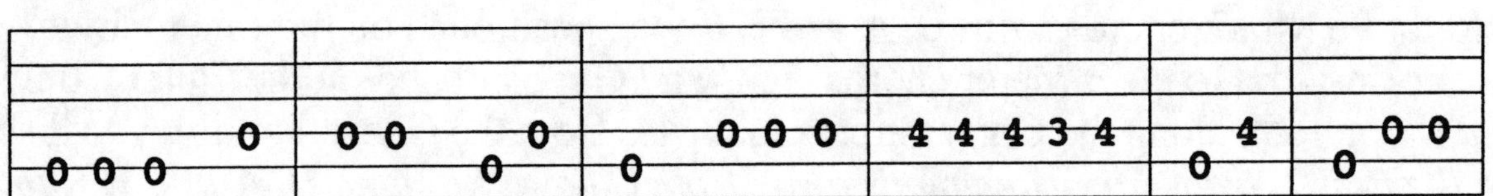

On the 5th day... O come all ye... O Christmas tree... O little town of... It came... We wish you...

Key of A

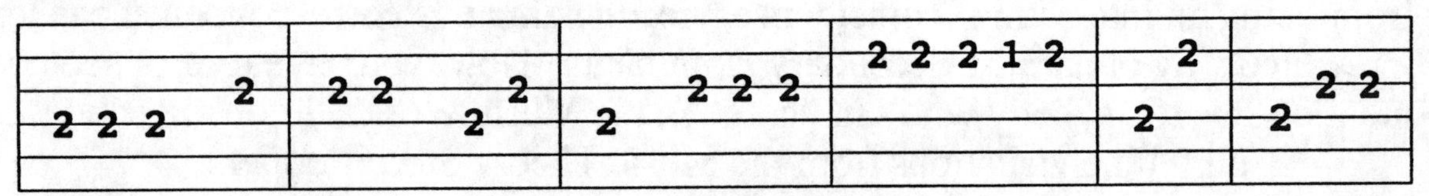

On the 5th day... O come all ye... O Christmas tree... O little town of... It came... We wish you...

Key of E

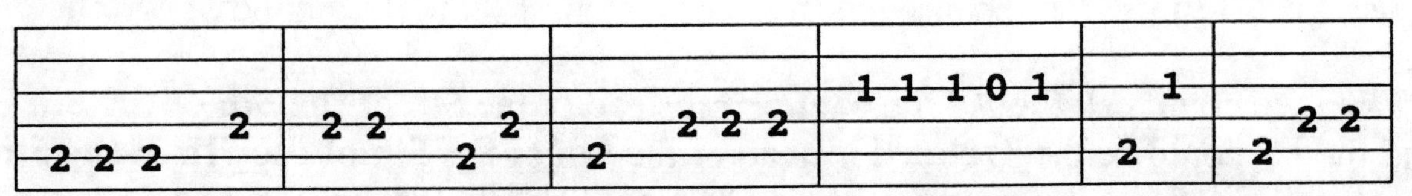

On the 5th day... O come all ye... O Christmas tree... O little town of... It came... We wish you...

Shortcuts in Terminology

I want to enlarge on something I said before, which was:

To summarize what has happened here, these songs consist largely of the **1 - 4 - 5** chords (C, F and G7), their Relative Minors (Am, Dm and Em), ***and the Dominant 7th counterparts of those Minors (A7, D7, and E7),*** which are also the first 3 Secondary Dominants away from C.

Let's look at the section of the Circle of Fifths that spotlights the Key of C:

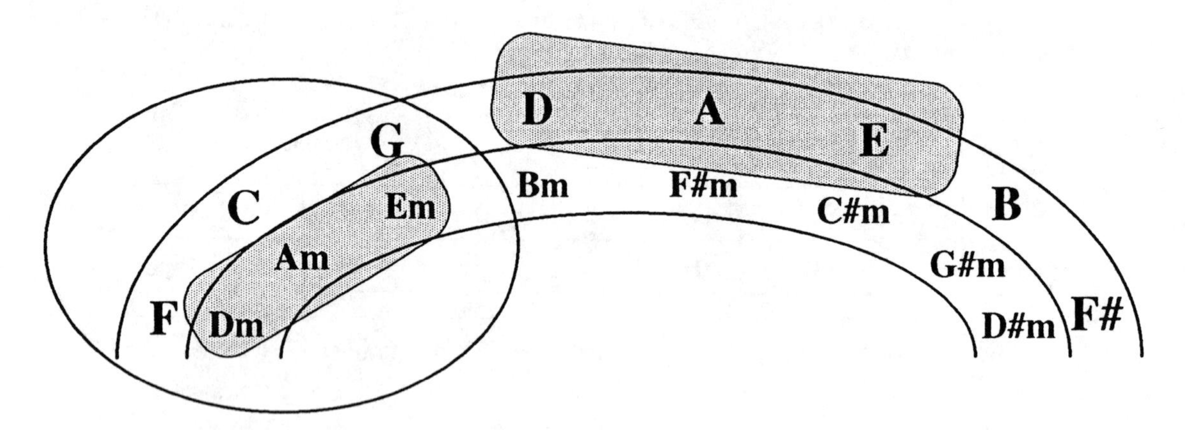

Look inside the oval at the C chord family. You can see the three Relative Minor chords, with D, A and E Roots, positioned on the Inner Circle, that correspond to the 3 Major chords (F, C and G) positioned on the Outer Circle. ***And*** if you look along the Outer Circle clockwise from the Chord Family, you'll see that *the first 3 Secondary Dominants away from C have* ***the same D, A and E Roots.***

So not only are D, A and E the ***Minor*** members of the C Chord Family, but they are also the most likely target chords, in ***Seventh*** form, of any Backcycling that might occur.

Apart from being an interesting "coincidence," recognizing this correspondence can lead to an abbreviated way of naming Secondary Dominants. Now, you have to promise not to mention this to anybody who's in charge in the Music World. I don't need any nighttime visitations from the Music Theory Stormtroopers.

It is rather awkward to keep talking about the **5th of the 5th of the 5th**, and so forth. So for the Key of C, why can't we just refer to D7 (the **5th of the 5th**) as the **2_7 chord**? By now, we all know that the **2 chord** in the Chord Family is really a *Minor* chord, so I don't think it will cause any *real* confusion. I think it's a handy shortcut.

Then we could call the A7 the **6_7 chord** instead of the **5th of the 5th of the 5th**, and the E7 could be the **3_7 chord** instead of the **5th of the 5th of the 5th of the 5th**. In Backcycling, the main sequence of chords would be labeled: **7_7 - 3_7 - 6_7 - 2_7 - 5_7 - 1**. Go ahead and express it this way, and if any classically-trained musicians ask you where you got this crackpot nomenclature, you tell them you made it up.

The 4th of the 4th

Yes, the **4th of the 4th**. The most common chord progression involving the **4th of the 4th** is **1 - 4/4 - 4 - 1**, where the **4/4 chord** passes through the **4 chord** on the way to the Tonic. But do you know what's *really* happening? This is **Root Movement *Upward By a Fifth!*** Yep, Upward By a **5th** works out to be the same as Downward By a **4th**, as you might have guessed. Jump 2 notches *backward* (counterclockwise) in the Circle of Fifths to the target chord, then travel up a **5th** to the **4 chord** (really the **minus-5 chord**), then up a **5th** to the Tonic. Check the Circle of Fifths (inside back cover) to confirm the following examples:

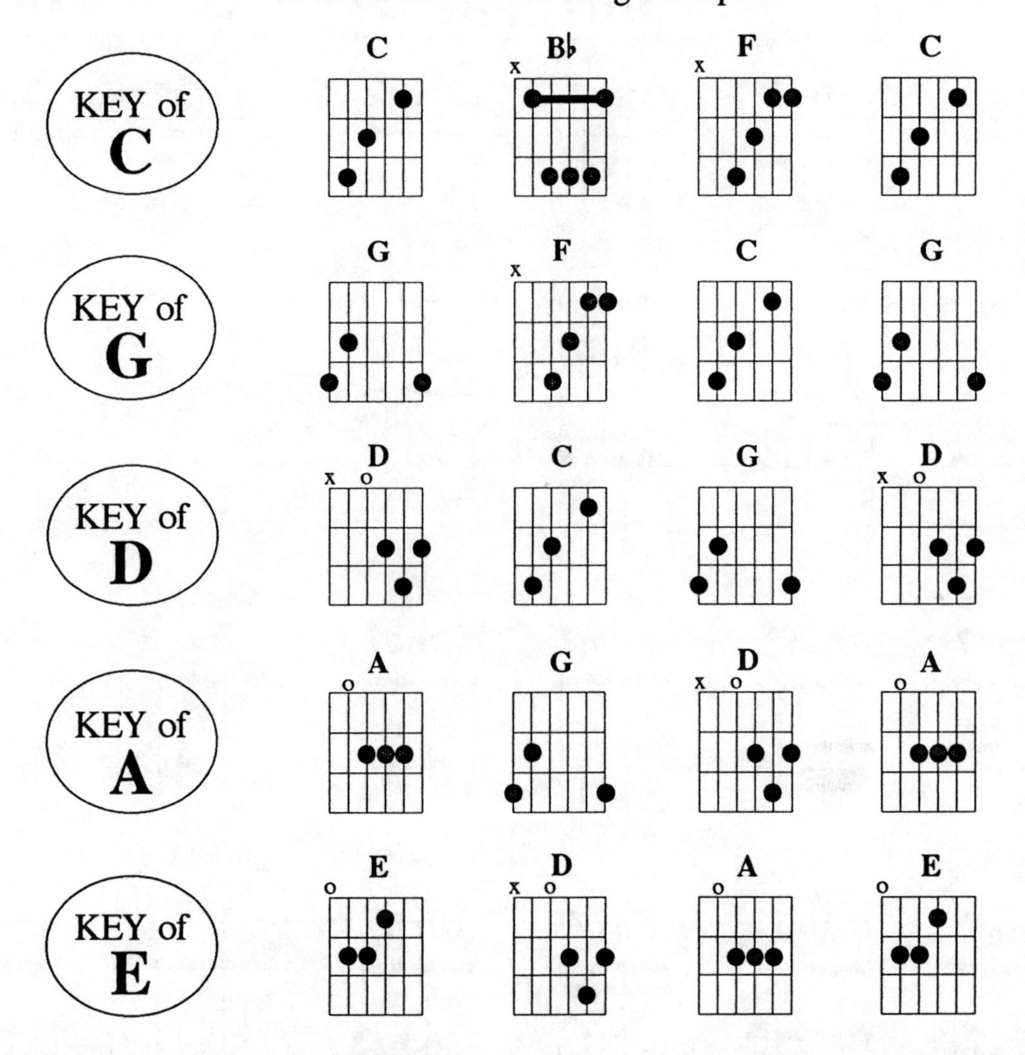

This is really just the opposite of Backcycling (so would this be called "Frontcycling?"). The *shortcut* is to move a Whole-step backward from the **Root**, which is just one letter in the Musical Alphabet. For the Key of G, you count backward from G to F. For the Key of D, you go from D to C. For C, you go back to B-**flat**. It's almost as popular in folk and rock music as Backcycling.

The **4 - 1** resolution even has a name---the **Plagal Cadence**, or "Church" Cadence. It's not as strong a resolution as the Perfect Cadence, but it is satisfying enough. Sounds like an "Ahhh - men."

Major 7th and Minor 7th Chords

Without going into any detail, I want to show you what happens if you extend ***all*** of the Major and Minor members of the Chord Family into 7th chords, or quadrads. All you need to do is to add the **7th** scale degree away from the Root onto the **1 - 3 - 5**. As you know, the **5 chord** assumes a Dominant 7th chord quality, but what about the other Chord Family members? Well, the **1** and **4 chords** become ***Major 7th*** chords, and the **2m, 3m** and **6m chords** become ***Minor 7th*** chords. Check 'em out:

	1ma7	**2m7**	**3m7**	**4ma7**	**5_7**	**6m7**
C	Cma7	Dm7	Em7	Fma7	G7	Am7
G	Gma7	Am7	Bm7	Cma7	D7	Em7
D	Dma7	Em7	F#m7	Gma7	A7	Bm7
A	Ama7	Bm	C#m7 4th	Dma7	E7	F#m7
E	Ema7	F#m	G#m7 4th	Ama7	B7	C#m7 4th

These Major 7th and Minor 7th chords are used as jazzy-sounding substitutions for their corresponding Major and Minor chords. We'll talk more about these jazz chords in later volumes.

For now, just think of the Major 7th chord as sounding "cool" and slightly dissonant. The Minor 7th chord is not quite as melancholy as the Minor chord; it's rather a bit more open and airy-sounding.

Here are the ***Rhythm Changes*** for the *C-A-G-E-D* Chord Families using these new chord qualities. Try singing some of those songs listed on p. 30.

	1ma7	6m7	2m7	5 7	1ma7
C	Cma7	Am7	Dm7	G7	Cma7
G	Gma7	Em7	Am7	D7	Gma7
D	Dma7	Bm7	Em7	A7	Dma7
A	Ama7	F#m7	Bm	E7	Ama7
E	Ema7	C#m7 (4th)	F#m	B7	Ema7

Minor Keys

We haven't explicitly talked about **Minor keys** yet, and that's because:

Each Minor key contains the same notes as its Relative Major key, *except that the Relative Minor Scale starts on the **6th degree** of the Relative Major Scale.*

So, for example, you know that the C Major Scale has the notes C-D-E-F-G-A-B. Well, the Relative Minor Scale of C, which is Am, has the notes A-B-C-D-E-F-G. Same 7 notes, no accidentals, but when you start on the A note, you produce a decidedly Minor-sounding scale. This is because the interval between the 1st and 3rd notes, A and C, is a ***Minor 3rd*** rather than a ***Major 3rd.*** Remember that from before? Somehow, all this stuff ties together. page 72

Here are the C Major and the A Minor Scales:

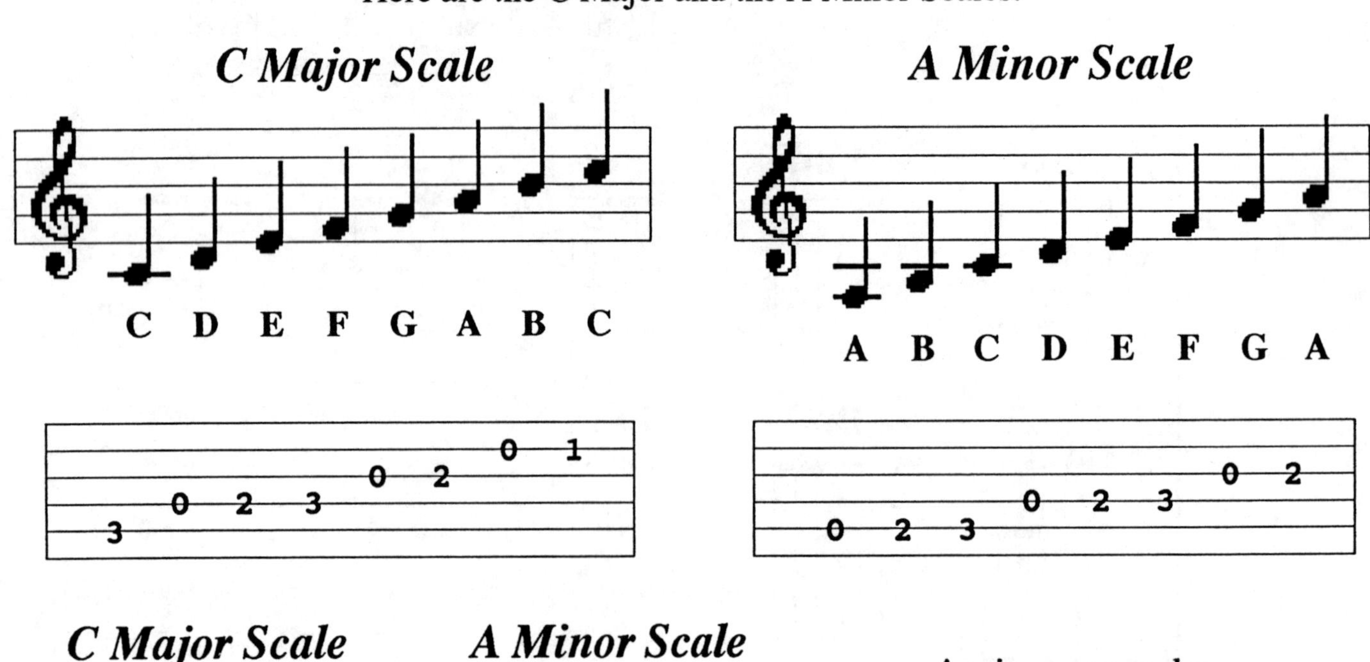

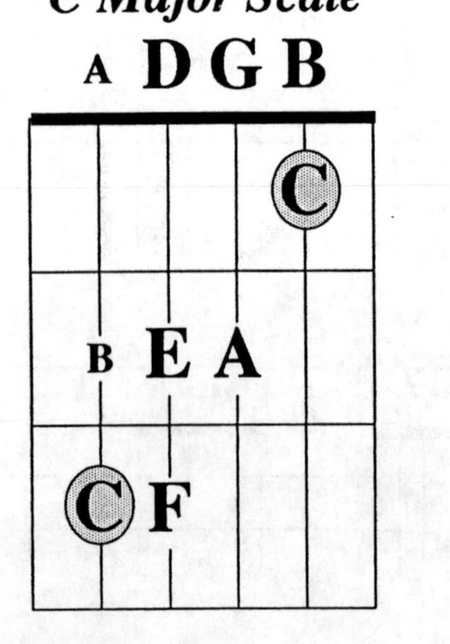

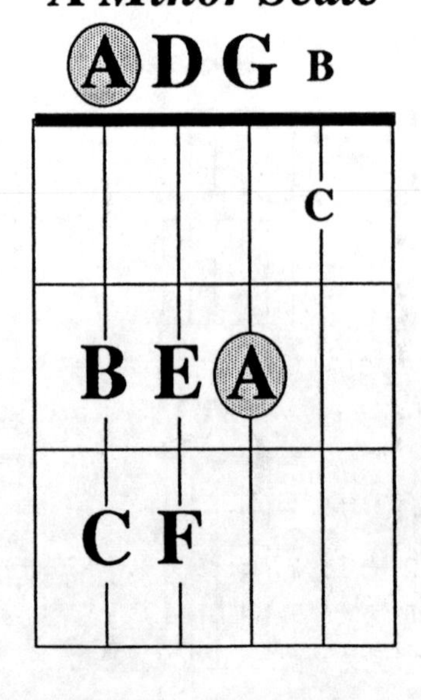

Again, same scales, different starting points.

But what is the relationship between the A Minor and A **Major** Scales? These are known as **Parallel Scales.** But the A Minor Scale has *so much more* in common with C Major than it does with A Major.

In fact, the Keys of A Major and A Minor differ by 3 accidentals and have no chords in common.

Since the C Major and the A Minor Scales are identical, it stands to reason that the two Chord Families are the same, except that in the Am Chord Family, we are calling Am the **1 chord**, Dm the **4 chord**, and Em the **5 chord**. The Major chords are the **3**, **6** and **7 chords**, and there is a **2dim chord**. Again, it's just a question of where you start counting:

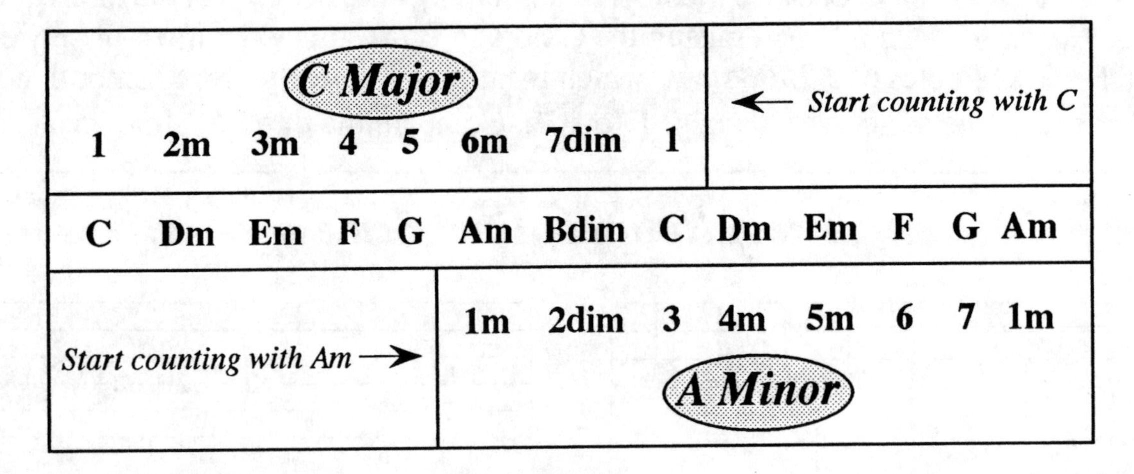

C Major								← *Start counting with C*				
1	**2m**	**3m**	**4**	**5**	**6m**	**7dim**	**1**					
C	**Dm**	**Em**	**F**	**G**	**Am**	**Bdim**	**C**	**Dm**	**Em**	**F**	**G**	**Am**
Start counting with Am →					**1m**	**2dim**	**3**	**4m**	**5m**	**6**	**7**	**1m**
					A Minor							

I usually think of a Minor key, not on its own terms, but in relation to its Relative Major key. So, beyond noting that the **1**, **4** and **5 chords** are Minor, it doesn't mean very much to me to refer to the other 4 chords by their *numbers,* as in "**3 major**" and "**2 diminished.**"

Try the **1m - 4m - 5m - 1m** progression in the Key of Am. It just sounds like a sad **1 - 4 - 5**.

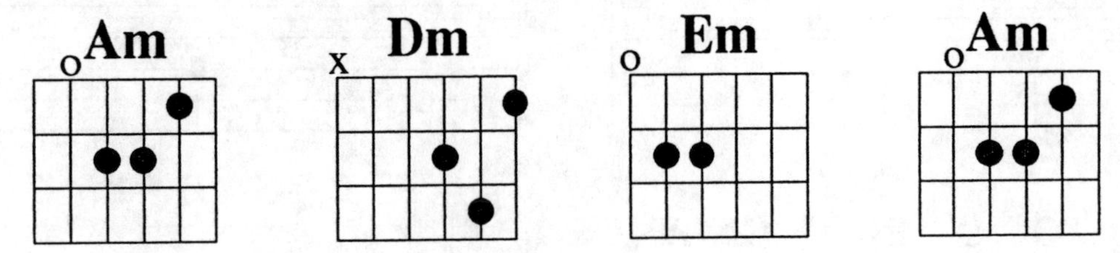

But there's one modification we might make. There seems to be something missing in the cadence from the **5m chord** to the **1m chord**. We are accustomed to hearing a more "dominant" sound in our **5 - 1** progressions. Notice that the cadence from Em to Am is just not quite as compelling as, for example, E to A in the Key of A Major.

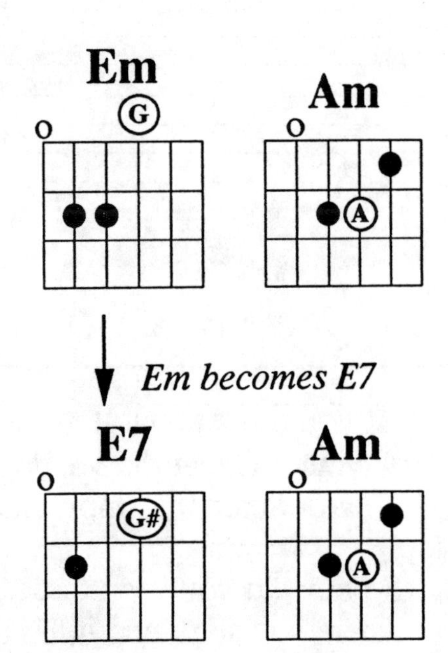

What we are missing is a **Leading Tone** between Em and Am. In the Key of A Major, the Leading Tone is **G#**, the note on the 3rd string, 1st fret, of the E chord. So let's replace the G note of the Em chord (E-G-B) with the G# note of the E chord (E-**G#**-B). Now we can have that *Half-step push* from G# to the Root Note A in the Am chord.

And just for good measure, why don't we make it an *E7* chord, to get that extra little bit of instability. Now, finally, in moving from E7 to Am, our musical craving is satisfied. You often see the **1m**, **4m** and **57 chords** in a song written in a Minor key.

By the way, we have created a *new scale* by replacing the G with a G#, and it is called the **A Harmonic Minor Scale,** A-B-C-D-E-F-**G#**-A, while the original, non-accidental version is called the **A Natural Minor Scale.**

There is one more variety of A Minor scale to know about: the **A Melodic Minor Scale.** This scale came about because it bothered somebody that, in the process of creating the A *Harmonic* Minor Scale, raising the G note to G# results in an interval between the F and G# notes of ***3 Half-steps,*** which is rather a lot, really. So to smooth out that gap in the scale, we also raise F to **F#**. Compare the three A Minor scales:

The A Natural Minor Scale

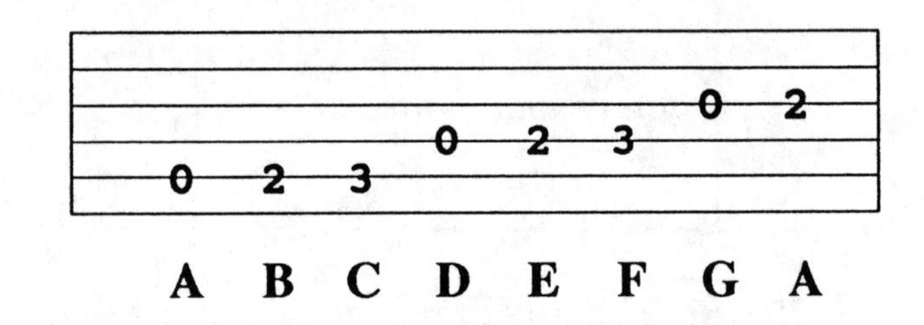

The A Harmonic Minor Scale

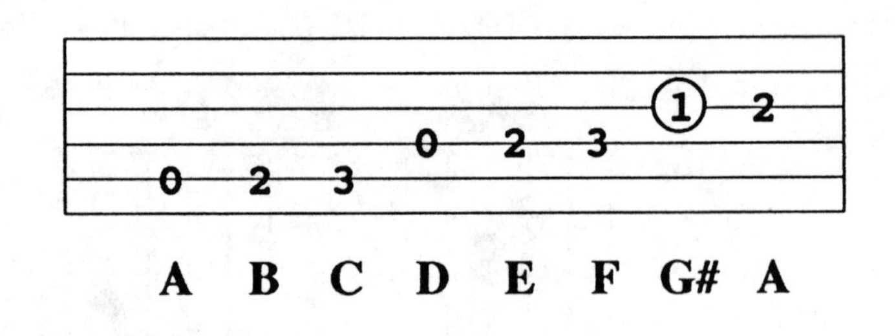

The A Melodic Minor Scale

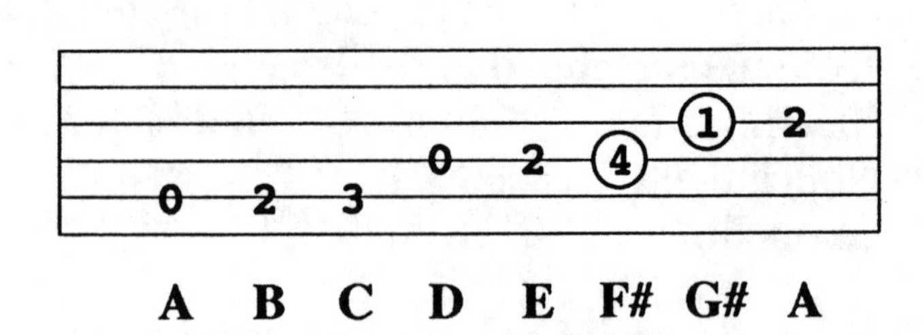

If you think about it, the A Melodic Minor Scale differs by ***only one note from A Major*** (C versus C#, at the 3rd degree). So here is a type of Minor Scale that we can generate from a Major Scale by simply flatting the **3rd** degree. It is used extensively in jazz improvisation.

So how do you keep these 3 Minor scales straight in your head? Well, the Natural Minor is where you start, and it has no push whatsoever. The ***Harmonic*** Minor is the one that makes the ***harmonies,*** or the chords, sound more dynamic. And the ***Melodic*** Minor goes back and fills in that 3-Half-step gap in the scale to help create smoother ***melody*** lines.

Let's use some more Christmas carols to explore the Key of A Minor. "What Child Is This?" (or "Greensleeves," same melody), sports both an Em *and* an E7 chord, so this song can't seem to decide whether to remain in the *A Natural Minor Scale* or the *A Melodic Minor Scale*. So it bounces back and forth between the two. (The notes for the words "rest" and "sweet" are G notes, while the second note in "sleep" and the first note in "watch" are G# notes.)

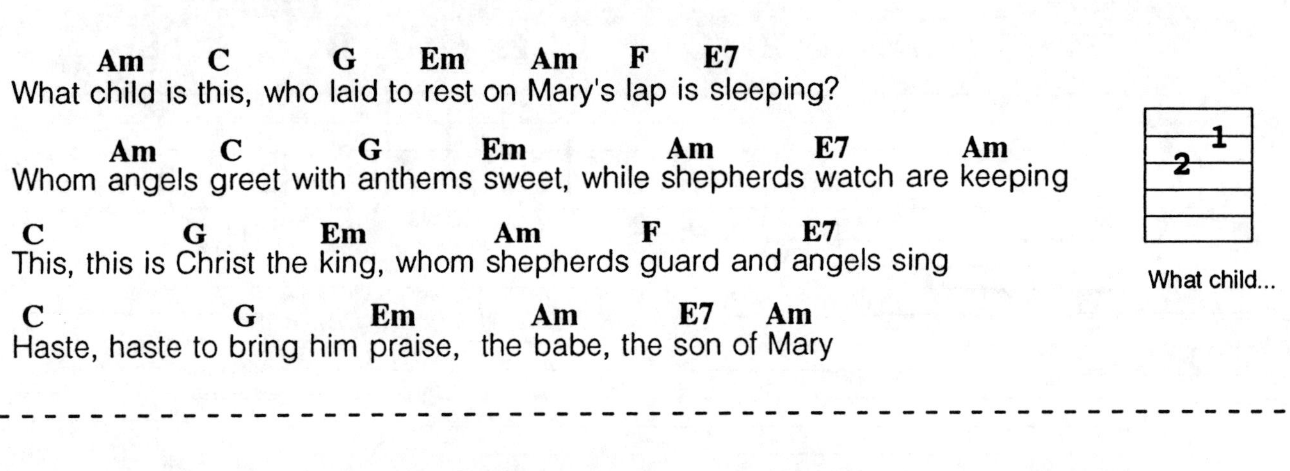

Next comes "We Three Kings," which has its own little identity crisis going. This one switches from the Key of A Harmonic Minor, with its *Am - Dm - E7*, (**1m - 4m - 5**7) to the Key of C Major, with its *C - F - G7*. You can really hear the Minor key in the first two lines and the Major key in the last two lines. By the way, this song ends with a Plagal Cadence (**4 - 1**).

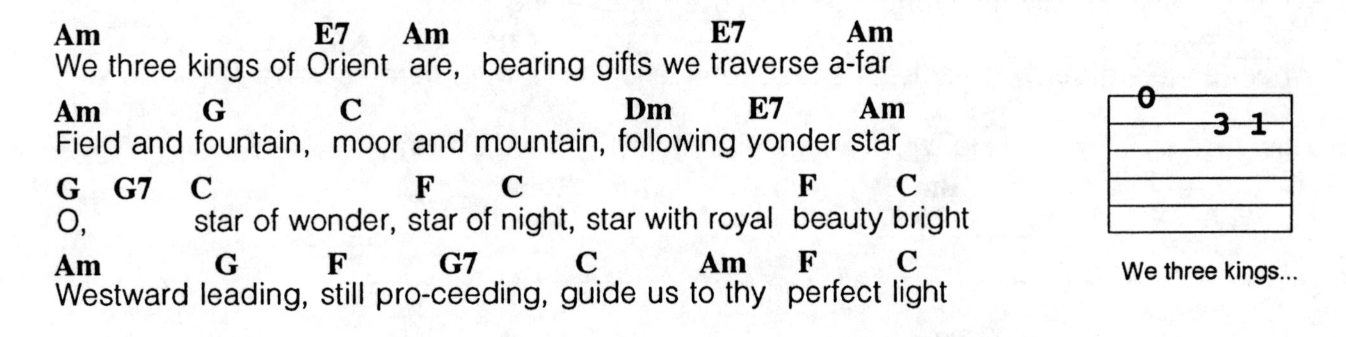

"God Rest Ye Merry, Gentlemen" switches back and forth several times between the Key of A Harmonic Minor, with all those E7-to-Am cadences, and the Key of C, with those G7-to-C cadences. (Can you spot the Secondary Dominant chord? I'll give you a hint: It's D7.)

```
     Am     E7     Am              Dm                   E7
God rest ye merry, gentlemen, let nothing you dis-may

      Am       E7         Am            Dm                      E7
Re-member Christ our Savior was born on Christmas Day

    Dm        G7        C          E7              Am          D7       G7
To save us all from Satan's power when we were gone a-stray

   C      F          E7                F                       G7
O tid  -  ings of comfort and joy, comfort and joy

   C      F          E7                Am
O tid  -  ings of comfort and joy
```

0
2 2

God rest ye...

Here are the 2 octaves of the **E Natural Minor Scale**, which is the Relative Minor of G Major (1 sharp, F#), along with the same three Christmas carols that we analyzed before in the Key of Am. Look for the same kinds of things: switching from Relative Minor to Relative Major, the Perfect and Plagal Cadences, and the Secondary Dominant chord.

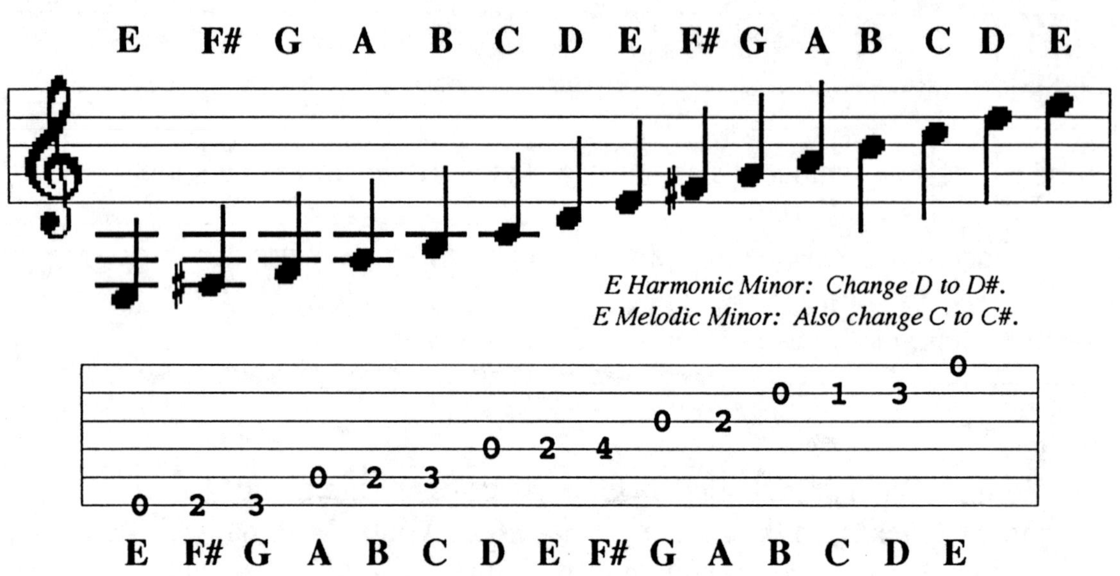

E Harmonic Minor: Change D to D#.
E Melodic Minor: Also change C to C#.

Em G D Bm Em C B7
What child is this, who laid to rest on Mary's lap is sleeping?
Em G D Bm Em B7 Em
Whom angels greet with anthems sweet, while shepherds watch are keeping
G D Bm Em C B7
This, this is Christ the king, whom shepherds guard and angels sing
G D Bm Em B7 Em
Haste, haste to bring him praise, the babe, the son of Mary

What child...

Em B7 Em B7 Em
We three kings of orient are, bearing gifts we traverse a-far
Em D G Am B7 Em
Field and fountain, moor and mountain, following yonder star
D D7 G C G C G
O, star of wonder, star of night, star with royal beauty bright
Em D C D7 G Em C G
Westward leading, still pro-ceeding, guide us to thy perfect light

We three kings

Em B7 Em Am B7
God rest ye merry, gentlemen, let nothing you dis-may
Em B7 Em Am B7
Re-member Christ our Savior was born on Christmas Day
Am D7 G B7 Em A7 D7
To save us all from Satan's power when we were gone a-stray
G C B7 C D7
O tid - ings of comfort and joy, comfort and joy
G C B7 Em
O tid - ings of comfort and joy

God rest ye

And here is one octave of the **D Natural Minor Scale**, which is the Relative Minor of F Major (1 flat, B-flat), along with the same examples. The Key of Dm is more popular on the guitar among the Minor keys than the Key of F is among the Major keys (especially in ***Drop D Tuning***, in which the 6th-string E note is lowered a Whole-step to D). The B-flat and Gm chords are diagrammed for you at the bottom of the page.

Appendix 1: Why the Number "Five"?

I'm sure this question has occurred to you by now. What is so blasted special about the number "**Five**" in music? And while we're at it, what about the "**1-3-5**" of the Major chord? Why, why, why? Well, there are some acoustic principles at work, and we're going to inspect them in a very general way. In a word, the answer to these question is **overtones.**

When you play a note by setting a string to vibrating, you are generating a complex pattern of wave motion in the string, and other higher pitched notes, known as overtones, are created. These overtones are hard to hear, because the main note, known as the **Fundamental** note, is so overwhelmingly loud. But they really do exist. Here's how to track them down.

On the guitar, there is a technique for revealing these overtones known as playing **harmonics**, or "chimes." There are various points along each string, called **nodes**, where, if you touch the string lightly with a finger while you strike the string with your thumb or with a pick, you expose the overtone to the human ear.

The First Overtone is found at 1/2 the string length, at the **12th fret**.
The Second Overtone is found at 1/3 the string length, at the **7th fret**.
The Third Overtone is found at 1/4 the string length, at the **5th fret**.
The Fourth Overtone is found at 1/5 the string length, at the **4th fret**.

There are more overtones than these, but these are the easiest to hear.

The First Overtone is the strongest, and the note you hear is exactly ***one octave*** above the Fundamental. (In effect, by touching the string at the 12th fret, you are knocking out the vibration of the Fundamental note.) So if you are playing the 6th string, the Fundamental is the E note, and so is the First Overtone. ***So the open E string "contains" its own octave.***

The Second Overtone is where it gets interesting. By playing the harmonic at the 7th fret, you are deleting both the Fundamental *and* the First Overtone and revealing a note that is, lo and behold, exactly a ***Fifth*** above the First Overtone. *Do you realize what this means?* It means that the Fundamental note contains its own **Fifth**. ***Every note contains its own Fifth!*** (This is true for both open and fretted notes.) So the open E string actually contains a B note. No wonder we subconsciously feel the downward pull of the mighty **Fifth**, from B to E.

The Third Overtone isn't so exciting: It's just ***a second octave*** above the Fundamental. So far, our open E string contains an E note, another E note, a B note, and yet another E note.

But the Fourth Overtone, G#, is (holy cow!) exactly a ***Third*** above the last overtone, E. That's a **Third** as in "**1 - 3 - 5**," as in "the Major Triad." *Do you realize what **this** means?* ***Every note contains its own Major Triad!*** No wonder this **1 - 3 - 5** business is so important.

I learned about this stuff over ten years ago, and I *still* get excited about it.

Appendix 2: Key Signatures

In Standard Music Notation, there is a shorthand representation, known as the **Key Signature**, which tells you the musical key for any given composition. The Key Signature is found at the beginning of each line of music, right after the Treble Clef, and it is composed of the number of accidentals that correspond to the key in which the composition is written. So if you see 2 sharps, the key is D, and if you see 3 flats, the key is E-flat. If there are no sharps or flats, the Key is C.

Here are the Key Signatures for the keys containing up through 6 accidentals:

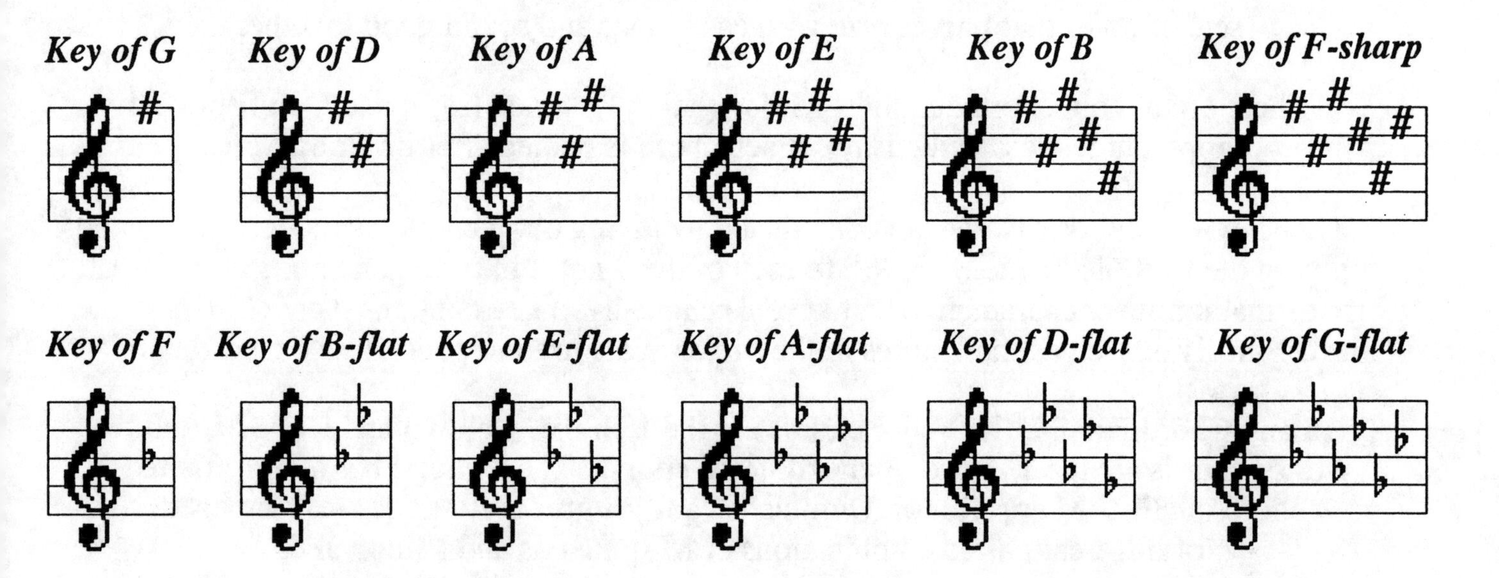

The symbols for the accidentals are not just thrown onto the staff randomly. They are placed on the lines and spaces that represent the notes that need sharping or flatting in that particular key.

Remember, the order of the sharp keys is: {Can} **G**uys **D**o **A**nything **E**lse **B**ut **F**lirt? The Key of G has 1 sharp, which is F#, the Leading Tone. Each additional sharp is added at the Leading Tone for the next key and all previous sharps are retained.

So what if you are looking through some Standard Notation, and you see a Key Signature with 4 sharps, but you have forgotten that this indicates the Key of E? Well, since the sharp symbol farthest to the right gives the Leading Tone for whatever key it is, and since that sharp symbol sits on the 4th line of the staff, which is D, then the keynote must be the note that follows D (that D *leads* to), which is E. (Page 53 gives the letter names of all the notes on the staff).

If you see flat symbols in the Key Signature, go to the one that is farthest to the right, ***and back up one***. That is the keynote. So if you see 3 flats, back up one from the last one to find E; so the key is E-flat. If you see 5 flats, check the 4th one, which gives you D-flat.

Volume One in a Nutshell

1. The 12 **notes** in the **Chromatic Scale** (which includes the entire **Musical Alphabet**) can be organized into 12 different **Major Scales**, each containing a unique subset of exactly 7 of the 12 notes. Each Major Scale is said to belong to its own **key**.

2. These 12 groupings of 7 notes each are pulled from the Chromatic Scale according to the formula "**2 Whole-steps, 1 Half-step, 3 Whole-steps and 1 Half-step.**"

3. On the guitar, we pay attention mostly to the 5 keys that are represented in the word ***C-A-G-E-D***, which are the keys having from 0 to 4 **sharps**. We like these keys because they let us use the most open strings when playing simple **chords** (sets of notes that **harmonize** with each other and sound good together).

4. There are 3 main chord qualities: **Major** (happy), **Minor** (sad), and **Dominant 7th** (happy but restless and pushy). Each chord is named after its **Root Note**.

5. The simplest chords, **triads**, are constructed by laying out the 7 notes in a given key and applying the formula "**1 (Root) - 3 - 5**" to each of the 7 notes in turn, generating a family of 7 triads that uniquely characterize that key. Technically, a key contains the 7 **chords** in the **Chord Family** as well as the 7 **notes** in the Major Scale used to generate the Chord Family.

6. In any Chord Family, the Major chords are the **1 chord**, **4 chord** and **5 chord**, and the Minor chords are the **2 chord**, **3 chord** and **6 chord**. The **7 chord** has a **Diminished** chord quality. Major, Minor, Diminished and **Augmented** triads are composed of different paired combinations of **Major 3rds** and **Minor 3rds**.

8. The **5 chord** can be extended into a **quadrad** (**1-3-5-7**) to become a Dominant 7th chord. The **5 chord**, whether it has a Major or a Dominant 7th chord quality, wants to **resolve** by an interval of a **Fifth** to the **1 chord**, which feels like coming home, musically. This **Root Movement Downward By a Fifth** is known as a **Perfect Cadence**.

9. Chord Families overlap with each other and share certain chords depending on how many **accidentals** the respective keys have in common.

10. "**C**an **G**irls/Guys **D**o **A**nything **E**lse **B**ut **F**lirt" gives the order of the sharp keys from C (no sharps) to F# (6 sharps). The closer together two keys are found in this memory aid, the more notes they have in common, the more closely **related** they are.

11. The Circle of Fifths lays out all 12 keys in order by accidentals. It also indicates which **Secondary Dominant** chords can be used to **Backcycle** between the most closely-related keys. And it shows, at a glance, the Major and Minor chords belonging to each Chord Family.

12. Each Major Scale has a **Relative Minor** Scale whose Root Note starts on the **6th** degree of the Major Scale. Similarly, every Major chord has a Relative Minor chord, its own **6m**. Man!

One Last Quiz --- Can You Do It?

Fill 'em in and play 'em!

1	6m	4	5_7	1	2m	3m	4	5_7	6m	2_7	5_7	1
C												
G												
D												
A												
E												

1	3_7	6m	6_7	2m	7_7	3_7	6m	5_7	1	4/4	4	1
C												
G												
D												
A												
E												

Preview of Volume Two...

Volume One is a "What-and-Why" book while **Volume Two** is more of a "How-To" book.

In **Volume One**, the guitar itself is secondary to the elucidation of the Principles of Music with a capital "M." These principles apply to all musical instruments equally; we just happen to be guitarists and want to see examples on the guitar, naturally.

But in **Volume Two** the primary focus is the fretboard of the guitar.

We begin by reviewing the C Major Scale and quickly moving into Chord Voicings, which are specific combinations of chord tones, for the C Major chord, and then for the other *C-A-G-E-D* chord forms. We then compare the different "personalities" that are exhibited by the different *C-A-G-E-D* chord forms and try moving some of them around the neck to find equivalent chords in different positions.

Next we take a side trip to learn how to create Complex Chords by incorporating the non-chord tones (the **2nd**, **4th**, **6th** and **7th**) into the Major Chords, producing the Suspended 2nd, Suspended 4th, Major 6th and Major 7th chord qualities.

Then it's back to the 5 basic chord shapes to see how you can find the C chord all over the neck of the guitar by using the A-shape, G-shape, E-shape, D-shape and C-shape again by knowing which positions on the fretboard to use. And we talk about how to use the capo to facilitate our work.

Next we change gears a bit and talk about the Major Scale "box patterns" that correspond to the *C-A-G-E-D* chord shapes that we just delineated. We see how to move between box patterns in the Key of C and then how to change keys.

Then it's back to the issue of chord quality, where we lay out all the Minor, Dominant 7th, Minor 7th and Minor 6th chords and see how they relate to the Quadrads of the Harmonized Diatonic Scale, harking back to Volume One. Then there are the oddball quadrads (Diminished, Augmented and so forth) and the Quadrad Extensions (9ths, 11ths and 13ths).

Now we really change gears and learn how chords and scales can be interwoven into "harmonized melodies," including a discussion of **Thirds**, **Sixths** and **Tenths**.

...and Volume Three

In ***Volume Three***, Part One, we focus on the **Blues**. We start by studying rhythm guitar parts (song accompaniment) with the classic Twelve-Bar Blues and Boogie-Woogie forms. Then we move in on the Pentatonic Minor Scale and all the little variations that can be thrown in to make an interesting Blues solo.

In Part Two, we look at **Jazz**---again, chords and chord progressions first, then the scales and modes used in soloing. This is not designed as an exhaustive treatise on Jazz, since there are a number of fine books written by Jazz masters already available. I am more interested in giving the average guitar player an introduction to and a feeling for Jazz, rather than trying to present all the intricate details (which I would need to learn first before I could teach you anyway!). But it's a good introduction.